RESEARCH DESIGNS
IN GENERAL SEMANTICS

RESEARCH DESIGNS IN GENERAL SEMANTICS

Edited by

KENNETH G. JOHNSON
*Department of Mass Communication
University of Wisconsin
Milwaukee*

GORDON AND BREACH SCIENCE PUBLISHERS

NEW YORK LONDON PARIS

Copyright ©1974 by

Gordon and Breach, Science Publishers Inc.
1 Park Avenue
New York, N.Y. 10016

Editorial office for Great Britain:
Gordon and Breach, Science Publishers Ltd.
41-42 William IV Street
London W.C.2, England

Editorial office for France:
Gordon & Breach
7-9 rue Emile Dubois
Paris 75014

Library of Congress Catalog Card Number: 74-121602　ISBN 0 677 14370 2

All rights reserved. No part of this book may be reproduced or utilized in any form or by any means, electronic or mechanical, including photocopying, recording, or by any information storage and retrieval system, without permission in writing from the Publishers. Printed in Great Britain.

PREFACE

This volume contains the papers presented at the First Conference on Research Designs in General Semantics held at Pennsylvania State University.

The Conference was made possible by contributions from The General Semantics Foundation, Harry Maynard, S. I. Hayakawa, Tore Browald, Ed Walther, and the Pennsylvania State University.

The Conference originated in the fertile brain of Elwood Murray. He planned the program, enlisted support, and invited colleagues throughout the country to attend. The success of the Conference is a tribute to his leadership. He is now Director Emeritus of the Institute for General Semantics.

KENNETH G. JOHNSON

Milwaukee, Wisconsin

CONTENTS

PREFACE v

INTRODUCTION xi

I BEHAVIORAL APPROACHES

Empirical and Experimental Research Possibilities in General Semantics—Alvin A. Goldberg 3

Korzybskian Models for Research—Kenneth G. Johnson .. 23

Relational Abstracting and the Structural Differential—Otto F. Bauer 37

Levels of Individuation in Semantic Structures—Charles F. Vick 41

Researching the "Intangible"—Charlotte S. Read .. 47

The Semantic Interaction Test—Rachel M. Lauer .. 55

Specifying the Structure of Our "Semantic Reactions"—C. A. Hilgartner, MD 61

Use of Psychological Scaling Methods for Quantifying Observable Aspects of Semantic Reactions—Franklin H. Silverman .. 69

Sociometric Measures of Semantic Reactions—Alton B. Barbour .. 77

The Measurement of Interpersonal Trust—Kim Giffin 89

The Situational Analysis of Urban Communication: An Extended-Case Study of Racial Tension—Russell W. Jennings, Thomas J. Pace, Jr. and Dennis E. Winters 95

II HUMANISTIC APPROACHES
Consciousness of Abstracting in Literary Research—
Donald E. Washburn .. 109
The Critical Approach—Robert G. Johnson 119
General Semantics as a Critical Tool in Literary Research—Paul Hunsinger 125
Rhetoric, General Semantics, and Ideology—
Lawrence W. Rosenfield .. 139

III PHENOMENOLOGICAL APPROACHES
Introduction to the OG Principle of Research—
Gerald M. Phillips .. 149
A Perceptual Approach to Rhetorical Study—
Richard B. Gregg .. 161

IV INTERDISCIPLINARY APPROACHES
Integration of the Integrative Disciplines—
Glynn Harmon .. 175
Linguistics and General Semantics: A Reappraisal—
Joseph A. DeVito .. 185
Psycholinguistics and General Semantics: Some Conceptual "Problems" and "Resolutions"—
Joseph A. DeVito .. 193
Possible Areas of Research in General Semantics: An Interdisciplinary Approach—George A. Borden .. 205
Research on Structural Design in Scientific Documents—
Bess Sondel .. 211

V CONCERNING RESEARCH
Semantic Factors in the Research Process—
D. David Bourland, Jr. .. 217
The Proper Study of Mankind Is Man—James M. Broadus 229
The Researcher and the Three "Laws of Thought"—
Elwood Murray .. 235

VI	**CONCERNING THE CONFERENCE**	
	An Evaluation of the Conference—James E. Roever	247
	Observations—Titus Podea	253
	Summary Session ..	257
VII	**NAME INDEX**	273
VIII	**SUBJECT INDEX**	278

INTRODUCTION

Dating from the publication of *Science and Sanity* in 1933, general semantics is a relatively new field of study. In the years since 1933 there have been seven national and international conferences, three congresses, and more than 116 major seminars and seminar-workshops which included occasional reports of research, but tended to emphasize applications of Alfred Korzybski's non-aristotelian methodology. These applications may be regarded as a kind of research, but generally they lacked the rigor necessary to produce demonstrably valid and reliable results.

The Conference on Research Designs in General Semantics in March 1969 brought together for the first time about 50 people who were specifically interested in the *research* aspects of general semantics. It readily became apparent that "research" meant quite different things to different participants, depending primarily upon their academic backgrounds, but also their personal interests and their theoretical training in general semantics. As the Conference progressed, the "cross-pollination" effect generally claimed for interdisciplinary fields was evident, but so, too, were the language and experiential barriers that emerge when a field is approached by people with diverse backgrounds.

The diversity is reflected in the papers in this volume. Their arrangement is arbitrary. Generally speaking, the authors of the papers in the "behavioral" section view general semantics as a discipline whose applications and implications are to be tested. The "humanistic" papers, on the other hand, report applications of general semantics as a research tool. One of the papers in this set takes a critical look at general semantics as an "ideology."

The "phenomenological" papers raise some serious questions about the limits of experimental and observational methods and particularly the statistical abstractions that tell us nothing about what is going on inside the subjects being observed. They suggest new methods of approaching research.

While many of the studies or research possibilities discussed in the other sections of the book are interdisciplinary, papers that emphasize this aspect are grouped together. The section "Concerning Research" includes papers that attempt to apply some of the principles of general semantics to the research process.

Evaluations and observations of the conference make up the section "Concerning the Conference." The Summary Session was transcribed from tape recordings and edited.

Perhaps "Conference on Research Designs in General Semantics" is something of a misnomer. The conference did not focus on "designs" as that term is usually used. Most of the participants apparently felt (rightly, I suspect) that a first conference on research designs, involving, as it did, participants from a variety of disciplines, was not an appropriate place to explain, discuss, or debate the details of any given design. It was, rather, a place to explore with colleagues the possibilities for research and to suggest possible designs.

Participants generally agreed that there has been "too little" research in general semantics. Josep DeVito suggested that this may be "a function of the failure of the field to have defined itself in research generating terms." Franklin Silverman mentioned measurement problems as a probable source of difficulty. Both suggested ways of overcoming these difficulties.

Another reason for the relatively small amount of research is that there are very few "full time" general semanticists. According to a study completed in 1960 by Prof. Cecil Coleman, 185 colleges and universities in the United States offer courses in this subject in some form or other, but none, to my knowledge, offers a major in the field. The University of Denver comes close with its graduate program in "Communication Methodologies," but most people in the field identify first with some other academic field and second with general semantics. Their research is likely to follow a similar set of priorities.

The Conference made it painfully clear that much of the research that has been done in this field is not widely known or generally available. What is needed is (1) a publication summarizing research to date in general semantics and (2) a periodical that would consistently carry articles or abstracts of all research in the field. The *General Semantics Bulletin* has attempted to meet the second of these needs, but apparently it is not known to all who would keep up with research in the field.

The Conference demonstrated potentialities for research in general semantics and a considerable interest in this aspect of the field. It is my hope that this publication will stimulate more research and more rigorous research in general semantics.

K. G. J.

BEHAVIORAL APPROACHES

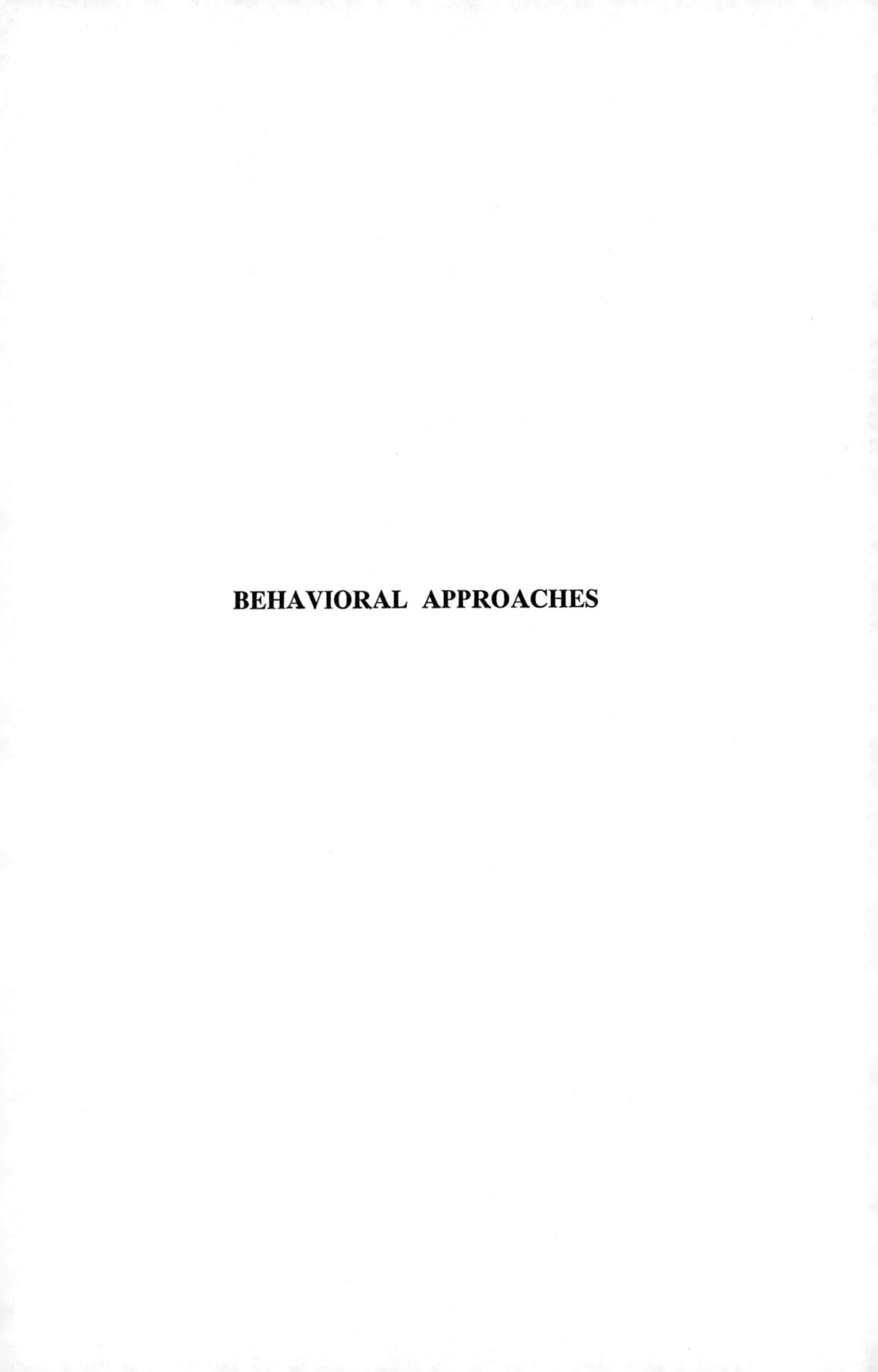

EMPIRICAL AND EXPERIMENTAL RESEARCH POSSIBILITIES IN GENERAL SEMANTICS

ALVIN A. GOLDBERG*
University of Denver

The problem with general semanticists, Lee Thayer once observed at a press conference,[1] is that too many of them spend their time trying to prove that they are right. If they really wanted to develop a scientific discipline, general semanticists would try to prove that they are wrong. A review of the fact territory would reveal that Thayer cannot easily be refuted. General semantics has many advocates, but relatively few of them have tested general semantics principles or methodology scientifically. Hayakawa, Weinberg, Chase, and others have done a fairly effective job of popularizing Korzybski, but relatively little to advance what Korzybski (1940) called the "empirical and natural science" of general semantics, a science that claims to reject "Aristotelian" or purely speculative approaches to knowledge (Rapoport, 1950). Some excellent research in general semantics has been reported by Weiss (1956 and 1959), Peters (1952), Minor (1964), Glorfeld (1965), and others, but for the most part, research in this area has not been very extensive. At the present time there is no elaborate body of research literature to turn to.

A few rather bold general semantics research projects were initiated by Johnson (1946), Rapoport (1958) and others and, as far as I can determine, not completed. In 1950, Irving J. Lee (1950) attempted to generate more research in general semantics by identifying specific

---
*The author is grateful for the assistance of Judy Goldberg, Michele Tolela Myers, and Gail E. Myers who read an initial draft of this manuscript and offered many worthwhile suggestions.
[1]*The Denver Post*, August, 1968.

problems that could be investigated, but a review of the literature would suggest that Lee stimulated more thought than action. After a lapse of eighteen years, I believe it's time to try once more.

The purpose of this paper is to generate more research in general semantics by identifying just some of the many problems that could be investigated by students of general semantics. The paper is limited to those problems that can be studied empirically and experimentally. Historical and critical research possibilities are not covered. The emphasis of the paper is on the "what," not the "how." Hence, only limited references are made to research design or measurement techniques. The paper also ignores research problems that deal with matters of importance to general semanticists but that would probably be identified as research in some other discipline.

General semantics research problems can be grouped into three broad categories: 1) studies that test fundamental assumptions that are essential to the entire system; 2) studies that focus on various aspects of general semantic theory; and 3) studies designed to measure the effectiveness of general semantics as a methodology for improving human interaction and adjustment.

Fundamental Problems

Like all sciences, general semantics is based on certain assumptions and values. It assumes that there is a reality outside of our skins, and inside too for that matter, and that man is capable of perceiving and dealing with this reality in a systematic way. Man commonly attempts to cope with reality by building language maps of it. The general semanticist asserts that man's adjustment, his sanity, even his survival is determined in large part by the "goodness of fit" between his verbal maps and "reality." Hence, accurate maps are valued. As Rapoport (1958) puts it, "an accurate map is more valuable than a beautiful map or one which is kept because it had belonged to one's ancestors" (p. 86).

On a gross level, the notion that inaccurate maps can get us into trouble seems to be rather obvious. Pilots with disorted maps have occasionally bombed their own troops rather than the enemy. Mislabeled mushrooms have killed many people. "Empty" barrels of gasoline have exploded when cigarettes have been dropped in them.

But what degree of isomorphism between map and territory is really possible or necessary? No matter how "accurate" a map or message may be, it will be distorted to some extent by the perceiver or receiver. So, in many contexts, there may be a point beyond which additional accuracy is no longer helpful.

If we operationalize "map" as an oral written message, a variety of studies could be done in the area of map-territory relationships. Individuals, for example, could be confronted with a mechanical construction task and slightly different directions for putting the pieces together could be given to the subjects in each of a number of conditions. If some directions are found to be consistently more helpful than others they could be analyzed to determine why. If we find that a number of differently designed maps are just as effective in getting the job done, we will know more about the level of accuracy or isomorphism between map and territory that is needed under certain circumstances.

Solomon Asch (1946) has done some relevant research along these lines. The Asch research consisted of dividing subjects into two groups and presenting one group with the following task :

Here is a list of characteristics that belong to a particular person. Read them carefully and try to form an impression of the kind of person described.

> intelligent—skillful—industrious—cold—determined—practical —cautious

Now select from the following list those traits which are most in accordance with the picture of the individual you have formed. Underline one in each pair.

1. generous—ungenerous
2. shrewd—wise
3. unhappy—happy
4. irritable—good natured
5. humorous—humorless
6. sociable—unsociable
7. popular—unpopular

8. unreliable—reliable
9. important—insignificant
10. ruthless—humane
11. good-looking—unattractive
12. persistent—unstable
13. frivolous—serious
14. restrained—talkative
15. self-centered—altruistic
16. imaginative—hard-headed
17. strong—weak
18. dishonest—honest

The second group of subjects in the Asch research was given the same task with one difference. The word "warm" was substituted for the word "cold" in the list of adjectives and this one change had a significant effect on the responses of the subjects. An unlimited number of studies could be done using Asch's basic design. What words other than "warm" and "cold" produce major differences in our perception of a fact-territory? What would happen if the fact-territory or referent were changed? That is, would the responses of subjects be the same if the adjectives used in the Asch study were applied, let's say, to a woman rather than a man? What adjectives influence the responses of subjects to cultures, nations, products, industries, minority groups, or educational institutions?

In the Asch research, the subjects responded only to verbal stimuli. Would the responses of subjects be the same if they are actually introduced to someone and then given a list of adjectives that supposedly describe that person? Would it matter if the adjectives described that person accurately or not? If subjects who were given an opportunity to observe someone, perhaps on film or videotape, were then given a list of adjectives that did not describe that person accurately, would their impressions of that person be influenced more by their observations or by the linguistic map they received? It is quite likely that subjects would differ from one another in this respect and we could call those who are influenced more by words "intensionally-oriented" and those who are influenced more by observations "extensionally-oriented." (Incidentally, if refined, this particular measurement technique could be used to measure the effects of general semantic training. Over time, general semantic students should become less intensional.) What would be the effect of giving subjects the verbal description of a person before they observed that person on film? Would they tend to see only those things that verified their map, as general semantic theory suggests? To what extent is the perception of an event biased by the commentary that accompanies it? Different sets of adjectives could be read aloud during the showing of a film and the reactions of subjects to the different "commentaries" could be compared.

The general semanticists tell us that the "universe is a product of the observer as well as the observed." This suggests that the personality, experience, or state of the perceiver will influence map-territory correspondence. That is, the same map may be accurate for individual A and inaccurate for individual B because A and B react to the "same" events differently. Empirical and experimental studies of the way different subjects deal with or respond to language would enable the general semanticist to say not merely that the map should fit the territory, but how that fit could be best achieved in different contexts and with different people.

Research by Ed Black (1955) suggests that in addition to map and territory the general semanticist should be concerned about the relationship between any particular map or message and those that precede and follow it. Black found some support for the hypothesis that group discussions are most likely to go astray when sudden shifts occur in levels of abstraction, but additional tests of this hypothesis are needed. Black's data also seem to indicate that group problem-solving is impeded when no group member uses language that is sufficiently abstract. This, too, could be studied. As a matter of fact, discussion groups are ideal for testing general semantic principles. A researcher, for example, could give a number of objective problems to hundreds of discussion groups and identify groups that are effective in solving those problems and groups that perform poorly. The language behavior of the groups on both ends of the effectiveness continuum could then be analyzed to determine if they differed significantly in their use of allness statements, failure to index, or along other dimensions general semanticists consider important.

Research that would go beyond a concern with map-territory relationships and focus more directly on the relationship between language and behavior is also needed. Korzybski believed, along with Sapir and Whorf, that human thought and behavior are a reflection of linguistic habits (Rapoport, 1958). Korzybski further believed that if an individual's language habits are modified in a significant way, his other patterns of behavior will change significantly also. The metalinguistic hypothesis (Hertzler, 1965)—that a person's language is a major determinant of his thoughts and actions—has been referred to as the Whorf, the Sapir-Whorf, and as the Korzybski-Sapir-Whorf hypothesis. This hypothesis, which is basic to the entire general semantic system, is extremely difficult to test directly. Much of the evidence in support of linguistic determinism relativity (Brown, 1958) or what Hertzler (1965) calls the "metalinguistic position" comes from anthropological linguistics. The data, however, are far from conclusive. They consist primarily of a comparison of modern European languages with Chinese, African, and American Indian languages. The differences in terminology and the way words are used by different language groups seem to suggest that language backgrounds and habits influence the way individuals see, hear, think, and otherwise behave. Korzybski applied the hypothesis that language habits are determinants of behavior not just to language groups, but to specific individuals as well.

Relatively few researchers have attempted to test the Korzybski-Sapir-Whorf hypothesis experimentally. Anatol Rapoport (1958) is an exception. In 1958 he reported the design of a fascinating experiment that was to be carried out at the Mental Health Research Institute at the University of Michigan. According to Rapoport, the research had been partially financed by the International Society for General Semantics. As far as I know, the research was never carried out. At least I have not been able to find published research findings related to this project.

Rapoport's design is a promising one, and since the study itself has apparently never been done, it remains a good research possibility. Briefly, the proposed study involves the use of a micro language consisting of 9 words or nonsense syllables; three subject words, three verbs, and three objects. Six grammars can be developed for these words; that is, six different rules for structuring a subject, verb, and object to form a sentence. The plan Rapoport reported involved teaching the six "languages" to six different groups of subjects. Some subjects would learn a language similar to English in structure (subject-verb-object), and others would learn something quite different. Pictures would be used to identify the territory that the various language structures refer to.

According to Rapoport, if the grammatical order that corresponds to English is learned faster, it tells us something about the effects of language structure on learning. If, instead of learning one grammar or language, subjects are taught a set of sentences from all six languages so that the actor is first in some sentences, second in others, and last in still others, and if the subjects of the sentences are learned quickest, then the verbs, with objects learned the slowest—no matter what position the words are actually in—it would be a sign that individuals carry the structure of their native language "in their heads" and lend support to the Sapir-Whorf hypothesis. Rapoport points out that the hypothesis would also be supported if, in a sentence where the actor and object are reversible (the woman kissed the child; the child kissed the woman), subjects learn the same word faster when it is an actor or subject than when it is an object. The hypothesis would be dramatically supported if it is discovered that subjects who internalize the nonsense syllable language with its unique grammar begin to learn nonsense words better when they are in a position that is grammatically appropriate for the experimental language and not for their native language.

The studies dealing with map-territory and map-thought-behavior relationships that have been suggested are merely a few of the unlimited number of investigations that could be conducted in these areas. At this point, let's consider research designed to test some of the basic formulations of general semantics.

Basic Formulations

Field or case studies of communication in many different settings would enable the general semanticist to make assertions about how language is used that are empirically based. How does communication break down in various situations and what happens when individuals make plans and reach agreements? Would the "bad" language habits that Korzybski identified, such as allness statements, signal reactions, or expressions of identification adequately explain what happens when things go poorly, and would such formulations as proper order of evaluation, consciousness of abstracting, and delayed reactions help us understand what happens when things go well? To what extent, in other words, will the general semantics map fit the territory?

An unlimited number of territories can be studied and analyzed from a general semantics point of view. How do people communicate in the home, the conference room, or the office? It was suggested earlier in this paper that interaction could be tape recorded and the tapes of groups on both ends of an effectiveness continuum could be analyzed and compared to determine if general semantic formulations can account at all for the differences. If it is discovered, for example, that participants in conference groups that are less effective (according to some commonly accepted criterion) make more allness statements and index less than participants in effective conference groups, we would have some empirical evidence to support certain aspects of general semantic theory. If we consistently found the reverse, or that allness statements and indexing have various effects depending on the circumstances, we could—in good scientific fashion—revise or refine the theory.

An alternative to ranking groups and analyzing the extremes is merely to study human communication in various kinds of situations. How do people communicate who are involved in divorce trials, strikes, sit-ins, door-to-door selling, counseling, research, teaching, mediation, decision-making conferences, and the like? How adequately do general semantic formulations explain the behavior of the participants caught up in these events? Do mediators and counselors exhibit certain language habits that are not characteristic of the speech of lawyers or salesmen? How does the language of advocacy in the courtroom and other conflict situations differ from the language of inquiry in, let's say, the research laboratory?

Instead of focusing on groups, the researcher could conduct case studies of individuals who exhibit certain behaviors or who are identified with particular roles. A general semantic theoretical framework could be used to study the speech of the mentally ill, the anxious, or the depressed. Researchers could study the language behavior of high achievers and low achievers, of conformists and deviants, of the highly motivated and those who don't seem to care, of leaders and subordinates, of the ororverbalized and the underverbalized, of—as Harvey, Hunt, and Schroder (1961) suggest —"abstract" persons and "concrete" persons, of those who tend to be thing-oriented and those who tend to be people-oriented. They could even study those who exhibit the "either-or" syndrome reflected in this paragraph.

A major concern of the general semanticist is the way problems in human affairs are generated. Descriptive studies of human interaction in groups could focus only on conflicts and misunderstandings to see if such difficulties are often the result of or at least influenced by the inappropriate use of language.

Many people, according to the general semanticist, believe that it is possible to determine the "real" meaning of every word, and this fallacious notion may get them into trouble. Surveys could be conducted to determine how prevalent this belief really is, and to see if believers and non-believers differ from one another in education, adjustment, flexibility, openness, or any other dimension. Surveys and group comparisons of a similar nature could be run to determine who and how many "falsely" think of words as unique events that can be considered apart from the sentences in which they appear; misunderstand the function of a dictionary; consistently fail to recognize how speakers are using multiordinal words; never seem to be aware that what is being said may not be what they assume is being said; believe that everyone perceives events the way they do; have no awareness of the abstracting process; often refuse to take action until "all" of the evidence is in; believe in single principles designed to solve all of life's problems; are totally committed to a specific religious or political dogma; believe only what they see or immediately understand perfectly what they read or observe. Many of these beliefs and attitudes may be part of the same "allness" syndrome. On the other hand, we may discover that there are many different combinations of beliefs about language and that holders of these beliefs are likely to have other characteristics such as rigidity or closed-mindedness.

12   Alvin A. Goldberg

General semantic theory claims that there is a relationship between language habits and sanity. Much of the research dealing with the language of schizophrenics would certainly support this belief. However, more research is needed to determine if the language behavior of the mentally ill is structured the way general semantic theory suggests. Is it true that the psychotic or the neurotic is, let's say, less conscious of abstracting, or fails to recognize that absolute sameness is impossible? A questionnaire instrument could be developed containing items that deal with many of the principles of general semantics, and the questionnaire responses of subjects could be correlated with their MMPI scores or other indicators of adjustment. The questionnaire responses could also be factor analyzed to identify the factors that comprise language attitude and belief systems.

According to general semantics, an awareness of both similarities and differences is important. Studies could be done to determine how individuals who tend only to see similarities differ from those who tend only to see differences. We would hypothesize, on the basis of theory, that strongly prejudiced individuals are less likely to see differences in others. On the other hand, "primitives," according to Irving J. Lee (1941), appear to be overly concerned with differences. Lee points out that the Bakairi of Brazil have names for different species of parrots but the generic name "parrot" is not part of their language. The effects of seeing or not seeing differences could be examined.

The mechanism of neglecting differences and identifying one situation with another can be investigated. Lee describes a student who obtained the signatures of his classmates on two worthwhile petitions. When he gave them a third, most of the students signed it without realizing that the petition, among other things, condemned the signers. How easy it is to establish such identification and what are the factors that influence the pattern?

Henry N. Peters (1952), and Gene Minor (1964) used the Stroop Test (1935) to study the behavior of individuals who are intensional and extensional in their orientations. Other measures of intension and extension could be developed. Individuals who respond to facts first could be compared with those who react to speech first and then facts, to determine if the two groups differ the way general semantic theory tells us they should. We may find that the same individuals are intensional under some circumstances and extensional under other circumstances.

Research by Robert Rosenthal (1966) and by Rosenthal and Jacobson (1968) provides strong support for the notion that intensional behavior can be easily generated and that it can have some rather disturbing effects. Rosenthal found that psychologists consistently perceived rats randomly labeled "bright" as outperforming rats randomly labeled "dull" and Rosenthal and Jacobson discovered that teachers perceived students arbitrarily given high IQ scores to be smarter than those arbitrarily given low IQ scores. Neil Friedman (1967), in his book *The Social Nature of Psychological Research*, reports that many of the psychological experimenters he observed unintentionally biased their results in a direction that supported their hypotheses. Gerald Marwell (1969) revealed an understanding of self-reflexiveness in his review of Friedman's book. "How do we know," Marwell asked, "that Mr. Friedman's 'experimenter effects' . . . . were not caused by the experimenter who instructed the experimenters?" Mr. Marwell's point is well taken, and his comments suggest that by studying aspects of intension and extension in research settings we may gain insight into self-reflexiveness.

In a sense, many of the studies in the area of ethos or source credibility deal with the effects of intensionality. It was discovered, for example, that women respond significantly less favorably to the same article if the author of the publication is identified as a woman rather than a man. Both male and female subjects react differently to a quote depending on the source it is attributed to. Research has also demonstrated that subjects are likely to respond more positively to the tape recording of a dull discussion if they are told that the discussants think highly of them and want them to become members of their group. It has been found that members of a political party respond more favorably to a speech if told beforehand that the talk supports their party's point of view. Much more research could be done along these lines to determine how a person's set or frame of reference influences his evaluations. Other studies of intensionality could focus on the extent to which individuals believe that Peyton

Place, Mission Impossible, Dick Tracy, Playboy, or various daytime soap operas accurately describe reality.

Individuals with two-valued orientations could probably be found by administering Lickert-type questionnaires to large numbers of subjects and selecting those who consistently score items on the extreme ends of the continuum. Once identified, studies could be run to determine if a two-valued orientation actually causes the difficulties general semantic theory claims it does. Groups could be formed, for example, of subjects with two-valued orientations and their problem-solving effectiveness or the number of conflicts they have could be compared with the performance of groups consisting of subjects with multivalued orientations.

The word is not the thing, the general semanticist tells us, but many people act as if it is. An unlimited number of studies could be done dealing with the emotional reactions people have to various words. One approach to this type of research would be to measure the GSR's of subjects when they hear the word; another would be to measure the connotative meanings of words by using Osgood's *Semantic Differential* (1957). A third approach might consist of empirical studies of individuals or groups who deliberately attempt to influence behavior with words, such as faith healers, witch doctors, voodoo practitioners, Trobrianders (who believe that magicians can say certain magic words to help grow plants), and the like.

"Four-letter words" have a tendency to generate strong reactions on the part of many people. It would be interesting to study the effects these words have on the reactions of people to the words that follow them. I suspect that if subjects were tested over the information in a particular statement, their test scores would be significantly lower than the scores of a control group if the statement presented to the experimental group was preceded by a "four-letter word" and the control group's statement was not.

Hayakawa (1941, 1964) and others refer to abstraction "ladders" and they assert that some words are more abstract than others. "Farm asset" is more abstract than "animal" and "animal" is more abstract than "cow." Although this seems to make a great deal of sense, it is conceivable that the abstraction ladder is meaningful logically and not psychologically. Studies could be done to determine if individuals tend to agree with one another on levels of abstraction. Farmers, perhaps, might agree that "cow" is less abstract than "farm asset," but bankers or accountants might put "farm asset" on a lower rung than "cows." Even if the ladder has little psychological validity, it might still be worthwhile. To test its theoretical value, studies could be done to determine if individuals differ from one another in the level of abstraction they generally operate at. If they do, differences between low and high level abstractors could be studied.

Research could be done on signal and symbol reactions. Can the two types of reactions be readily distinguished? If they can, do individuals characteristically react one way or the other? If they do, symbol reactors could be compared with signal reactors to determine if they operate more effectively and manage to avoid the kinds of problems general semantic theory associates with undelayed, automatic, impulsive behavior.

The general semanticist is interested in more than how man uses language and the relationships between reality, language, thought, and action. He not only wants to understand language behavior, he wants to improve it. Hence, the final section of this paper is devoted to possible research studies dealing with the effectiveness of general semantics as a methodology for improving man's personal adjustment and capacity for survival.

Methodology

General semantics identifies the inadequacies of our language structures and the problems it causes us. It also contains a methodology for improving our language behavior so we can, as it were, lead more satisfying and productive lives. The methodology consists essentially of the extensional devices (indexing, dating, the use of etc., hyphens, quotes, etc.,) and a variety of what Wendell Johnson (1946) called "practical devices and techniques" (p. 237).

Korzybski (1940) once wrote that approximately ninety per cent of his seminar students derived "definite benefits in their professional work, as well as in personal life" from a knowledge of general semantics. Others who have taught the subject claim to have noted similar effects. The Coleman (1963) survey of college teachers on general semantics revealed that thirty-eight per cent felt they observed "discernible changes in student attitudes and behavior as a result of the study of general semantics" (p. 463). The remaining respondents indicated that they did not have enough data to judge. A number of systematic attempts to investigate the effects of a course in general semantics have been reported (See Trainer (1938), Johnson (1958), Croft (1960), Hansen (1962), Lauer (1963), True (1964), Minor (1964), Goldberg (1965)).

Wendell Johnson (1961), once summarized the responses of his students to a course in general semantics. He found that students improved significantly during a semester in their knowledge of the subject. His students also reported that they benefited in many personal ways from the experience. Class members indicated that the course made them less rigid, dogmatic, and opinionated; they felt that they were better able to understand and accept others and themselves. Some of Johnson's data were obtained from a final examination which included a question that asked the students to describe and discuss the personal meaning general semantics had for them.

Experimental research dealing with the effectiveness of general semantics has many pitfalls. Among other things, it is difficult to randomly assign subjects to control and experimental groups; keeping everything the "same" in the experimental groups and control groups except for the independent variable is almost impossible; determining exactly what the independent variable—the training approach—should consist of is a major problem; and subject improvement or change is very difficult to measure. Nevertheless, such research is vital if the value of general semantics as a methodology or therapy is to be determined on the basis of anything other than a priori grounds.

General semantics is often used to enhance a course dealing primarily with some other subject matter. Units on general semantics can be found in English courses, speech courses, sociology courses, etc. The value of these units should be studied. A good model for such research is provided by Glorfeld (1965) who found that general semantics was helpful in teaching freshmen composition. It would also be worthwhile to do research on the effectiveness of different approaches to the teaching of general semantics itself. Is it better, for example, to teach it inductively or deductively? Should the principles be taught first, should they be taught after the extensional devices are considered, or is a non-linear approach best? Should a student's age, maturity, personality and expectations be taken into consideration? There no doubt is a difference between an intellectual knowledge of general semantics and a gut level knowledge. How can it be taught so that students develop more than just a superficial understanding of the subject?

If general semantics has some therapeutic value, if the insights it offers and the language devices and techniques it recommends really make a difference, this difference should be measurable. Research is desperately needed in this area to determine if the claims made for general semantics as a therapy and methodology are legitimate. Testimonials are not enough. Scientific evidence of its effectiveness is needed, and if the evidence does not fully support the claims, the claims should be properly qualified and new devices and techniques should be tested.

The basic question is—do individuals who have received training in general semantics and who exhibit an appropriate change in their consciousness of abstracting and language behavior, improve in other ways? Do they have less anxiety, solve problems more effectively, engage in fewer conflicts or misunderstandings with others, experience more personal satisfaction, or develop a better self concept? Are they perceived by others as being better adjusted or easier to get along with? Do they communicate more effectively as measured by the technique based on the game "Password" developed by Charles Vick (1967)? In other words, what are the effects of training in general semantics? A basic design for experimental research in this area could consist of randomly dividing subjects into control and experimental groups, giving the experimental subjects a course in general semantics and the control subjects a course in something else such as phonetics or the sociology of language or linguistics, and then placing experimental and control subjects in a variety of situations where their behavior or test performance on many different dependent variables could be measured and compared. (Michele Tolela [Myers] (1967) used a variation of this design to study the effectiveness of T-group training.) Incidentally, the experimental and control subjects could consist of individuals labeled "mentally ill" or "neurotic" or "healthy."

A number of hypotheses related to the effectiveness, not of the entire methodology but of different aspects of it, could also be tested. What do people experience, for example, when they deliberately refrain from speaking? What are the effects of knowing that a word may have many uses or that our assumptions about what another person means may be wrong? Does consciousness of abstracting or the awareness that one can't say all about anything make a difference in one's behavior? What are the effects of deliberately taking the other side for a few minutes of an issue we feel strongly about or of trying to admire someone we hate? Does the use of etc., or of the hyphen or dating actually reduce conflicts or heated arguments? Do people act differently toward others if they refrain from labeling them? Will training people to recognize that "identity" or "absolute sameness" is impossible make a difference in their behavior? What are the effects of seeing more differences and fewer similarities?

If trained, individuals can tell the difference between colors that they normally would not be able to differentiate. Would training in color differentiation cause an individual to differentiate among people and avoid lumping all Jews or all Negroes or all college students together? Would the tendency to overgeneralize about groups be overcome by training people to describe the unique characteristics of events? What are the effects of training people to avoid responding emotionally to words? How can people be trained to be aware of non-verbal levels and what are the effects of such training? Is training in symbol as opposed to signal reactions beneficial?

Count Korzybski felt that general semantics was an important part of what will one day be a science of man. If individuals who are interested in general semantics as a theory, a philosophy, or as a methodology can be encouraged to actually conduct research in general semantics, Korzybski's description of general semantics as an empirical science with material content could in time become an accurate map of the territory.

REFERENCES

Arnold, William E. and James C. McCroskey, 1968, "The Application of Behavioral Research Methods to the Study of General Semantics Principles," paper presented at the International Conference of General Semantics, Denver Hilton Hotel, August 8, 1968.

Asch, Solomon J., 1946, "Forming Impressions of Personality," *Journal of Abnormal and Social Psychology,* 41, 258-290.

————, 1946, "Forming Impressions of Personality," *Journal of Abnormal and Social Psychology* (1946) 41, 258-290.

————, 1952, *Social Psychology,* New York: Prentice-Hall.

Black, Edwin B., 1955, "A Consideration of the Rhetorical Causes of Breakdown in Discussion," *Speech Monographs* (1955), XXII, 15 ——.

Brown, Roger W., 1958, *Words and Things,* Glencoe, Illinois: The Free Press.

Case, Keith E., 1952, "General Semantics: A Technique in Reading Social Relationships." *General Semantics Bulletin* (1952), 8/9.

Chase, Stuart, 1952, *The Power of Words,* New York: Harcourt Brace.

Coleman, Cecil J., 1963, "Courses in General Semantics in American Higher Education," *ETC.* (1963) XIX (4) 463.

Croft, Wilfred F., 1960, "General Semantics and the Teaching of Science," *ETC.* VII, December.

Friedman, Neil, 1967, *The Social Nature of Psychological Research,* New York: Basic Books, Inc.

Glorfeld, Louis E., 1965, "The Relation Between the Study of the Principles of General Semantics and Writing Ability in Freshman Composition," Unpublished Dissertation, University of Denver.

Goldberg, Alvin, 1965, "The Effects of a Laboratory Course in General Semantics," *ETC.* (1962), XXII, 19-24.

Gorman, Margaret, 1962, *General Semantics and Contemporary Thomism,* Bison Book 131, Nebraska Univ. Press.

Hansen, Helen M., 1962, "A Study of Applications of General Semantics Made by Students During a Course in Interpersonal Communication," Unpublished thesis, University of Denver.

Harvey, O. J., D. E. Hunt, H. M. Schroeder, 1961, *Conceptual Systems and Personality Organization,* New York: Wiley.

Hayakawa, Samuel I., 1964, *Language in Thought and Action,* New York: Harcourt Brace.

Hertzler, Joyce O., 1965, *A Sociology of Language,* New York: Random House.

Johnson, Kenneth G., 1958, "Patterns of Response to a Semantic

Differential Test Before and After Training in General Semantics," *General Semantics Bulletin* (1958), 22 & 23, 28-34.

Johnson, Wendell, 1946, *People in Quandaries,* New York: Harper & Brothers.

—————, 1961, "Some Effects of a Course in General Semantics," *ETC.* (1961), XVIII (3) 315-346.

Korzybski, Alfred, 1940, "A Memorandum," Chicago: Institute of General Semantics.

—————, 1958, *Science and Sanity,* Lakeville, Connecticut. The International Non-Aristotelian Library Publishing Co., 4th Ed.

Lauer, Rachel M., 1963, "Effects of a General Semantics Course Upon Some Fifth Grade Children," *General Semantics Bulletin* (1963/64) 30 & 31, 106-112.

Lee, Irving J., 1941, *Language Habits in Human Affairs,* New York: Harper.

—————, 1950, "On the Varieties of Research in General Semantics," *ETC.* (1950), VII. Spring 170-179. Also in *General Semantics Bulletin* (1949/50) 1 & 2, 10-15.

Livingston, Howard, 1965, "An Investigation of the Effect of Instruction in General Semantics on 'Critical Reading' Ability," *General Semantics Bulletin* (1965/66), 32 & 33, 93-94.

Marwell, Gerald, 1969, "Capsule Commentaries," *Psychiatry and Social Science Review,* 111, February, 30.

Minor, Gene, 1964, "The Relationship of Various Characteristics to the Stroop Color-Word Test," Unpublished Thesis, University of Denver.

Murray, Elwood, 1953, *Integrative Speech,* New York: Dryden Press.

Osgood, Charles E., George J. Suci, Percy H. Tannenbaum, 1957, *The Measurement of Meaning,* Urbana, Illinois: U. of Illinois Press.

Peters, Henry N., 1952, "Supraordinality of Association and Maladjustment," *ETC.* X, 1952, 37-45.

Rapoport, Anatol, 1950, *Science and the Goals of Man,* New York: Harper and Bros.

—————, 1958, "General Semantics: Its Place in Science," *ETC.* (1958) XVI, 1, 80-97.

Rosenthal, Robert, 1966, *Experimental Effects in Behavioral Research,* New York: Appleton-Century-Crofts.

—————, and Lenore Jacobson, 1968, *Pygmalion in the Classroom,* New York: Holt, Rinehart.

Stroop, R., 1935, "Studies in Interference in Serial Verbal Reactions," *Journal of Experimental Psychology* (1935) XVIII, 1935, 643-661.

Tolela, Michele, 1967, "Effects of T-Group Training and Cognitive

Learning on Small Group Effectiveness," Unpublished Dissertation, University of Denver.

Trainer, Joseph C., 1938, "Experimental Results of Training in General Semantics Upon Intelligence" (Test Series), *Papers from the First American Congress on General Semantics,* New York.

True, Sally Ralston, 1964, "A Study of the Relation of General Semantics and Creativity," *General Semantics Bulletin* (1963/64) 30 & 31, 100-105. (Abstract of doctoral dissertation, University of Wisconsin.)

Vick, Charles F., 1967, "Similarity and the Communication of Meaning," Unpublished Dissertation, University of Denver.

Weinberg, Harry L., 1959, *Levels of Knowing and Existence: Studies in General Semantics,* New York: Harper.

Weiss, Thomas M., 1956, "Experimental Study Applying Non-Aristotelian Principles in Measurement of Adjustment and Non-Adjustment," *Science Education* (1956) XL, October, 312-316.

—————, 1959, "The Construction and Validation of an 'Is of Identity' Tests," *General Semantics Bulletin* (1959) 24 and 25, 69-80.

KORZYBSKIAN MODELS FOR RESEARCH

KENNETH G. JOHNSON
University of Wisconsin-Milwaukee

In the course of his teaching, 1934-1950, Alfred Korzybski developed and used a variety of diagrams in his lectures and seminars. The best known, of course, is the structural differential (Figure 1) (Korzybski, 1933, 1958), which he described as "a structural summary of the whole non-aristotelian system" (p. 13). Beginning in 1943 the "Silent and Verbal Levels" diagram (Figure 2) became a focal point of his seminar presentations (Korzybski, 1950, 1951).

What I propose to do is to examine these two diagrams as models and as sources of research possibilities.

Evaluating the models

A good model symbolizes the essential features of what we are talking about in a simple, parsimonious way. It might be considered a map of a "universe of discourse" and, like any map, its value depends upon how well it represents those aspects of the territory we are interested in.

There is, then, no single or simple standard for judging models; the value of any given model depends upon our purpose. The information theory model (Shannon and Weaver, 1949), for example, may be adequate and useful as a model of electronic communication, but because it assumes a perfect correspondence of symbol systems encoded and decoded, it is a naive model of human communication. Johnson and Klare (1961) surveyed the development of general models of communication research. They summarized and to some degree evaluated a variety of models, some of which might be useful in general semantic research, and provided a bibliography of articles on models of communication. More recently King (1968) developed

24   Kenneth G. Johnson

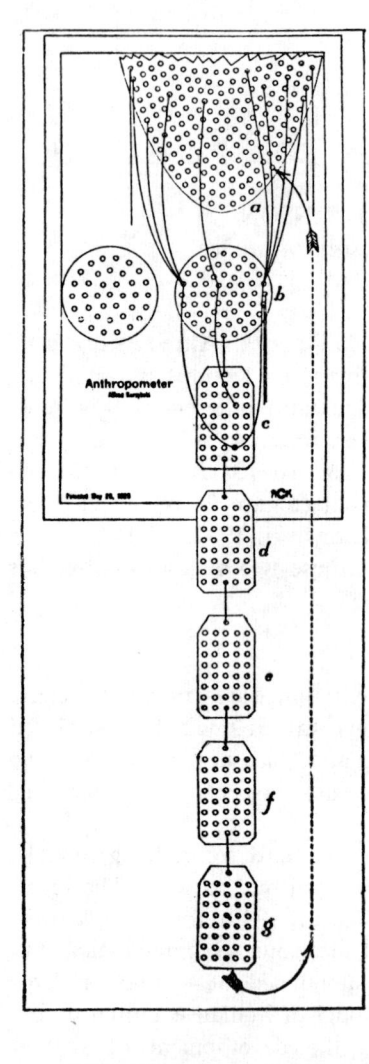

(A) EVENT LEVEL (*Silent*) (1) The deeper process level "a mad dance of electrons, something acted upon by everything else and reacting upon everything else"; (2) a variable *different* all the time; (3) "something" which we do not recognize directly; (4) given as result of tested inferences; (5) the broken-off line indicates that the parabola could be extended to infinity; the holes represent characteristics, infinite in number.

(B) OBJECTIVE LEVEL (*Silent*) (1) What a nervous system abstracts from the *event*, fairly permanent, which we recognize directly; (2) finite size, with large, yet definite number of characteristics, fewer than the event; (3) a first-order abstraction; (4) our life facts, extensional facts (including "feelings" inside-our-skin); (5) each "object" unique a relative variable different for every observer, and in process (sometimes slow); (6) the level of ordinary sense impressions.

(C) DESCRIPTIVE LEVEL (1) Labels and statements (second-order abstractions), which are used to represent the above first-order abstraction; (2) words standing for *some* characteristics of the object, the "meaning" of the term here being fixed by definition, any term being used in many ways subject only to explanation by example; (3) for predictability these statements must be similar in structure to the event and object levels.

(D) INFERENTIAL LEVEL (1) Labels and statements (third-order abstractions) which are used to represent the second-order verbal abstractions; (2) come from speaking about descriptive statements; (3) more general statements applying more widely than (C); (4) since more tentative and less probable they are to be tested by going back to lower-order abstractions; (5) inferences made by human nervous systems must not be projected out on to (A) and (B); inferential terms must not be objectified and made to stand for "things" (A and B) when they arise as statements about other statements.

(E) INFERENTIAL LEVEL Higher-order abstractions, statements about statements, etc.

(F and G) INFERENTIAL LEVELS Higher-order abstractions, statements about statements about statements, etc.

Figure I.   Structural Differential.
This diagram of the structural differential is reproduced from *Time-Binding: The General Theory* (Korzybski, 1954, p. 35) with the kind permission of the Korzybski estate. The descriptions of the levels are adapted from *Language Habits in Human Affairs* (Lee, 1941, pp. 264-265).

Korzybskian Models for Research

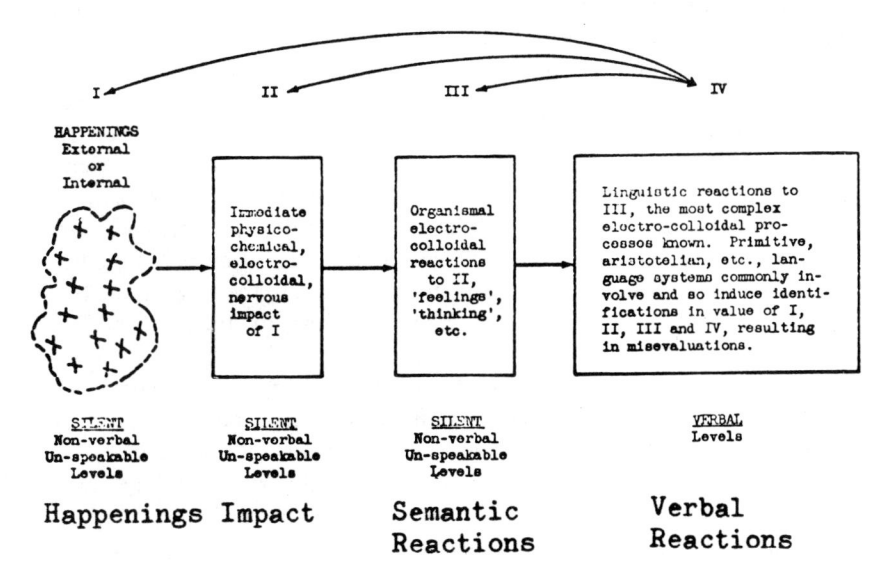

I	II	III	IV
HAPPENINGS External or Internal	Immediate physico-chemical, electro-colloidal, nervous impact of I	Organismal electro-colloidal reactions to II, 'feelings', 'thinking', etc.	Linguistic reactions to III, the most complex electro-colloidal processes known. Primitive, aristotelian, etc., language systems commonly involve and so induce identifications in value of I, II, III and IV, resulting in misevaluations.
SILENT Non-verbal Un-speakable Levels	SILENT Non-verbal Un-speakable Levels	SILENT Non-verbal Un-speakable Levels	VERBAL Levels
Happenings	**Impact**	**Semantic Reactions**	**Verbal Reactions**

Figure 2. Korzybski's "Silent and Verbal Levels" Diagram[*]

Note: The words set in bold face at the bottom of the diagram have been added by the author to serve as convenient labels for the four stages.

---

[*] "...even though it becomes necessary to investigate different aspects of the processes of abstracting for purposes of analysis, we should be aware that these different aspects are parts of one whole continuous process of normal human life." (Korzybski, 1951, p. 172.)

an "event-structure model for communication" which, more than any previous model, attempts to explore the development of "meaning."

My purpose is not to compare models but to evaluate the two Korzybskian models against certain criteria and to generate a number of research possibilities from them.

First, a good model should *define the universe of discourse* and provide a unified framework for discussing that universe. The "universe of discourse" of the structural differential is broad indeed, ranging as it does from sub-atomic "events" to the highest orders of abstraction man can generate. It focuses on *orders of abstraction,* an aspect neglected in other models, and provides a framework for discussing that universe. The "Silent and Verbal Levels" diagram (to be referred to here as the SVL diagram) covers the same universe but from a somewhat different point of view; it focuses on the individual perceiver-reactor.

Second, a good model should be *similar in structure* to the structure or process it attempts to map. Both Korzybskian models seem to meet this criterion at a rather high order of abstraction. There are undoubtedly an almost infinite number of sub-structures that they make no attempt to map. And, like linguistic maps, these models are static representations of dynamic processes.

Third, the model should *aid communication* by providing an efficient vocabulary. We can save time and effort by talking about "events," "semantic reactions," etc., once these terms are defined. The model should permit us to talk at high orders of abstraction, yet be reasonably sure that these abstractions refer to the same events or relationships. The extensive use of the structural differential at this conference suggests that it can indeed aid communication. The SVL diagram is less widely used, but I have found it a most useful aid in communicating in the classroom.

The fourth characteristic is closely related to the third: the model should be *general* enough to map a variety of situations, yet detailed enough to be relevant to specific problems. For many purposes the two diagrams seem to meet this criterion. Each focuses on somewhat different aspects of the process of abstraction and represent different orders of abstraction. It might prove valuable to make a series of models representing different orders of abstraction: detailed models could be designed to "plug in" to the more general, abstract models.

Fifth, a good model should *include all of the major variables* in the universe of discourse. Just what constitutes a "major" variable depends on the purpose of the model (or the user of the model). In one area of research or theory, selective perception may play a major role; in another area it may be unimportant. Feedback is a major variable in some models; in others it is absent or can be added if it seems important.

Both of the Korzybskian models focus on the process of abstracting, which is only a part of the process of evaluating or communicating. Neither, as drawn, bring in interaction between individuals or the feedback such interaction would necessarily involve. However, interaction and feedback can be added to the SVL diagram by linking two or more such diagrams to create a communication "chain." Wendell Johnson (1946, 1948) presents an elaboration of this kind. Other writers have modified these basic diagrams to include additional variables. Bois (1966) has added the "semantic reactor" to the structural differential. Meyers (1966) and Payne (1968) have created minor modifications of the SVL diagram.

Sixth, much of the value of a model lies in its ability to *clarify relationships* among variables. A graphic model, like a map, can often do a better job of showing structure and relations than a verbal description. It has the advantage of being easily remembered and readily reproduced. Korzybski developed both of these diagrams specifically to clarify relationships in the process of abstracting and emphasized the importance of *using* the structural differential as a training device in developing "consciousness of abstracting."

The seventh criterion, the *heuristic value* of a model, is the one I am most concerned about in his paper. To what extent does the model suggest new relationships, new variables, new direction for research? This criterion may be difficult to apply, however, because a model that appears sterile to one research may prove pregnant to another. The second part of this paper will explore research possibilities suggested by the two models.

Models have certain other values that cannot readily be made into criteria for evaluating them. For example, model A may be similar in structure to model B in an entirely different field of study; reasoning by analogy may then lead to new hypotheses and new directions for research. General Systems theory is based on just such a search for similarity of structure.

As we use models we should be aware that a scientist, like an artist, may fall in love with his model and become blind to its flaws.

Hueristic Value: An Examination of the Models for Research Possibilities

What follows is a kind of one-man brainstorming session using the two models as stimuli. Since the resulting "research possibilities" will reflect the observer fully as much as the observed, I should begin by admitting my biases. My experience is primarily with behavioral research using experimental or survey methods. Other papers in this volume reflect quite different approaches.

The suggestions for research are by no means fully developed "designs" for research. Considerable ingenuity may be needed in some cases to devise testable hypotheses, to define terms operationally, to design tests or observational techniques, to select effective analytic schemes, etc. Nor do I mean to imply that these suggestions could emerge only from these models. Many of them might just as readily emerge from other models or no model at all. And finally, I do not mean to imply that none of this research has been done. In some cases I refer to specific studies as examples of what has been done, but I have not made a search of the literature to find out the present state of research on all of these topics. With these limitations clearly in mind, let us examine the SVL diagram.

The four stages in the SVL diagram (Figure 2) could be studied separately or, more profitably, by relating each stage to the other stages in the diagram. We are seeking relationships: what varies with what. If we find two phenomena varying together, we cannot assume a cause-effect relationship. However, with careful design of our research and with replication, cause-effect relationships may be established. As Johnson (1946) points out, "Whether in the laboratory or from moment to moment in everday life, what one aims to accomplish through scientific method can be summarized in one word: *prediction.*" Westley (1958) claims, "Science does not blush at attempting to establish and confirm causal connections. When we have found invariances between classes of event and have cast them in a form in which the conditions consistently yield the predicted events, there is no reason to back away from the implication of causality. Perhaps no feature of scientific inquiry so sharply distinguishes it from other branches of scholarship."

"Happenings," then, as the term is used in this diagram, are of interest primarily for their effect on the later stages. They may be naturally occurring, staged, or filmed happenings, depending upon our purpose. They may consist of words or other symbols, written or spoken, if we look upon these as triggering impacts and reactions. Because of the problem of replication, we frequently prefer happenings that can be reproduced, e.g., taped, filmed, or printed materials. However, happenings of this kind may be obvious "experimental conditions" to the subjects, and the results of our research may be questionable or of limited generality for this reason.

Stage II as defined by Korzybski (the "immediate physio-chemical, electro-colloidal, nervous impact of I") calls for research by biochemists or neurologists or at least the use of tools they might provide to measure such things as the galvanic skin response, EEG, etc. In a broader sense, stage II and some aspects of stage III (these are not mutually exclusive categories; the organism responds as a whole) constitute what we generally call perception. Selective perception (abstraction) seems a fertile area for research in general semantics, particularly if we relate it to attitudes, semantic reactions, characteristics of messages selectively perceived, the language structure of such messages, or of the receiver of such messages (See Korzybski, 1951).

As a journalism teacher I am especially interested in what might be called "perceptual efficiency." Is it possible to measure "perceptual efficiency"? How is it related to extensionality? To attitude, purpose, motivation, dogmatism, etc.? To the habitual language structure of the perceiver? Can "perceptual efficiency" be improved?

The news reporter is taught to selectively perceive and selectively encode in terms of "news values." What "happenings" are ignored as a result? Which are overemphasized to the point of distorting the picture of the world that is relayed through the media? The process of abstraction is as natural and unavoidable as digestion, but we may wish to know the effects of various frames of reference, attitudes, motivations, or assumptions on the process.

Semantic reactions (Stage III) can be measured in a variety of ways, none of which are entirely satisfactory. We may accept the spontaneous or elicited verbal reports of subjects concerning their "thoughts," "feelings," "tensions," etc. Or we may base our research on the judgments of observers as Silverman and Hilgartner suggest in this volume. Or we may use devices to measure galvanic skin response, pulse rate, breathing rate, eye movements, etc., as indicators of semantic reactions. In any case, we must make certain assumptions about and inferences from our data.

Again, the interesting research possibilities lie in relating semantic reactions to other variables. We may, for example, wish to compare semantic reactions to certain happenings with reaction to words about those happenings, or to compare reactions to descriptions with reactions to categorical statements as Nunnally (1961) did in his study of *Popular Conceptions of Mental Health*.

Does a person who is aware that he is projecting his evaluations on happenings react differently from one who believes he "sees things as they really are"? And can we determine "awareness of projecting" or "consciousness of abstracting" from the language structure used in describing a happening?

Higher order semantic reactions—that is, reactions to reactions, thoughts about thoughts, feelings about feelings—should provide a multitude of research possibilities. Korzybski (1933, 1958, p. 440) argues that some of these reactions (analysis of analysis, reasoning about reasoning, evaluation of evaluation, etc.) may be considered positive, while others (worry about worry, fear of fear, belief in belief, etc.) represent morbid semantic reactions.

The labeling of a reaction is, in itself, a higher order reaction and may influence the first order reaction. For example, a student might say, "I am a failure." A teacher or counselor, in his best non-directive manner, may reply, "You feel you are a failure." What effect does labeling this "statement of fact" (from the student's point of view) a *feeling* have on the feeling?

Cognitive dissonance can be considered a kind of semantic reaction. Do the extensional devices or an extensional orientation provide a way of resolving dissonance? Do they increase dissonance? Or is the relationship, as I suspect, too complex to be answered in either-or terms?

At stage IV, verbal reactions, there is no shortage of measurable variables: nouns, verbs, type-token ratios, self-reference words, quantifying terms, positive or negative evaluational terms, qualifying terms, terms showing consciousness of projection, abstraction or inference, etc. The problem is to find meaningful relationships among measurable variables or to find ways to measure more significant variables. Johnson (1946) described a number of possible studies and some of these were carried out under his direction at the University of Iowa.

With proper programming computers can be "taught" to count most of the variables listed above. Because of this, studies of much greater complexity are feasible than would be if using older counting methods. But beware of the OG Principle; a study is not necessarily worthwhile merely because it is feasible. (See article by Phillips in this volume.)

Perhaps using a computer-assisted content analysis, studies could be made of the verbal output of members of a sensitivity group. How do the members of the group differ in their verbal output? Does the language structure of a person correlate with personality variables? With judgments about him by other members of the group? Does a change in language structure cause corresponding changes in personality variables? In judgments about him by other members of the group?

The computer might also be used in comparing the verbal output of groups classified on the basis of other criteria. For example, we may wish to compare self-actualizers (Maslow 1954, 1962) and those considered least self-actualizing, "open" and "closed" minded people (Rokeach, 1960), the top 10% and the bottom 10% on any test that on theoretical grounds might be related to verbal output or language structure. Maslow's descriptions of self-actualizing people include descriptions of their language behavior which suggest that they tend to be extensional, non-aristotelian, and quite conscious of abstracting.

In other contexts we may wish to study the relationship of message variables to reactions to messages as I did in a study of linguistic correlates of judgments of science news stories (Johnson, 1960). One of the message variables of special interest would be "level of abstraction" if we can adequately operationalize that term.

The sensitivity of minority groups to certain labels suggests a study of the linguistic correlates of prejudice. Francis (1968) argues that "nouns are attitudes," pointing out that an attitude is normally defined as a "predisposition to act."

Many studies would involve communication between two or more individuals which might be diagrammed by linking two or more SVL diagrams, with appropriate arrows to indicate feedback. (Since statements about statements, reactions to reactions, etc., may be regarded as higher order abstractions, we may, for some purposes, find the structural differential, Figure 1, a more useful model. From this point on, the research suggestions may be based on either model.) Interviewers, from journalists to personnel managers to psychiatrists, might be interested in the effects of specific kinds of feedback on verbal output, message variables, attitudes toward self or the interviewer, etc.

As a journalism teacher I am concerned about the transmission of news along a communication chain—from observer to reporter to editor to reader. Frequently many levels of abstraction are involved between the event and the reader. Since each person in the communication chain brings to the situation different experiences, different assumptions, different language patterns, different vocabulary, etc., what kinds of distortion creep into the mapping and remapping and re-remapping of the event? With a greater awareness of the sources of distortion, would it be possible to train "high fidelity" reporters who would not only distinguish observations from inferences, but would insist that their sources do the same; who would be sensitive to linguistic differences and careful to recheck their understanding through feedback; who would be fully aware that their news stories represent abstractions, that they cannot say "all," that they *must* (indeed, *do* whether they are aware of it or not) decide what is relevant? Perhaps the first step is to define, operationally, a "high fidelity" reporter. Then we may go on to study "invariance under transformation" along the communication chain.

The problems I am talking about are not limited to a journalistic context; communication chains abound in the business world, in academic circles, I suspect in most areas of human endeavor. In each of these contexts some people operate as "gatekeepers," controlling the flow of information. Who are these gatekeepers? How do they operate? What are their assumptions about their roles? Their criteria for making selections? David Manning White (1950) conducted the first of many studies of gatekeepers in journalism, but much remains to be done in this and other contexts. In a study of the flow of science news I found that editors, the gatekeepers in the system, used different criteria or "dimensions of judgment" in judging science news than scientists, science writers, or the readers of science news! (Johnson, 1960, 1963).

The effects of feedback on the transmission of information along a communication chain offer many possibilities for research. We might also investigate the effects of assumptions about the expectations of other people in the chain on the kinds of messages transmitted. For example: to what extent does a reporter's assumptions about the editor's expectations determine what the reporter will write? To what extent do these "assumed expectations" match the actual expectations of the editor? Here we are dealing with the effects of higher order abstractions on the relatively low order "reports of events." In a similar way we might investigate the effect of a "verbal preview" of a happening on reports of the happening (i.e., a reversal of the natural order).

Earlier, in discussing "higher order semantic reactions," I dealt with some research possibilities specifically concerned with higher order abstractions. Perhaps research of this kind will make us more fully aware that there are no "final answers," no "highest order" abstraction, no research that cannot trigger research on research.

We might also become aware (and perhaps demonstrate for our own edification and for the edification of others) that the responses we get from subjects are a function of the level of abstraction on which they are operating. What happens, for example, when the subject of an experiment suddenly becomes aware that he is indeed the subject of an experiment? A related problem is that of the discrepancy between the stimulus (happening, event) as defined by

34   Kenneth G. Johnson

the experimenter and the stimulus as defined by the subject.

Similarly, a parent may use "psychology" on his child and it works. Fine! But at some point the child may become aware that the parent is "using psychology" and, armed with this new level of awareness, change his response. The parent, knowing that the child has become aware, tries a new technique. The child, sooner or later, becomes aware, etc., etc., etc. (I am reminded here of the song "I can't get adjusted to the you who got adjusted to me," and of the mental gymnastics of people playing the game of "Prisoner's Dilemma.") What I am suggesting is (1) an awareness of this problem and (2) the possibilities of research dealing with it. Studies of this kind will require a long methodological leap from (relatively) simple stimulus-response research, but certainly we must make that leap if we are to go beyond animal psychology to study that most human of all human characteristics—man's ability to generate higher order abstractions.

Along these lines, I wonder if we can devise means of testing students not on what they know but on their ways of gaining knowledge?

"Consciousness of abstracting" provides us with another level of awareness. Can we isolate verbal indicators of this awareness? Nonverbal indicators? Is a "delayed reaction" a natural outcome of "consciousness of abstracting" as Korzybski suggests? Do "consciousness of abstracting" and the extensional devices help reduce conditioned behavior? Make conditioning more difficult? More selective? Perhaps what we need in this age of instant communication is applied research on how to resist conditioning.

In more subtle ways than I am prepared to suggest, we might explore the effects of "higher order awareness," e.g., "How do you feel?" "How do you feel about how you feel?" "How do you feel now that you are aware of how you feel about how you feel?"

Responses to Rachel Lauer's "Semantic Interaction Test" described in this volume might be analyzed to determine the frequency of metalinguistic statements (statements about the nature of the statement rather than expressions of agreement or disagreement). Her report suggests that students trained in general semantics respond in this way more often than those with no such training—a finding consistent with DeVito's definition of "prescriptive general semantics" as "an applied science, concerned with how metalanguage can be taught and how it can be most effectively utilized" (this volume, p. 196).

The implications of general semantics, dealing as it does with human evaluational behavior, are so broad that almost any human activity could conceivably be the subject of research. Yet this broadness may blind us to the specific, feasible research we should be doing. While research in many fields—psychology, sociology, neurology, psychiatry, etc.—have a relation to general semantics and we should try to keep abreast of developments in these fields, I believe there are some unique emphases in general semantics that require special research attention. One of these, I believe, is an emphasis on the *role of language structure* in perception, evaluation, communication, etc.—indeed in all of human behavior. Another is an emphasis on *higher order abstractions* and *higher order reactions*. These two special emphases alone should provide research opportunities for years to come.

REFERENCES

Bois, J. Samuel, 1966, *The Art of Awareness,* Dubuque: Wm. C. Brown Co.

Francis, Roy G., 1968, "Talking About Bread," in *Perspectives On Communication,* Milwaukee: Speech Communication Center, University of Wisconsin-Milwaukee.

Johnson, Kenneth G., 1960, *Differential Judgments of Science News Stories and Their Structural Correlates.* Ph.D. Dissertation. Ann Arbor: University Microfilms. Abstracted in *General Semantics Bulletin* 26/27: 93.

─────, 1963, "Dimensions of Judgment of Science News Stories," *Journalism Quarterly* 40 (3): 315-322.

Johnson, F. Craig and George R. Klare, 1961, "General Models of Communication Research: A Survey of the Developments of a Decade," *Journal of Communication,* 11 (1): 13-26.

Johnson, Wendell, 1946, *People in Quandaries,* New York: Harper and Brothers.

─────, 1948, "Speech and Personality," in *The Communication of Ideas,* New York: Harper and Brothers. pp. 53-78.

King, William A., 1968, "An Event-Structure Model for Communication," *Journal of Communication* 18 (4): 389-403.

Korzybski, Alfred, 1933, 1958, *Science and Sanity: An Introduction to Non-Aristotelian Systems and General Semantics*, Lakeville, Conn.: International Non-Aristotelian Library Publishing Co. (4th Ed. 1958).
————, 1950, "An Extensional Analysis of the Process of Abstracting from an Electro-Colloidal Non-Aristotelian Point of View," *General Semantics Bulletin* 4 & 5 (1950) 9-12.
————, 1951, "The Role of Language in the Perceptual Processes," in *Perception, An Approach to Personality*, New York: The Ronald Press.
————, 1954, *Time-Binding: The General Theory* (Two Papers, 1924 and 1926), Lakeville, Conn.: Institute of General Semantics.
Lee, Irving, 1941, *Language Habits in Human Affairs*, New York: Harper & Brothers.
Maslow, Abraham H., 1954, *Motivation and Personality*, New York: Harper & Brothers.
————, 1962, *Toward Psychology of Being*, New York: D. Van Nostrand Co.
Meyers, Russell, 1966, "On the Dichotomy of 'Organic' and 'Functional' Diseases," *General Semantics Bulletin*, 32 & 33 (1965-66): 21-37.
Nunally, Jum, 1961, *Popular Conceptions of Mental Health*, New York: Holt, Rinehart and Winston.
Payne, Buryl, 1968, "Extraverbal Techniques and Korzybskian Formulations," *ETC.* 25 (1): 7-15.
Rokeach, Milton, 1960, *The Open and Closed Mind*, New York: Basic Books.
Shannon, C. and W. Weaver, 1949, *The Mathematical Theory of Communication*, Urbana: University of Illinois Press.
Westley, Bruce H., 1958, "Scientific Method and Communication Research," in *Introduction to Mass Communication Research*, Baton Rouge: Louisiana State University.
White, David Manning, 1950, "The 'Gate Keeper': A Case Study in the Selection of News," *Journalism Quarterly*, 27: 283-90.

RELATIONAL ABSTRACTING AND THE STRUCTURAL DIFFERENTIAL

OTTO F. BAUER

Bowling Green State University

Let us repeat once more the two crucial *negative* premises as established firmly by *all* human experience: (1) Words *are not* the things we are speaking about; and (2) There *is no* such thing as an object in absolute isolation (Korzybski, 1958, pp. 60-61).

All languages are composed of two kinds of words: (1) Of *names* for the somethings on the un-speakable level, be they external objects, or *internal feelings*, which admittedly are *not* words, and (2) of *relational terms*, which express the actual, or desired, or any other relations between the un-speakable entities of the objective level (Korzybski, 1958, p. 250).

But names alone do not give propositions. We need *relation-words*, and it is here where our undefined terms become important (Korzybski, 1958, p. 155).

Korzybski's Structural Differential

In his description of the structural differential, Alfred Korzybski gives principal attention to the first of his two negative premises. By calling the first order of abstraction the "objective" level, he is able to emphasize that "this *is not* this"—that the word is not the object. He states, "The disk . . . symbolizes the human object," and "The label . . . represents the higher abstraction called a name (with its meaning given by a definition)" (1958, p. 399).

How does the structural differential symbolize the second negative premise, that no object exists in absolute isolation? How does it symbolize the relationship between relational terms and the un-speakable relations that occur on the "objective" level? Identifications in this area are probably just as harmful semantically as identifications of word and object.

An additional complication results from his stating that the object has "a finite number of characteristics," which he, in turn, symbolizes with a circle or disk (1958, p. 389). If he intended the circle or disk to represent only one object, then how can its relationship to other objects be symbolized? An obvious solution, which is implied by Korzybski, is to talk about the objective *level* and to include "all" objects in the same disk. However, if this is done, how can the infinity of relations among objects in space-time be then described as having "a *finite* number of characteristics"?

Bois' Version of the Structural Differential
While reviewing some of my materials on these problems, I came upon some notes in which I suggested that Korzybski's "parabola" should not be limited to symbolizing a submicroscopic world of events, but rather should be extended to include the "infinite world at *all* levels." The first order abstraction I then described as "every happening or occurrence of which I am conscious on a given date."

Although these observations were made prior to my reading of Bois' *The Art of Awareness,* the similarity to Bois' version of the structural differential is obvious. For example, he describes the larger parabola as a "symbolic picture of *what is going on* at all known levels of existence, from atomic elements to galactic spirals racing away from one another" (Bois, 1966, p. 65), and his first order experience or abstraction includes a "limited number of 'infinities' of a lower order." (1966, p. 79.)

While Bois' version virtually eliminates the infinite-finite quandary, the place of relational terms and their unspeakable referents is still in question. His high regard for "relational abstracting," however, reveals his concern for relational formulations and their significance as descriptions and interpretations of invariant structures (1966, pp. 89-90). I prefer to think of relational abstracting as a process that is applicable to all levels of abstraction.

Toward a Solution
As indicated in the opening statements by Korzybski, relation-words, along with names, are needed to create propositions. And here is where undefined terms become important. Of special signi-

ficance are the various prepositions, numbering more than seventy. Many of them have "meanings" that are based in a context of language, such as "contrary to orders," "in spite of the law," and "as to your interest." But many of them also portray a kind of physical, *relational* existence that is not only difficult to define but is also difficult to point to. For example, "the pencil is *on* the desk," and "he is *with* the team." Other kinds of relation-words can be described and pointed to, but most of them are actional verbs, such as "Smith kicks Brown." At this point, however, I am concerned with the representation of these relation-words and their unspeakable counterparts in the structural differential.

If Korzybski's differential is to be used, at least two "objects" will need to be suspended and lines or strings will be needed to connect the "objects" horizontally. Similarly, additional lines will be needed to connect separate "name" words, in order to portray a horizontal relationship. If Bois' differential is to be used, lines will need to be inserted within the structure used for each level of abstraction in order to show horizontal relationships.

Eventually, it would be appropriate to develop relational lines that describe the relationships as symmetrical, non-symmetrical, asymmetrical, transitive, non-transitive, or intransitive. In short, we can find more ways to emphasize relational abstracting at all levels in the structural differential and in this way make it a more useful model for research.[1]

REFERENCES

Bois, J. Samuel, *The Art of Awareness*, Dubuque, Iowa: Wm. C. Brown Company. 1966.
Korzybski, Alfred, *Science and Sanity*, Lakeville, Conn.: International Non-Aristotelian Library Publishing Company, 1958.

---

[1] Editor's note: For a discussion of some of these elements see D. D. Bourland, Jr., 1952, "Introduction to a Structural Calculus: A Postulational Statement of Alfred Korzybski's Non-Aristotelian Linguistic System," *General Semantics Bulletin*, Nos. 8 and 9, 16-22, and Bourland, 1963, "Semantic Construction: A Time-Binding Mechanism," *General Semantics Bulletin*, Nos. 30 and 31, 74-77.

LEVELS OF INDIVIDUATION IN SEMANTIC STRUCTURES

CHARLES F. VICK
Temple University

The major focus of this paper is on semantic structures. It may be helpful, however, to first clarify my view of interpersonal communication in order to provide a context for these more specific concerns.

In a recent survey of the National Society for the Study of Communication, Minter (1968) found that the most preferred definition of communication was that of Ruesch and Bateson (1951). In terms of attempting to say what communication is, perhaps such a broad definition, including as it does any influence of one organism by another whether there is intent or not, is a reasonable approach. If, on the other hand, we are interested in defining a particular class of behavior for theory building and research, it seems to me that a more narrow definition has greater utility. Otherwise, we are left with the impossible task of studying nearly all behavior under a single classification.

One way of approaching such a definition is to examine what investigators have commonly studied when they regarded their research as being concerned with interpersonal communication. It has been my observation that most such research is concerned with the process of consciously sending and receiving a message. Interpersonal communication, then, may usefully be defined, in my view, as the exchange of symbols between two or more persons, when each consciously intends to interact with the other and is aware of the other's intent to interact with him. While such a definition presents problems in identifying intent and awareness, it does set aside those behaviors in which we are primarily interested.

If the above definition is accepted, it provides a further benefit in that it points to the central problem confronting the student of human communication. How do we account for the variance between the intended meaning of the message producer and the obtained meaning of the message receiver? The extent to which this problem is solved will determine in large part our ability to specify the requirements of effective communication.

While the above definition and stated problem do not, in themselves, tell one what the student of interpersonal communication ought to study, they do provide a framework for specifying the task confronting him. It is easy to feel that the communication scholar is duplicating the efforts of psychology, psycholinguistics, and other highly related disciplines. There is, in my view, however, a subtle but important difference between their interests and ours. The psychologist is primarily interested in individual behavior even though he may look at it in a social context; the psycholinguist is primarily interested in the relationship between characteristics of language and verbal behavior. The communications scholar is primarily interested in how the relationships between the characteristics and behaviors of one individual and those of another affect the process of communication. It is for the most part a matter of similarities and differences between any two individuals that determines the effectiveness of their communication with each other.

Having defined interpersonal communication, stated the central problem to be solved, and specified the relationships to be studied in solving that problem, I can now turn to the main concern of this paper, individual semantic structures. Perhaps the most widely and uncritically accepted idea in the area of communication is that meaning is not in the message but in the individual. The validity of this assumption is clear when we examine any one of the more accepted theories of meaning acquisition. Whether we look to association theory, behaviorist theory, or mediation theory, the basis of meaning is found in the experience of the individual. Since meaning comes not from language, but from the individual's interaction with his environment (including language), it is evident that his interpretation of a message is an internally determined event.

I have then no argument with the basic notion that meaning is in the individual. The problem is, that, taken at face value, such a formulation presents a very considerable difficulty for the student of communication. If meaning is an entirely individual matter, then the probability of successful communication, that is of obtaining similarity between the intended and received meaning, is extremely low. We all have different experiences and we all interpret the "same" experiences somewhat differently. Therefore, on the face of it, one would expect considerable difference in the semantic structures of any two individuals.

While I accept the notion that meaning is indeed in the individual, I would argue that the basis for meaning, that is experience, is not an entirely individual phenomenon. Certainly part of our semantic structures is built on the foundation of our private interaction with our environment, but not all of our experience is private. A goodly share of our experience comes in the form of social interaction. Therefore, part of a person's semantic structures is socially rather than individually determined. Semantic structures are not the result of the simple translation of experience into memory trace which can be usefully analyzed at a single level. Rather, they are complex, in part socially determined, dynamic and interactive and demand multi-level analysis.

How, then, can a multi-level analysis best be conducted? It seems to me that, if our primary concern is one of similarities and differences which affect the process of communication, then these levels can best be categorized by their degree of individuation. The categories presented below are tentative and not fully developed, but they do provide an idea of what such an analysis might look like.

The level with the highest degree of individuation is the object-event level. Here, the concern is with the individual's private interaction with objects and events in his environment. It is well established that a child forms concepts; that is, parts of his environment have recognized significance for him, prior to the time that he acquires language. This non-verbal and essentially non-social experience/concept phenomenon no doubt continues after the acquisition of language. It is at this level that meanings are most individuated, and, therefore, probably most different from one person to another.

A second level, still containing a high degree of individuation, is the primary group level. Probably the family is the best example here. The individual's semantic structures are influenced by the amount of interaction he carries on with other members of the group and by the potency of that interaction. If, over time, an individual primarily interacts with a particular group of individuals, his perceptions and indirectly his memory traces (the bases of his semantic structures) will be influenced by that group. The potency of that influence is determined in part by the importance the individual attaches to the group. It is not, of course, contended that the semantic structures of such group members will be the same. The point is that between any two group members one would expect more similarity of meaning than between a group member and a non-group member.

Closely related to the primary group level, but with a considerably lower level of individuation, is the sub-cultural level. Here, the concern is with larger groups where all members do not interact with each other, but where chains of interaction between sub-groups create the appearance of groupness. Some examples at this level would be ethnic groups, economic groups, geographic groups and so on. The influence of the sub-culture comes in part from the individual's direct interaction with other members and groups connected with the sub-culture and from the representation of the sub-culture in his primary groups. Particular experiences are associated with such sub-cultures, such as special food, ceremonies, language and so on, and these tend to build similarities into individual semantic structures.

Finally, there is the cultural level where individuation is at its lowest. Through mass media, education, national governmental programs, cultural traditions and so on, certain concepts and ideas are transmitted at a culture-wide level. Conventions of language usage, such as accepted grammar and dictionary definitions, have their influence at this level. It is a level of indirect interaction, although the individual, of course, is also influenced by the extent to which culture-wide norms and standards are accepted by his sub-cultural and primary groups.

It is not the intent of this paper to argue that socially determined semantic structures are the *same* between members of the group in question. The argument is that members of such groups have more similarity of meaning between them than would any member and a non-member. It is clearly recognized that prior experience influences our perception of present experience, and that the levels specified above interact with each other allowing for a great deal of individuation in semantic structures. On the other hand, these structures appear to be subjected to a considerable amount of social influence. It may, therefore, for particular messages relevant to particular groups or cultures, make sense to talk about "meanings" in messages.

In terms of research, then, we need first to define, at least loosely, those areas where there is apt to be low individuation (high cultural similarity) in semantic structures. Studies from linguists and word-associationists may be helpful here. Once having established some measure of low individuation, one can better analyze the effects of high individuation in semantic structures on interpersonal communication since they can be identified and contrasted more easily. The important point is that the researcher dealing with meaning must be aware of social similarities operating in the interpersonal process as well as individual differences. Our view has been too narrow and, consequently, too pessimistic in so far as human communication is concerned.

REFERENCES

Minter, Robert L., 1968, "A Denotative and Connotative Study in Communication," *The Journal of Communication* (1968) XVIII (1), 26-35.

Ruesch, Jurgen, and Gregory Bateson, 1951, *Communication, The Social Matrix of Psychiatry,* New York: W. W. Norton Company, Inc.

RESEARCHING THE "INTANGIBLE"

CHARLOTTE S. READ
Institute of General Semantics

To research the "intangible," what we classify as "intangible" on one level of abstraction would need to be translated into tangibles on other levels. A few examples occur to me: empathy, concern, trust, love, sincerity, warmth, etc., and their opposites. Since much investigating has already been done in this direction, in the context of this conference we may ask: If we study "intangibles" in a Korzybskian framework, will new light be shed, new relationships be uncovered? Where will it lead? I have not carried out any formal research along these lines, but I should like to consider some possibilities, and to raise some questions which seem basic to me.

First, an organism-as-a-whole-in-an-environment point of view would include as many different levels or aspects as feasible, not only verbal, but non-verbal as well, such as gestures, movements, unconsummated movement patterns held as tensions, chemical changes, breathing, brain waves, voice, perceptual behavior, etc. Data on any of these, or their combinations, would be pertinent, since they are all a part of our evaluating.

Second, at the foundation of our investigating we would need to come to grips with a clearer description of what the terms "intensional orientation" and "extensional orientation" refer to behaviorally. These seem to me particularly important intangibles for us. In what ways are they related to the variables mentioned above?

Third, taking into account work which has already been done, especially by Maslow and Humanistic psychologists, we would need to qualify the intangibles (as between growth and deficiency-motivated, for instance), to index and date, to distinguish between habitual *general* orientations (loving, hostile, etc.) and manifestations in *specific* instances.

Fourth, we would want to know whether the study of the principles and methods of general semantics over a period of time makes any difference in the intangible behaviors studied.

With regard to the first statement, a number of recording procedures are possible. Words and voice can be recorded, movements can be recorded on videotape or movies, chemical changes can be measured on instruments such as psychogalvanometers, etc., brain waves can be taken, electrical activity in muscle fibers can be measured, etc.

Perhaps the first, and what may now be considered classic, detailed and many-faceted experimenting was done in the 1920's and 1930's by Trigant Burrow. Working day after day for years with a group of colleagues studying their behavior in a group, he found that it became possible to discriminate between two different patterns of tension, which he named "cotention" and "ditention." In ditention, a person was in a divided, conflictual condition, showing self-centered defensive behavior, concerned with his limited "I-persona"; in cotention, he functioned harmoniously without need to defend himself or to justify himself, he felt expansive, etc. In discovering and studying these two very different states during his experimental group-analytic work, he instrumentally recorded the characteristics of various physiological functions in both ditention and cotention. The following positive correlations were found: in cotention there was a deepened and slowed respiratory rhythm, a decrease in frequency and range of eye movements, and a reduction in percentage and amplitude of the alpha waves of the electrical brain potentials. When a person was in a ditentive state, Burrow noticed certain tensions around the region of the eyes and forehead. "Cotention is synonymous with functional balance, organismically and intraorganismically. It is identified with ease, quiet, clarity and preparedness, both in feeling and in thought . . . the outlook becomes broad, impersonal, affirmative," he said (Burrow, 1949, p. 222).

In seeking to understand the broad categories of intensional and extensional orientations, not only the verbal patterns are significant, but also the accompanying organismal behaviors: the manner of movements, bodily expressions, tone of voice, the actions taken or withheld, the feelings experienced.

The way we speak about ourselves, and our feelings, is especially revealing in indicating our attitudes. A study was made of the verbal behavior of clients in therapy by Dr. Francis Henry Mitchell (1952), who wrote his doctoral dissertation on "A Test of Certain Semantic Hypotheses by Application to Client-Centered Counseling Cases: Intensionality-Extensionality of Clients in Therapy." The thesis of his report was that extensional types of reactions tend to replace intensional in the semantic behavior of clients progressing positively through a therapeutic relationship. The Counseling Center at the University of Chicago made transcriptions of counseling interviews available for ten cases, where a Rogerian approach was used. The clients' statements were critically analyzed according to certain criteria of intensional and extensional attitudes. Some of the criteria for extensional attitudes were, for example, lack of identifications; differentiating past, present and future; awareness of differences; conditional statements; awareness of non-allness, etc. The clients' statements were rated on a scale by three different judges who were acquainted with writings on general semantics, and who also received some training preparatory to their rating of the data.

Mitchell found that "progress in counseling is concomitant with movement toward increased extensional evaluation" and "regression in counseling is concomitant with movement toward increased intensional evaluation." Some of his conclusions were that: "1) A general semantics framework is applicable to transcribed counseling data. It provides a reliable and sensitive basis for measure of client change. 2) Experienced judges are able to make reliable and valid estimates of the degree of client intensional-extensional orientation from units of data. 3) Measures of intension-extension are consistent in trend with other measures of client progress. 4) Client intensional-extensional evaluation undergoes change in psychotherapy as predicted by proponents of general semantics."

To my knowledge another study such as Dr. Mitchell's has not been made. A client-therapist relationship offers an excellent opportunity for the study of recorded verbal evaluations changing (hopefully) over a period of time. I wonder if it would not be possible to use the type of rating scale formulated in his investigation to analyze tape recordings of group discussions in sensitivity sessions. If group sessions could also be recorded on videotape, we would have the additional correlations with movements, facial expressions, etc.

Does an extensionally-oriented person show more loving behavior than one with intensional attitudes? Does he have characteristics in common with a "self-actualizing" person? (Maslow, 1954, 199 ff.). Would persons who could be called "self-actualizing" also be exceptionally "conscious of abstracting" in the Korzybskian sense?

In a review of Maslow's *Religions, Values, and Peak Experiences* (1964), Henry Winthrop (1965) remarked that "peakers [persons who tend more than the average to have peak experiences] are more likely to be extensional in their thinking." This judgment has not been investigated as far as I know, though many of Maslow's observations suggest this relationship.

If we could delineate the characteristics of persons who we classify as "extensionally oriented" by means of available tests and ratings, personal questioning and observations, these could be compared with similar data or descriptions of "self-actualizing" persons recorded in the psychological literature, or with those who tend to have more than usual peak experiences.

We have an excellent example of some qualifications of that "ideal extensional man" in "Irving J. Lee: The Semantic Man" based on lectures by the late Irving J. Lee and formulated in writing by Dr. Sanford Berman (1955) as a tribute to Lee (who he believed fitted the description). This profile shows what Lee believed such a man would look like were he to behave in terms of the principles of general semantics, and the description may well serve us as a guide in our investigations. One also may turn to the description of man at the fifth stage of human development—the "unifying stage"—as characterized by J. S. Bois (1957, 1966).

Would those rare persons who come close to being an "ideal extensional man" have characteristics in common with the "self-actualizing" person or the man in the "unifying stage" in relation to such intangibles as love, trust, etc.? Burrow found that there were two quite different states in "cotention" and "ditention," and Maslow

(1953) found that in their love relationships, as well as in many life activities, self-actualizing people behaved differently from others. We very much need more actual data on extensionally and intensionally oriented persons. We would then be in a position to correlate our findings with other studies. Such studies should take into account not only verbal, which remains very important, but also physiological, perceptual and other available data. I have explored some of these questions previously with emphasis on physiological aspects, and will not repeat here (Schuchardt, 1952).

Trust, for example, can be expressed with words, but our behavior on other levels may or may not correspond with our words. For instance, the way we move or stand or sit can belie our words. Our verbal trusting, our postural trusting, trusting the support of another person, trusting another person to behave in a predictable way (or even if in an unpredictable way, still trusting in a deeper respect), etc.—these trustings may be found to be related to our other ways of behaving, for instance, our habits of speech. Although this may seem obvious, in my experience working with groups it is usually a new experience for persons actually to sense kinesthetically their trusting or non-trusting attitudes. We may feel quite trusting as a general attitude, and non-trusting in a particular situation (See paper by Kim Giffin in this volume).

It appears that our genuineness, the degree to which we are "fully functioning," is connected with how "total" our functioning is; that is, whether at all levels (feeling-thinking, physiological, chemical, muscular, verbal, etc.) we function harmoniously.

In investigating whether or not training in the principles of general semantics has an influence on the intangible behaviors studied, several kinds of variables enter. What constitutes "training in general semantics"? We would need to consider the type, the length and intensity of study, the depth of understanding gained, etc. Those who have studied and taught the work will appreciate the time needed. Learning how we function and how our nervous system works will eventually make it more possible for us to be our own guides.

Searching in vain in Berelson's and Steiner's excellent "inventory of scientific findings" about human behavior (1964) for information on studies in the areas discussed in this paper, we see their own recognition of the lack forthrightly stated : "This book has rather little to say about central human concerns; nobility, moral courage, ethical torments . . . happiness, love and hate, death, even sex. . . . Why the lacunae? Partly because of the youth of the field : it takes time to accumulate the scientific means to study such matters. Partly, perhaps, this is the price paid for method, for system, for abstraction : the concern of science for concepts, for replicability, for objectivity, for rates and patterns. . . . Not yet, anyway, do the behavioral sciences see life steadily and see it whole" (pp. 666-667).

Perhaps a greater concentration on the expression of our highest potentialities will enable us also to explore them more fully scientifically, as indeed work is begun in this direction. If we want to hypothesize that terms we use for different "intangibles" are but names we give for different relationships felt toward each other, aspects of one larger "single 'fund' of love-energy capable of endless transformations of quality or aim," (Suttie, 1952), this seems to be not inconsistent with a holistic point of view. Or we may choose some other hypotheses. In any case, the extensionalizing methods of general semantics and awareness of the time-binding process should be able to help us to see relationships between higher and lower order abstractions, to see life less "split" and more "whole", to know the importance of our underlying premises, whatever they may be, for the consequences that follow. Perhaps no research would be more valuable at this time than in the realm of the "intangible".

REFERENCES

Berelson, Bernard, and Gary Steiner, 1964, *Human Behavior; An Inventory of Scientific Findings,* New York: Harcourt, Brace, and World.
Berman, Sanford I., 1955, "Irving J. Lee: The Semantic Man," *General Semantics Bulletin,* (1955) 18 & 19, 22-25.
Bois, J. Samuel, 1957, *Explorations in Awareness,* New York: Harper & Bros.
——————, 1966, *The Art of Awareness,* Dubuque, Iowa, Wm. C. Brown.
Burrow, Trigant, 1949, *The Neurosis of Man : An Introduction to a*

Science of Human Behavior, New York: Harcourt, Brace & Co.

Maslow, Abraham, 1954, "Love In Healthy People", in *The Meaning of Love,* New York: The Julian Press.

——————, 1954, *Motivation and Personality,* New York: Harper & Bros.

——————, 1964, *Religions, Values and Peak Experiences,* Columbus, Ohio: Ohio State University Press.

Mitchell, Francis Henry, 1952, "A Test of Certain Semantic Hypotheses by Application to Client-Centered Counseling Cases: Intensionality-Extensionality of Clients in Therapy," *General Semantics Bulletin* (1952-53) 10 & 11, 23.

Schuchardt, Charlotte, 1952, "Some Aspects of Behavior: Comments on Several Physiological Approaches," *General Semantics Bulletin* (1952) 8 & 9, 100-107.

Suttie, Ian D., 1952, *The Origins of Love and Hate,* New York: The Julian Press. Originally published in 1935.

Winthrop, Henry, 1965, Review in *Journal of Humanistic Psychology* (1965) (Spring).

THE SEMANTIC INTERACTION TEST

RACHEL M. LAUER
Chief School Psychologist
Bureau of Child Guidance
New York, N.Y.

To my knowledge there are few tests which are designed specifically to reflect degrees of integration of general semantics principles. Researchers who have attempted to measure the effects of general semantics training have used such instruments as Torrance's Creativity tests (True, 1964), The Watson-Glaser Critical Thinking Appraisal (Livingston, 1965), tests of dogmatism, opinionation, rigidity, and authoritarianism (Goldberg, 1965), and student compositions (Glorfeld, 1965). Weiss' "Is of Identity" test (1956) and Haney's tests of "Uncritical Inference" (1961) do focus directly upon the subjects' grasp of the principles of non-identity and of the distinctions between fact and inference.

The Semantic Interaction Test was designed by the author to elicit a subject's ability to respond spontaneously to common conversational gambits with some evidence of having integrated a wide variety of general semantic formulations. In "real life" people do start an interaction by such challenges as, "You can't change human nature," or "It's a sign of weakness to change your mind." The responses people give to these statements probably reflect their ability to recognize thinking disorders and to reply discriminatively.

History of the Semantic Interaction Test

After having given a 26-session course in general semantics to a class of white, middle-class children in suburbia, I decided to risk testing the effects of the course upon something as close as I could get to "real life" behavior with a paper and pencil instrument. Hence, the Semantic Interaction Test. In addition to the two items mentioned above, there are 18 others such as, "That's a really ugly picture," "Let's get even with Billy after school," "I'll never be able to divide fractions," and "I hope no Negroes ever move in around here." The statements were designed to present the subject with examples of absolutistic thinking, failure to date and index, failure to timebind, stereotype of male-female roles, authoritarianism, confusion of fact, inference and generalization, etc. Each subject was instructed to imagine that a child his age had made the statement to him and to write down a "good reply." To compare the replies of children with general semantic training with those without such training, the same test was administered to all the fifth grade children in two elementary schools, including two classes of "fast learners."

On Scoring the Semantic Interaction Test

With a mass of data before me (teachers reported that the children appeared to take the test quickly and with gusto) the problem was how to score the replies. What exactly constitutes a "general semantic" reply to the remark. "You can't change human nature"? A scoring system of adequate validity and reliability had to be worked out *before* comparing the trained and untrained groups. Influenced by the need for simplicity in scoring, by what appeared to stand out in the data, and by my familiarity with forms of scoring in the Stanford-Binet and the Wechler Intelligence Scale for Children, I developed a three-category method of grouping the replies, attaching scores of 0, 1, or 2 to each category as follows:

0 for a reply revealing agreement with the remark
1 for a reply showing some recognition of the thinking disorder in the statement by negating it in some way
2 for a reply showing recognition of the thinking disorder, plus an attempt to provide mediation, alternatives or modification.

For example, to the remark, "You can't change human nature" the following replies were scored 0:

"I agree, you can't."
"Who wants to try, anyhow."
"People are born the way they are."

A score of 1 was given to replies such as the following:
"What makes you think you can't?"
"Oh yes, you can."
"Don't be so sure."
"Maybe you couldn't, but I could!"

A score of 2 was given to replies such as the following:
"It depends upon what you mean by human nature."
"Some people learn a lot in school."
"What about the head shrinkers?"
"My dad says he's not nearly as smart as he used to be."
"It might be possible."

As another example, to the remark, "That's a really ugly picture," 0 was credited to the following:
"It makes you sick to look at it."
"Let's not look at it."
"It's ugly all right. I hate art."
"That's because it's modern art."

1 was credited to the following:
"Who are you to judge?"
"I think it's pretty."
"You just don't like art."
"Let's not argue about it."

2 was credited to the following:
"Some people might like it."
"What do you mean by 'ugly'?"
"I used to think that, but you can change your mind."
"What's ugly to you might not be to me."

Reliability

To check my own scoring reliability, I re-scored all the responses after a two-weeks' interim. All replies were separated from the names of the children; thus, I did not know whether I was scoring an experimental or control subject. My own reliability as a rater of replies with the above scale was over 95%. No attempt has yet been made to determine the extent to which other scorers would be consistent with themselves, each other, or me.

Other methods of scoring this test could be developed. For example, a more refined scaling technique might result in scores ranging from 0 to 5 or 7. No assumptions should be made that a score of 2 is twice as good as a score of 1.

Validity

To what extent does this test measure what it purports to measure? With the scoring method used, the general semantics trained children as a group were clearly (.01 level of statistical significance) superior to all other fifth grade classes including the two fast-learner groups. All items, except two, discriminated between the experimental and control groups at an equally high level of significance. These same general semantics trained children also showed superiority over the controls on a variety of other general semantics tests, although before the course their scores were not significantly different. The children were similar to each other in intelligence, socio-economic background, and reading levels. The children had had the same teacher the year before the course was given; thus, her influence upon the children had already affected the children before the course began. One cannot, however, use a test to indicate the validity of a course of study, and then use the effectiveness of the course of study to validate the test. More research must be done. But, there is enough evidence to indicate that such research would probably be fruitful.

Further, the scoring system has a kind of a priori or face validity. Most adults with a knowledge of general semantics would probably agree that a reply, "What do you mean by that?" is "better" than "You're wrong about that!" This, too, needs more study. If a group of highly trained general semanticists got together, they might determine the extent of their agreement on just what constitutes a "general semantic" response. I would anticipate that such a group might, however, find all kinds of complexities to confuse the issue. For example, they might think that a "good" response would depend upon the nature of the relationship between the conversationalists; e.g. the appropriate response, the one which fits the responder's desire to facilitate the relationship or to end it, might be considered the "good" general semantic response. But for the purposes of creating a test designed to measure the effectiveness of a course in general semantics, validity might best be determined empirically; that is, by using the items and the scoring system which differentiate significantly between trained and untrained subjects.

Summary and Conclusions

The Semantic Interaction Test has been described as an attempt to meet the need for a tool which reflects capacity to respond to "real life" situations with a spontaneous show of integrated general semantic principles. In its application to a group of fifth grade children, the test was found to be interesting for them to take and reliably scored. It differentiated very successfully between the children trained and untrained in general semantics. The test will not be ready for publication until more data on reliability and validity are obtained. For those who wish to experiment with it, a copy can be obtained from the author.

Versions of this test could be created in language appropriate to older children and adults.

REFERENCES

Glorfeld, Louis E., 1965, "The Relation Between the Study of the Principles of General Semantics and Writing Ability in Freshman Composition," Unpublished Dissertation, University of Denver.

Goldberg, Alvin, 1965, "The Effects of a Laboratory Course in General Semantics, *ETC.* (1962) XXII, 19-24.

Haney, William V., 1961, "The Uncritical Inference Test: Applications," *General Semantics Bulletin* (1961/1962) 28/29, 26.

Livingston, Howard, 1965, "An Investigation of the Effect of Instruction in General Semantics on 'Critical Reading' Ability," *General Semantics Bulletin* (1965/66) 32 & 33, 93-94.

True, Sally Ralston, 1964, "A Study of the Relation of General Semantics and Creativity," *General Semantics Bulletin* (1963/64) 30 & 31, 100-105. (Abstract of doctoral dissertation, University of Wisconsin.)

Weiss, Thomas M., 1956, "Experimental Study Applying Non-Aristotelian Principles in Measurement of Adjustment and Non-Adjustment," *Science Education* (1956) XL, October, 312-316.

SPECIFYING THE STRUCTURE OF OUR "SEMANTIC REACTIONS"

C. A. HILGARTNER, M.D.*

Center for Theoretical Biology
State University of New York at Buffalo
Amherst, N.Y.

In my opinion, the problem of conducting research so as to specify the structure of our "semantic reactions" involves tangled and interrelated sets of practicalities, of personal problems, and of fundamental theoretical issues. In effect, in order to make profitable use of the holistic, non-elementalistic notion of "semantic reactions," we must so sharpen our wits, our vision, and our expectations that we become able to see-and-understand the human events which occur right before our eyes or in our own lives.

The practical issues we must deal with include the problem of producing examples of the class of entities (behavioral sequences) we wish to study, and the problem of recording these human events in a form which permits us repeatedly to re-examine these events.

In this era of advanced technology, we can handle many recording problems relatively easily, for example, by the use of sound movies or video tapes. But as Condon & Ogston (1968) point out:

> Confrontation with a sound film of human behavior overwhelms the observer with a rapidly flowing and shifting scene of sound and motion. There seem to be no clear boundary points dividing the flow of events into discrete segments. An under-

---
*The author acknowledges the support of NASA Grant NGR-33-015-016.

standing of what is said provides a segmentation of the sound stream into words, phrases, and utterances. But where is the location of this segmentation? Is it now clear where a word begins and ends, or is where a word begins and ends as sound somehow not the same as where an understanding of the word begins and ends? . . . What does a lowering of the voice, "while" the eyes lower, "while" the face flushes, "while" the head turns aside, "while" a leg and foot shift, have to do with what is being said? How is this modified by or the immediate result of the equally complex configurations which immediately, and not so immediately, precede and how do they anticipate those which follow? And how are all of the above changes, in turn, related to the equally complex behaviors of the other person or persons in the interaction?

Before we can make useful decisions concerning the handling of the "practical" problems, we need an adequate "map" of the "territory" we wish to survey. No matter how formidable the barriers to the construction of a theoretical language similar in structure to human behavioral sequences may appear, we must overcome these barriers before we can design and execute significant research on our own "semantic reactions."

I don't know how to tell anyone else how to conduct research on the structure of our "semantic reactions," but in an important sense, I have been working on precisely this problem for the past nine years, and I feel I have achieved some successes in this direction. It seems to me that I can do no better and no worse than to present my own story as a case study, in the form of a very personal account of what I have done and how I have done it.

My own story has involved a sustained dialogue between theory and personal experience, theory and experiment. Although I first encountered general semantics before I entered college, and started reading *Science and Sanity* (Korzybski, 1933) in February 1950, about one week before Korzybski died, my own concerted use of general semantics for the amelioration of my own life did not begin until 1960. That summer I attended the Seminar-Workshop of the Institute of General Semantics as recipient of the 1960 Fulkerson Memorial

Scholarship. And at that point in my life, I discovered that I did not have to *remain* the way I had "turned out." Rather, I found that there exist reliable methods for making one's own life more to one's own liking, and I had a chance to try out some of these methods in the safety of the group and see for myself how they worked. Since that time, I find I have committed an important part of the passion of my life to this peculiar endeavor, to make my own life more to my liking. The results of my efforts could not possibly have been predicted beforehand.

One sequence which occurred in our "D-group" (permissive discussion group) at that seminar proved particularly important for me. At one point (as I saw it) a young man verbally "attacked" an older woman whom I particularly liked. I "rose to her defense," and ended up in a sharp quarrel with the young man. Thereafter, for the next few days, feeling that I had "made a fool of myself in front of the group," I experienced a considerable amount of anxiety. Finally, I mentioned my anxiety symptoms in the D-group. In the exploration which followed, (among other things) our group leader challenged me to make explicit the assumptions which underlay my discomfort. This I was able to do. Then, to my great astonishment, he acidly asked, "Well, are you going to put these assumptions to test, or not?" I found a way to do so, and my assumptions turned out untenable, which proved a relief. But more important, by my own actions I convinced myself that the testing of one's own assumptions constitutes a *procedure,* a *process,* which I could make use of any time I wanted to. During the next few years, through reading and through assiduous practice, I began to build up something of a repertory of methods by which to test my own assumptions.

One morning in the spring of 1963, Prof. Ernst W. Caspari remarked that general semantics has proved fruitful as a source of hypotheses concerning human behavior, but as a discipline it is severely deficient and will never become "academically respectable" until it remedies this deficiency. According to Caspari, general semantics lacks adequate methods of hypothesis-falsification. To be able to come up with new ideas is laudable enough, but what good are new ideas if one cannot prove at least some of them wrong?

Reflecting upon this comment, I realized that I could make sense of much of my own experience by regarding human behavior-and-experience as showing a postulational structure: human beings constitute mechanisms for generating and testing behavioral hypothesis, and human behavior-and-experience is therefore intrinsically self-correcting in the same sense that scientific research is self-correcting. In these terms, the key operation common to the psychotherapy of any therapeutic school comprises the process of hypothesis-falsification. I wrote a paper in the summer of 1963 to express this insight; a portion of this paper was recently published (Hilgartner, 1968).

I continued to pursue my own self-scrutiny, and by the spring of 1965, I found I was able to extend this Korzybskian viewpoint on psychotherapy to explore the way that our expectations or "theories" concerning human behavior are *socially shared*. In the resulting paper (Hilgartner, 1965), I developed and documented the empirical observation that at present throughout the human race there exists a mode of behavior involving a shared disorientation, a species-wide social context of psychodynamically stabilized distortions of behavior, self-perpetuating in one individual and mutually reinforcing from one individual to others. Like my prolonged anxiety attack several years before, each of these behavioral distortions constitutes a set of repetitious, stereotyped, physically painful maneuvers by which the individual blocks his own ongoing activities, and in the process blinds himself to *what he is doing* and *why he is doing it*.

But if human organisms comprise fundamentally self-correcting structures, how is it possible for us to display distortions of behavior which do not get eliminated by our own spontaneous self-correcting activities? Well, it seems that these distortions of behavior constitute self-paralyzing maneuvers which serve to put out of operation our own self-correcting activities. Furthermore, since these self-paralyzing maneuvers prove physically painful, the difference between moments of distorted and of relatively undistorted behavior remains in principle detectable, in both inter-personal and intra-personal transactions. Anyone who learns to distinguish between these behavioral modes can then at will challenge the assumptions underlying moments of distorted behavior, whether the distorted behavior comprises his own or somebody else's. The challenged person will respond with anxiety, hostility, or other emergency-functions, as if his very life were at stake, and thus will try to persuade, manipulate, or coerce the challenger to cease challenging. If the challenge cannot be defeated, the challenged person (oneself or somebody else) will go through a crisis marked by stark terror, for in his own judgment, not to succeed in paralyzing himself *this time* will result in his total destruction. But when he realizes that the maximum of his terror was not followed by his own death or dismemberment, he will in effect find himself thrown out of his habitual pattern of behavior, and will find he has to (or at least has a chance to) work out a new solution to the problem, which was previously stabilized in an insoluble form by the distortion. And in the process of this working-out, the distortion will disappear. This kind of working-out involves pain and suffering, but it is not the meaningless suffering of trying to adapt to the unendurable. Instead, it stands as the price of growth.

At this point, this thesis comprised a far-reaching doctrine of the spatio-temporal structure of human psychodynamics. When I presented this paper in August 1965 at the Ninth International Conference on General Semantics in San Francisco, I made two large logical claims for that doctrine: a) since it is based on Korzybskian premises, I claimed that it stems from assumptions more parsimonious than those in general use by students of behavior, and b) I claimed that the doctrine itself is free of self-contradiction.

In order to test these claims, in collaboration with John F. Randolph, Fayerweather Professor of Mathematics at the University of Rochester, I translated this theory into the form of an axiomatic system stated in a set-theory notation (Hilgartner & Randolph, 1969 a, b, c, d). Thus I can support the claim that there now exists at least one general theory of human behavior which starts from first principles, and which has survived extensive logical scrutiny and so demonstrably meets logical and epistemological standards of adequacy.

Scientists cannot afford to ignore logical criteria, e.g. topics such as self-consistency or parsimony; but in the evaluation of a theory, scientists properly regard the topics of scientific accuracy and correctness as more important than logical claims alone. But the formulations of this theory offer such explicit pictures of the structure of human inter-personal transactions that it appears feasible to put this theory to test by recording actual human inter-personal transactions, as by movies or video tapes, and then subjecting these recorded transactions to intensive analysis from the viewpoint of the theory.

One pilot study designed to test this theory has already been performed. In one of the theoretical papers (Hilgartner & Randolph, 1969c), I use our logical calculus of behavior to analyze a fabricated "encounter" in which two strangers meet in an otherwise deserted hallway, and exchange a glance and a warm smile, but no words. This "encounter" is shown as being important to the two participants, and in the notation, I show just how and why it proves important. But it constitutes also a "commonplace" situation, which can be closely approximated experimentally. For this experimental study, a concealed camera was set up, and was used to record the actual encounters between a "known participant" standing in a corridor and those unselected strangers who happened to pass down the corridor toward the camera during the time it was in use. These recorded encounters were then shown to independent judges, who were asked to classify them according to a rating scale derived from the theory. Statistical procedures were then used to estimate the degree of inter-judge agreement, and to establish the probability that this degree of inter-judge agreement could occur as a result of chance alone.

On the basis of our findings, we must conclude not only that our judges showed highly significant agreement in assigning encounters to the different categories of our scale, but they also showed highly significant agreement concerning which encounters approximate "unimpaired" behavior and which encounters include the contact-avoiding (self-paralyzing) maneuvers which constitute overtly "impaired" behavior.

That crucial point of our Korzybskian theory which was subjected to test by this study constituted precisely the question of the appropriateness of using *Korzybskian* assumptions in the study of human behavior. In order to test this question, we set up a null-hypothesis based on the traditional Aristotelian assumptions—and the results unequivocally disconfirmed the Aristotelian view, and did not disconfirm the Korzybskian view. To quote our conclusion:

"If the relations with ourselves-and-others, such as the processes of 'forming an association' and 'continuing the association' or the various means of avoiding contact, were somehow 'mental' and thus did not constitute observable physical activities, then they could not be observed by independent observers; and if they could not be observed by independent observers, then the ratings recorded by independent observers viewing movie records of encounters would show no greater degree of inter-judge agreement than could be accounted for on the basis of chance alone. This, however, is clearly not the case: Our judges showed highly significant inter-judge agreement. Therefore our study appears to have disconfirmed the Aristotelian view of inter-personal transactions, and appears not to have disconfirmed the Korzybskian view." (Hilgartner & Johnson, 1968.)

At present, my plans include attempts further to extend our logical calculus of behavior, in an attempt to account for the structure of human inter-personal transactions which involve verbal as well as non-verbal interchanges. I already have other movies and video tape records of inter-personal transactions, as well as audio tape records of the entire proceedings of a weekend seminar on the topic of Inter-Personal Transactions, which await analysis. Furthermore, I have designed a series of studies of two-person groups, where not only the visible and audible aspects of the transactions are studied, but equipment is used to measure and record several physiological variables on both participants. Furthermore, the results of the measurements are to be displayed so both participants can easily see them. By methods like these, perhaps we can begin to improve our understanding of the "semantic reactions" which occur when two people deal with themselves-and-each-other.

Summary

I have given a brief, personal account of some of the efforts I have made to increase my own understanding of the happenings which make up my own life. In the course of these efforts, I have had to shift my attention from the "nutty-gritty" details of my own life, to matters of fundamental theoretical import, to informal and formal experimentation, and back again. I suggest that this paper deals with the structure of the "semantic reaction" of trying to specify the structure of my own "semantic reactions."

REFERENCES

Condon, W. S., and W. D. Ogston, 1968, "Speech and Body Motion Synchrony of the Speaker-Hearer," presented at the Perception of Language Conference, Pittsburgh, Pa., 12 Jan. 1968.

Hilgartner, C. A., 1968, "General Semantics, Psychotherapy, and the Logic of Science," *ETC.*: A Review of General Semantics (1968) 25: 315-324.

―――――, 1965, "Feelings, Orientation, and Survival", presented at the Ninth International Conference on General Semantics, San Francisco State College, August 1965.

―――――, and William R. Johnson, 1968, "Encounters in a Corridor: Human Inter-Personal Transactions", presented at the Tenth International Conference on General Semantics, Denver, August 1968.

―――――, and John F. Randolph, 1969, "PSYCHO-LOGICS: Human Behavior in the (Organism Environment) Field "
a. "A Logical Calculus of Behavior", *J. Theoretical Biology* (in press).
b. "The Structure of 'Unimpaired' Human Behavior", *J. Theoretical Biology* (in press).
c. "The Structure of Empathy", *J. Theoretical Biology* (in press).
d. "The Structure of 'Impaired' Behavior" (submitted for publication).

Korzybski, Alfred, 1958, *Science and Sanity: An Introduction to Non-Aristotelian Systems and General Semantics.* Fourth Edition, Lakeville, Conn.: International Non-Aristotelian Library Publishing Co.

USE OF PSYCHOLOGICAL SCALING METHODS FOR QUANTIFYING OBSERVABLE ASPECTS OF SEMANTIC REACTIONS

FRANKLIN H. SILVERMAN
Marquette University

The "semantic reaction" (Korzybski, 1958) is of considerable interest to general semanticists. Alfred Korzybski (1958), Benjamin Lee Whorf (1956), Wendell Johnson (1946) and others have offered numerous hypotheses regarding various aspects of this formulation. Although these hypotheses have profound implications with respect to understanding and modifying individual and group behaviors, they have stimulated relatively little systematic research. This may be due in part to the fact that many of the "entities" referred to in these hypotheses, such as signal-symbol reactions and evaluational rigidity, are difficult to quantify or measure. Since most investigators seem to desire data that can be treated statistically—i.e., numerical data—they tend to gravitate to areas where such data are obtainable. Hence, it is highly probable that measurement problems have impeded the development of general semantics as a research area. The solving of these problems, then, appears to be a prerequisite to systematic research based upon the semantic reaction formulation.

Methodologies will be discussed in this paper which should prove useful for quantifying some aspects of semantic reactions. These methodologies are referred to collectively in the educational, psychological, sociological, and speech literatures as psychological scaling techniques. Included in this group are the methods of constant sums (Guilford, 1954), direct magnitude-estimation (Stevens, 1956), equal-appearing intervals (Edwards, 1957), paired (pair) comparisons (Edwards, 1957), rank order (Guilford, 1954), and successive intervals

(Edwards, 1957). The semantic differential (Osgood, Suci, and Tannenbaum, 1957) is a related methodology which can be viewed as an extension of the method of equal-appearing intervals in which each stimulus is rated for more than one "attribute."

The term "measurement" has been variously defined. One of the more frequently cited definitions refers to measurement as ". . . the assignment of numerals to objects or events according to rules" (Stevens, 1951, p. 1). With psychological scaling methods, the assignment of numerals is accomplished by means of judgments from a panel of observers. Depending upon the scaling method, these judgments may be of either *direction only* (e.g., specifying which of two stimuli possesses the greater amount of an "attribute") or of *both direction and magnitude* (e.g., specifying the relative amount of an attribute possessed by each of two stimuli). In the case of judgments of *direction only,* the numerals would theoretically satisfy the conditions for a "quasi-serial order" (Hempel, 1952) and result in a scale with ordinal "properties." In the case of judgments of *both direction and magnitude,* the numerals might in addition to satisfying the conditions for a quasi-serial order satisfy the conditions of "extensiveness" (Hempel, 1952) and thus result in a scale with either interval or ratio "properties."

The "objects or events" which would serve as stimuli for scaling aspects of semantic reactions would generally fall into one of two categories. The first would consist of "live," audio-taped, and video-taped segments of individual or group behaviors. Included in this category would be segments from interviews, segments of verbal and nonverbal group interactions, audio and video tapes of subject's responses to experimental treatments, etc. The second would consist of objects or events which had been "created" by man. Included here would be words, essays, drawings, sculpture, music, etc.

Specific aspects or "attributes" of semantic reactions which can be reliably quantified through the use of psychological scaling methods need to be identified. However, before scaling methods can be incorporated into research designs for quantifying an "attribute" of semantic reactions, various methodological questions need to be answered including the following:

1. Can scale values for the "attribute" be obtained which possess a degree of reliability adequate for the research design(s)?
2. Which scaling method is most advantageous to use to rate the "attribute"?
3. What "properties" of the stimuli may be influencing judges' ratings?

For illustrations of research designs which could be used to answer each of these questions, I would recommend a paper by Sherman, Shriner, and Silverman (1965) for the first question, one by Sherman and Silverman (1968) for the second question, and one by Shriner and Sherman (1967) for the third question.

What specific observable aspects of semantic reactions might be quantifiable by means of scaling methods? Several which I feel are quite likely to be quantifiable by these methods are (1) "consciousness of abstracting" (Korzybski, 1958); (2) "idealism," "frustration," and "demoralization" (Johnson, 1946); (3) "extensionalization" (Korzybski, 1958); (4) "delay of reaction" (Korzybski, 1958); (5) use of "allness" terms (Johnson, 1946); (6) "relaxation" (Johnson, 1946); and (7) "evaluational rigidity" (Johnson, 1946). In the near future, I hope to begin a program of research at the University of Illinois do assess the scalability of several of these aspects of semantic reactions.

One of the most important determiners of the success or failure of scaling experiments is the instructions given the judges. What specific kinds of instructions might one give to panels of judges for scaling aspects of semantic reactions? I will attempt to partially answer this question by presenting a set of instructions which could be used for scaling "idealism" (Johnson, 1946) by the method of equal-appearing intervals. The first, third, and fourth paragraphs of these instructions are similar in structure and content to those used by Moodie (1957) for scaling articulation defectiveness.

"You are asked to listen to a series of five-minute segments from tape-recorded interviews. The interviewer in all of the samples is the same. The segments will be presented to you one at a time. You are asked to judge the *interviewee* in each segment in relation to a nine-point scale of degree of *idealism*. Make your judgment on the basis of the whole segment."

"The term 'idealism' is discussed in a paper by Wendell Johnson entitled *Verbal Cocoons* which you were asked to read before this session. If you are uncertain about the meaning of this term, reread *Verbal Cocoons* before beginning the scaling task."

"The scale is one of equal intervals—from *1* to *9*—with *1* representing *lowest* degree of idealism and *9* representing *highest* degree. Interval *5* is the middle between *1* and *9* in degree, with the other numbers falling at equal distances along the scale. Do not attempt to place segments between any of two of the nine points, but only at these points."

"After listening to each segment, you will record immediately the number of the scale position you think the sample should have. The next segment will be played after a short pause. Each segment will be announced by a number. You will record your scale number to the right of the segment number on your response sheet. Notice that you will start at the top of the column and work down toward the bottom."

"Before you record any judgments, play the entire tape to acquaint yourself with the experimental task and to acquaint yourself with the range of the samples with respect to the degree of idealism of the interviewee which you are asked to judge."

"After you have acquainted yourself with the task and the range, make a judgment on every sample. If you are somewhat doubtful, make a guess as to the most suitable scale position."

The assumption has been made in these instructions that the judges will perform the scaling task individually by means of the sequential procedure described by the author (Silverman, 1968). Considerable attention should be given to the second paragraph since the approach used to "define" idealism may prove useful for defining other aspects of semantic reactions. In order to maximize the probability that the judges will adequately acquaint themselves with the "attribute" to be rated before beginning the task, they could be asked to read the article in the experimental room (within view of the experimenter), rather than prior to coming to it.

The fact that these instructions were written for the method of equal-appearing intervals should not be construed to mean that this would necessarily be the best scaling method to use. It is quite possible that one of the other methods would be more advantageous. If an interview segment approximately in the middle of the range for idealism could be identified to use as a "standard," then the method of direct magnitude-estimation could be used. Direct magnitude-estimation would not require that the judges listen to the entire set of interview segments before beginning the task (see paragraph five of the equal-appearing-intervals instructions). Hence, the time required to rate the segments could probably be reduced by a third to a half if direct magnitude-estimation were used.

The following instructions, which with the exception of the second paragraph are similar in content and structure to a set used by Prather (1960) for rating articulation defectiveness, could be used to rate the interview segments for idealism by the method of direct magnitude-estimation:

"You are asked to listen to a series of five-minute segments from tape-recorded interviews. The interviewer in all of the samples is the same. The segments will be presented to you one at a time. You are asked to estimate the relative degree of *'idealism'* exhibited by the *interviewee* of each segment in relation to the degree of *'idealism'* exhibited by the *interviewee* in a *standard* segment which will be played for you soon. You will do this task by assigning the number of points you believe represents the relative degree of idealism for each segment."

"The term 'idealism' is discussed in a paper by Wendell Johnson entitled *Verbal Cocoons* which you were asked to read before this session. If you are uncertain about the meaning of this term, reread *Verbal Cocoons* before beginning the scaling task."

"Now you shall hear what we call the *standard segment*. (Play it once.) You will assign 100 points to this segment. The point assignments you will be asked to make on the succeeding segments should represent the relative degree of idealism exhibited in each segment. For example, if you believe that the interviewee in the second segment exhibits twice the degree of idealism as the interviewee in the standard segment, you will assign 200 points to the second segment. If you believe that the degree of idealism exhibited in the segment is half that exhibited in the standard segment, you would assign 50 points. Of course, you may use any point assignment you choose to represent the degree of idealism; you need not limit yourself to even fractions and multiples of the 100 points assigned to the standard. You might use the quantity 85 or 65 or 20 or even 57, or 112 or 120 or 215 or any number you choose so long as it represents the degree of idealism exhibited in the segment in relation to that exhibited in the standard segment."

"Now you will hear the standard segment followed by several segments similar to the ones you will soon be judging. Do not record judgments—merely listen. You might think about the point assignments you would make if you were recording judgments. (Play the standard segment followed by several interview segments.)"

"You are now ready to judge the experimental segments. The first segment is your standard segment so when it is played you will record the number 100 on your response sheet. With the remainder of the segments, you must record the number which represents the degree of idealism exhibited in the segment in relation to the 100 points assigned to the standard segment. If you are somewhat doubtful about what number to assign, make a guess. You will record your number to the right of the segment number on your Rating Sheet. Notice that you start at the top of the column and work down. After listening to each segment, you will record immediately the number of points which you think the segment should have."

These instructions could be recorded on the same tape as the segments to be rated. The assumption has again been made that the judges will perform the scaling task individually. With minor modifications both these instructions and the ones for equal-appearing intervals could probably be used to scale other observable aspects of semantic reactions.

I have attempted in this paper to suggest ways in which psychological scaling methods could be incorporated into research designs in general semantics. While there is to the best of my knowledge no data available on the scalability of general semantic formulations, it should be noted that formulations which are as "abstract" and difficult to define as many in general semantics have been successfully quantified through the use of psychological scaling methods.

ACKNOWLEDGMENT

This paper was supported by PHS Training Grant No. TI-NG-5479 from the National Institute for Neurological Diseases and Blindness.

REFERENCES

Edwards, A. E., 1957, *Techniques of Attitude Scale Construction,* New York: Appleton-Century-Crofts.
Guilford, J. P., 1954, *Psychometric Methods* (2nd Ed.), New York: McGraw-Hill.
Hempel, C. G., 1952, *Fundamentals of Concept Formation in Empirical Science,* Chicago: Univ. of Chicago Press.
Johnson, W., 1946, *People in Quandaries,* New York: Harper & Row.
Korzybski, A., 1958, *Science and Sanity: An Introduction to Non-Aristotelian Systems and General Semantics* (4th Ed.). Lakeville, Connecticut: Institute of General Semantics.
Moodie, Catherine, 1957, "A Comparative Study of Four Psychological Scaling Methods Applied to Articulation Defectiveness," M.A. thesis, Univ. of Iowa.
Osgood, C. E., G. J. Suci, and P. H. Tannenbaum, 1957, *The Measurement of Meaning,* Urbana: Univ. of Illinois Press.
Prather, Elizabeth M., 1960, "Scaling Defectiveness of Articulation by Direct Magnitude-Estimation," Ph.D. dissertation, Univ. of Iowa.
Sherman, Dorothy, T. Shriner, and F. Silverman, 1965, "Psychological Scaling of Language Development of Children," *Proceedings, Iowa Acad. Sci.* (1965) 72, 366-371.
Sherman, Dorothy, and F. H. Silverman, 1968, "Three Psychological Scaling Methods Applied to Language Development," *J. Speech Hearing Res.* (1968) 11, 837-841.
Shriner, T., and Dorothy Sherman, 1967, "An Equation for Assessing Language Development," *J. Speech Hearing Res.* (1967) 10, 41-48.
Silverman, F. H., 1968, "An Approach to Determining the Number of Judges Needed for Scaling Experiments," *Percept. Mot. Skills* (1968) 27, 1333-1334.
Stevens, S. S. (Ed.), 1951, *Handbook of Experimental Psychology.* New York: Wiley.
Stevens, S. S., 1956, "The Direct Estimation of Sensory Magnitudes —Loudness," *Amer. J. Psychol.* (1956) 69, 1-25.
Whorf, B. E., 1956, *Language, Thought, and Reality,* New York: Wiley.

SOCIOMETRIC MEASURES OF SEMANTIC REACTIONS

ALTON B. BARBOUR
University of Denver

Man's relations with his fellow men are crucially important for his personal and social survival.—*H. H. Remmors*

As with a number of useful ideas which have come to us, it will probably not surprise anyone that Aristotle said it first. Speaking about man, the "political" (social) animal and his relations with others, he said, "Birds of a feather flock together." Empirical and experimental evidence support Aristotle's assertion and further suggest that those "birds" have a "pecking order," and that "flocking together" *makes* "birds of a feather." Social scientific investigations since World War I have revealed that groups are formed and rank their members because of a similarity of norms, standards, and values of the group members. The description and measurement of such interpersonal relationships are the subject of this paper.

Theoretical Considerations

Group formation and ranking might be explained in this way. Shutz (1960) has said that an individual in a group will want to achieve a sense of comfort and balance in three areas, (1) inclusion, (2) affection, and (3) control. That is, the extent to which he personally wants to be included in the group, to show or be shown affection, to control or be controlled by others. The extent to which this individual's comfort level exhibits itself in behavior that represents group norms (the group's comfort level) will be a determiner of ranking in the group for that individual.

Another way of explaining group formation and ranking is with the internal-external systems analysis of George C. Homans (1950). Homans would say that we rarely determine our goals, norms, standards, or values on an individual basis, but rather, they are determined for us by the groups we are members of; that there is a tremendous pressure exerted by the group to conform; that the groups which exert the strongest pressure are those which have the strongest ties to members, e.g., those where sentiment (affection) is greatest, where there is more frequent interaction, where activities allow for interpersonal communication.

It might be said, then, that ranking in groups is determined by how well the individual comfort level described by Shutz fits the group system described by Homans. The individual will want to satisfy his sense of balance, harmony, and equilibrium. The group will want to determine its norms, standards, and values. Group structures and ranking will be a function of how well these two systems coincide. It is important to note that, according to Homans, sentiment is the major factor in strength of group ties. One's measure of inclusion is based on reciprocal feelings, and inclusion and affection are, according to Shutz, two major elements of the individual comfort level. The feeling-affection-sentiment overlap of the two systems is obvious, at least on the theoretical level, and is central in the sociometric measurement of group relationships.

Ranking in Groups

In nearly all established groups, members are ranked and in turn rank others. The ranking may be implicit or explicit, may be rough or very precise. But one thing is virtually certain: the more a group member represents the norms, standards, and values of the group, the higher he will rank (see "Summary" in Berelson and Steiner, 1964, p. 339 ff.).

Middle-status persons are most likely to conform. They have the most to gain by conforming and the most to lose by deviating. They are most likely to be criticized for deviating or ostracized under strict and continuous social control. A high premium of group membership has a direct relationship to conformity. This means that people will tend to go along with the group. I believe that we are all familiar with the autokinetic effect explored by Sherif in 1935 and the Asch experiments done in 1951. The individual will normally resist conforming to group norms only if there are strong countervailing influences from another group to which he is conforming. For instance, highly popular teen-age girls tend to conform closely to neighborhood norms for popular music and disc jockeys. Fad and fashion norms are anchored in small groups of friends (Johnstone and Katz, 1957, p. 563).

However, there is an exception to this rule. Very secure, high-ranking members do not conform *as strictly* as others and are not subjected to such serious pressure to conform. Tolerance of "eccentricity" is normal in some groups because high-status people provide services for the group and have more freedom from control (Riecken and Homans, 1954, p. 793).

High status is more innovative than low or mid status. A responsibility for innovation is assumed with leadership. Innovation brings esteem and authority. Low status non-conformity, on the other hand, is more apathetic and deviant against the norm rather than setting or extending the norm (Homans, 1961, p. 163).

The closer a person conforms to the norms of a group, the better liked he will be (Affection-Shutz; Sentiment-Homans). The better liked he is, the more he will conform. The less he conforms, the more disliked he will be. "Deviants are rejected while conformists become popular" (Argyle, 1957, p. 155). People want to be liked, so they will engage in actions that will tend to increase the esteem they receive from those around them, i.e., conformity.

Finally, different groups will have different norms and will rank their members differently depending upon group objectives, clarity of goals, member access to information, etc. (Bales, 1959, p. 299). It is clear, however, that groups rank their members based on feelings (affection, sentiment) arising out of the extent to which individuals represent group norms, standards, and values.

Sociometric Theory
Social scientists have long been concerned about the problems

80 Alton B. Barbour

inherent in man's interpersonal relationships because social relationships have a significant bearing on individual and group effectiveness. Moreno (1960 *et al.*) has developed sociometric concepts and tools that have yielded new and important understandings of complex social microcosms. (See Gage, 1963, p. 347 ff. and Hare, Borgatta and Bales, 1965, p. 99 ff.) Moreno did not originate the idea that groups had structures. Olson (1929), Loomis (1931), and Challman (1932) all had studied group structures on the basis of observation. However, Moreno, as early as 1931, was the first to develop a sociometric "test" and to structure a group according to expressed preference.

A sociometric "test" is a technique for eliciting responses from members of a defined social group about each other. The responses have direction and are essentially rankings. The results, once obtained, are usually presented in some diagrammatic or sociomatrix form. Moreno is responsible for the systematic development of this method for obtaining verbal choice responses and their subsequent representation. Most reports of the development of the sociometric "test" appeared in *Sociometry,* a journal which was under Moreno's direct control until 1956 when it was taken over by the American Sociological Association.

Sociometric theory involves a special vocabulary to specify the way in which it describes interpersonal relationships. Two important words are *tele* and *transference*.

> *tele:* A fundamental unit of attraction between members of a group and having two dimensions, projective or outgoing and retrojective or returning.

According to Moreno, "The trend toward mutuality of attraction or rejection many times surpasses chance probability." Moreno described it as being mathematically in direct proportion to the number of pair relationships, and in inverse proportion to the number of unreciprocated relationships.

> *transference:* A "passing over" of tele or "identity." Increases in direct proportion to the number of un-

reciprocated relationships and in inverse proportion to the number of paired relationships.

A psychiatrist named Sullivan called transference a "parataxic distortion" because it is a "carry-over" from past experience, largely false-to-fact, more misleading than reliable, based on incident, accident, and irrelevancy.

social atom: The smallest living social unit, itself not further divisible (Moreno, 1953, p. 291).

As related to tele, the networks of the social atom are composed of tele (attraction, rejection, flow of feeling). Once a sociometric "test" has been devised and a sociogram or sociomatrix constructed, there are several other terms used to describe the configurations and occurrences within the structures of the social atom. These can be found in any standard reference on sociometry (see "Bibliography").

Sociometry and Psychometry
The word "sociometry" is often confused with "psychometry," but there are fundamental differences between the words and formulations. Psychometry is individual mental-psychological measurement. Sociometry is a testing of social structure and social sentiment. Psychometry doesn't measure group structure but sociometry does (Crisswell, 1949, p. 288). Sociometry focuses on the individual as part of a group rather than on the individual as an entity (Pepinsky, 1949, p 39).

Lindzey and Borgatta (1954) say that a sociometric "test" is a rating scale in that members of the group are asked to rate the other members of the group in terms of their social desirability for sharing activities, but there are fundamental differences between sociometric "tests" and rating scales. Sociometric measures are more limited than rating scales in the variables they can be used to assess, and more restricted in the settings in which they can be employed. There is usually no need to train raters to engage in sociometric ratings. The rater is asked to use the same criteria he has been using all his life to do something he is an expert in: to indicate whom he likes or dislikes and to what degree; to decide those with whom he would wish to interact or avoid. There are differences even in the ratings. Sociometric ratings are not impersonal, but are thought to be the result of rater-rated interaction. Because of these differences, Crisswell (1949) suggested that "test" not be used to describe sociometry, but that "technique" be employed instead.

Sociometric Validity and Reliability

Scientific evaluation carries with it the conventional notions of validity and reliability. There are some limitations of scientific reliability applied to sociometric data. It is difficult to distinguish between the effects of memory and change. If a test-retest interval is long, real changes in group relationships will have taken place and the reliability coefficient will have been lowered. In this example, "low reliability" is preferred because it distinguishes the modification of group relationships manifested in changed choice patterns. In fact, Lindzey and Borgatta (1954) say that high reliability may mean an insensitive instrument. Crisswell (1949) suggests comparing the instrument scoring to some other criterion and measuring the extent to which error variance is reduced.

Sociometric validity is also difficult. In most psychometric tests a trait is measured by eliciting related responses. For example, attitude is measured by asking opinions and the answers can be compared to data gathered by psychological testing. But in a sociometric test, the sample is drawn *from the behavior studied.* Under such conditions, the predictor is the same as the criterion. However, once sociometric choice behavior is used to describe more general traits, it becomes, for scientific purposes, the same as a psychometric test, and can be subjected to validation against a suitable criterion.

Pepinsky (1949) says that sociometric validity finally rests on being sure that the responses obtained are not falsified. This would mean that the tests have face (appearance) validity, that there be rapport between the experimenter and subjects, that Moreno's criteria of actual reorganization (for "built-in" validity) actually take place.

Gronlund (1959) reviewed literature on sociometric validity and reliability. He found the internal consistency of sociometric tests to be high and stability over time to be high also, varying with time interval. As to validity, Gronlund reported that sociometric tests have been found to be sufficiently related to subject behavior outside the testing situation. He found it to be more related to social adjustment than to personal adjustment.

Sociometric-semantic Synthesis

At the cost of oversimplifying, it would appear that Korzybski (1921, 1933) was essentially concerned about two things: (1) that people behaved as if words were things, and (2) that people assumed that their abstractings and meanings were the same as everybody else's. It is important to note that instead of talking about "meanings," Korzybski referred to "semantic reactions." He suggested that a great number of the ills of the world were traceable to a lack of correspondence between the perceivable world and the "semantic reaction" inside. He further suggested that a greater harmony in interpersonal relations might be achieved if the world were more "scientific" and hence more "sane." That is, if people observed objectively, defined operationally, and judged rationally. He held that science was sane, and that the applicability of the scientific method to social ills was bound to improve the *status quo*. Korzybski's suggestion was largely ignored, and the *status quo* has sadly degenerated from chaos to catastrophe.

It would appear that there is considerable overlap between the methodologies of Moreno and Korzybski. That which Korzybski advocated is what Moreno accomplished. In very simple terms, Moreno made objective, scientific, and measurable that which was subjective, personal, and emotional. He opened the door on the science of interpersonal relationships by describing interpersonal "meaning," by measuring "semantic reactions" of attraction and rejection that people have toward each other.

Obviously, we don't only react to words: we react to people depending upon what we abstract about them. Let me specify. Tele is a semantic reaction based on a factual relationship. Let me remind you of the importance both Shutz (1960) and Homans (1950) ascribed to feelings-affection-sentiment, and say that tele is that relationship scientifically defined and measurable. Transference is, again, a semantic reaction, but one which is non-scientific, based not on

Korzybskian fact-territory abstractings, but upon faulty abstractings and identifications of an un-indexed and un-dated variety. Clearly, training in general semantics holds considerable promise for reducing transference in interpersonal relations, for making them more "sane."

Secondly, it seems to me that the presentation of sociometric data in sociogram or sociomatrix form is again an example of making objective and scientific that which is subjective and emotional. Changes in time and in relationships (dating and indexing) can be rendered in elaborate overlays, three dimensional models, or with matrixalgebra. It seems rational to want to understand relationships before tampering with them. These display techniques describe the relationships so they then can be treated experimentally.

Which leads to a third point. Sociometry is not only a research methodology, but an action methodology. Once the relationship is exposed, it can (if deemed appropriate) be changed. The methodology has direct application to daily living in the world around us because it tells us:

1. How to organize large aggregates into small face-to-face groups.
2. How to develop compatible groups.
3. How to organize efficient groups with members who get along with one another.
4. How to adapt a group to a specific task.
5. How to identify group leaders, followers, etc.

But there is a reciprocity apparent in the works of the two men, Moreno and Korzybski. For all of the scientific promise sociometry has for objectifying the "semantic reactions" of interpersonal relations, there is also the potentiality of the application of general semantics to sociometry. An obvious example would be the tendency of a researcher to identify his symbols on a chart or numbers on a line as if they were more than high-order abstractions.

It would also appear that the two methodologies could be used conjointly and that such a usage could be productive. Both men were concerned about the problems and ills of the world. Such problems, so far as I see, tend not to be content problems but "people problems." It is apparent that sociometry can describe aspects of interpersonal relationships essential to group structure and that this "meaning in people" is one of the provinces of general semantics. The relationships as well as the "reactions" can be understood and, hopefully, remedied.

But there is still much to know. Both methodologies are in their infancies and need development. Apart from the critical synthesis already implied here, I would also suggest factor analyses of the relationships between sociometric choice and psychological profiles. I suggest investigation into the relationships between sentiment-affection-liking and conformity. I suggest the investigation of transference as a semantic disorder. I suggest correlation investigation between sociometric choice and sociological attitude data. I suggest that new instruments for measuring meanings be developed and that instructional instruments be developed for moving the findings from the academic world to the streets. The infinite variety of social ills are too enormous to undertake totally, but a semantic-psychometric-sociometric investigation of *conflict* looms before us so importantly on the local, national, and international scene that it can hardly be ignored. It appears to me that general semanticists have long overlooked the potentiality of sociometry for accomplishing the goals of general semantics. They can only overlook the potential now at a tremendous cost in time and effort.

Such research as I've suggested should yield insights into who ought to communicate what, when, and to whom, to alter Aristotle's "birds of a feather" from "hawk" or "dove" into man, the social animal who is able to see the grey between the black and the white, and cope with his feelings about it.

REFERENCES

Argyle, Michael, *The Scientific Study of Social Behavior*, New York: The Free Press, 1957.
Bales, Robert F., "Small Group Theory and Research" in Robert K. Morton, *et al.* (eds.) *Sociology Today: Problems and Prospects*, New York: Basic Books, 1959.
Barbour, Alton, "Making Uncommon Sense" in Louis E. Glorfeld *A*

Short Unit on General Semantics, Beverley Hills, Cal: Glencoe Press, 1969.

Berelson, Bernard and Gary A. Steiner, *Human Behavior, An Inventory of Scientific Findings,* New York: Harcourt, Brace and World, Inc., 1964.

Challman, R. C., "Factors Influencing Friendships among Pre-school Children," *Child Devel.* (1932) 3, 46-158.

Criswell, J. R., "Sociometric Concepts in Personnel Administration," *Sociometry* (1949), 12, 287-300.

Gage, N. L. (Ed.), *Handbook of Research in Teaching,* Chicago: Rand-McNally, 1963.

Gronlund, N. E., *Sociometry in the Classroom,* New York: Harper, 1959.

Hare, A. Paul, Edgar F. Borgatta, and Robert F. Bales, *Small Groups: Studies in Social Interaction,* New York: Knopf, 1965.

Homans, George C., *The Human Group,* New York: Harcourt, Brace Inc., 1950.

Horst, P., "A Generalized Impression of the Reliability of Measures," *Psychometrika* (1949), 14, 21-32.

Jennings, H. H., *Leadership and Isolation,* New York: Longmans, Green, 1943, 1950.

Korzybski, Alfred, *Manhood of Humanity,* Lakeville, Conn.: International Non-Aristotelian Library Publishing Co. (2nd Ed., 1950).

—————, *Science and Sanity,* Lakeville, Conn.: International Non-Aristotelian Library Publishing Co. (4th Ed., 1958).

Lindzey, G. and E. F. Borgatta, "Sociometric Measurement" in G. Lindzey (ed.) *Handbook of Social Psychology,* Cambridge, Mass.: Addison-Wesley, pp. 405-448, 1954.

Loomis, A. M., "A Technique for Observing the Social Behavior of Nursery School Children," *Child Develop. Monograph* No. 5, 1931.

Moreno, J. L, "Sociometry in Action," *Sociometry* (1942) 5, 298-315.

—————, "Sociogram and Sociomatrix," *Sociometry* (1946) 9, 348-349.

—————, "The Three Branches of Sociometry, A Postscript," *Sociometry* (1948), *11,* 121-128.

—————, *Sociometry, Experimental Method and the Science of Society,* New York: Beacon House, 1951.

—————, *Who Shall Survive* (Rev. Ed.), New York: Beacon House, 1953.

—————, and H. H. Jennings, "Statistics of Social Configurations," *Sociometry* (1938), *1,* 342-374.

—————, H. H. Jennings, and J. Sargent, "Time as a Quantitative Index of Interpersonal Relations," *Sociometry* (1940) *3,* 62-80.

————, H. H. Jennings, and J. Sargent, "Time as a Measure of Interpersonal Relations," *Sociom. Monograph* No. 13, 1947.

————, et al. (eds.), *The Sociometry Reader*, Glencoe, Ill.: The Free Press, 1960.

Olson, W. C., "The Measurement of Nervous Habits in Normal Children," *Univ. of Minnesota Inst. Child Welf. Monograph* No. 3, 1929.

Pepinsky, P. M., "The Meaning of 'Validity' and 'Reliability' as Applied to Sociometric Tests," *Ed. Psych. Meas.* (1949) 9, 33-49.

Riecken, Henry and G. C. Homans, "Psychology Aspects of Social Structure," in Gardner Lindzey (ed.) *Handbook of Social Psychology,* Cambridge, Mass.: Addison-Wesley, Vol. II, 1954.

Shutz, William, *The Interpersonal Underworld,* Palo Alto, Cal.: Science and Behavior Books, Inc., 1960.

THE MEASUREMENT OF INTERPERSONAL TRUST

KIM GIFFIN
The University of Kansas

The problem of identification of different levels of abstraction for research purposes is one of extreme importance to all scholars of human bahavior as is the relationship between two behavioral elements. An example of two such behavioral elements might be (1) instructional communication on the part of a job supervisor and (2) the implementation of these instructions on the part of an employee. However, the determination of the *attitude* of the employee toward the supervisor (for example, the degree to which the employee *trusts* the supervisor) is also of extreme importance because the use of such a construct as "trust" can *explain the relationship* between the two behavioral elements.

Trust is referred to as a "construct" because it cannot be observed *per se*; it can only be *inferred* from observed behavior of two types: (1) the degree to which the instructions were followed, or (2) responses on an introspective questionnaire or interview schedule. Such a questionnaire or schedule may be highly sophisticated, such as those using a summated ratings scale or a semantic differential or even a behavioral differential as that developed by Triandis (1964a). In any event, such an instrument produces only introspective data which implies the existence of a construct, that is, an object or event whose existence is inferred but *not directly observable*. A very great danger to a behavioral scientist is that he may confuse his thinking by failing to recognize the limited research value of construct-measurement, and thus engage in reification; he may come to believe that the construct itself is behavioral reality. An excellent detailed discussion of this problem is given by Mellinson (1967).

The nature of this problem is exemplified in the research on interpersonal trust. Avoidance of reification is illustrated below; at the same time, the construct, "trust," is shown to be useful in explaining the connection between related behaviors in a trusting situation.

Trusting Behavior

The attempt to operationally define trusting behavior in the interpersonal situation was pioneered by Morton Deutsch (1958). He noted that it involves more than predictability—expectation is also involved. He noted that risk or personal investment is requisite and that, when trust is not fulfilled, the trusting individual suffers an unpleasant consequence which is greater than the gain he would have received if the trusted person had proven to be reliable.

It appears that the following elements are requisite for a condition of interpersonal trusting behavior:

(1) A person (P) *is relying* upon another person (O).
(2) P *is risking* some potential loss.
(3) P *is attempting* to achieve some goal or gain.
(4) This desired goal is *uncertain*.
(5) P's *potential loss* if his trust is violated *is greater* than his potential gain if his trust is fulfilled.

Note that each of the elements listed above is requisite for a trusting situation to occur; however, even when all of them are present, they do not guarantee that an *attitude* of trust is also present. Note, too, that each of the elements in trusting behavior can, when present, be ascertained by a competent observer. Such is not the case with "trust" which here is identified as an attitude or construct.

Interpersonal Trust: A Construct

Trust is here defined as an attitude in the sense of involving cognitive, cathectic and conative tendencies (cf. Triandis, 1964b). It involves *cognition* of a situation (cf. Newcomb, 1953); it involves *cathect* in terms of degrees of positive or negative affect (cf. Thurstone, 1946); it involves *conation* as a "latent variable," a potential for action under certain conditions (cf. Edwards, 1957).

It is important to distinguish the difference between an attitude of trust (the introspective orientation which is a potential for action) and the action itself (trusting behavior). It is common knowledge that one's attitude toward another person may not always be reflected by one's observable actions. Thus, behavior which may appear to be based upon an attitude of trust may not always be so, and an attitude of trust may not always be reflected by observable trusting behavior.

Note that trusting behavior is a sub-set of reliant behaviors; trusting behavior is always reliant, but reliant behavior is not necessarily trusting behavior. Reliant behavior can include a situation of ignorant dependency, such as that of a one-year-old child in his father's arms; the child may not be *attempting* to achieve any personal goal as identified by item 3 in the trusting behavior paradigm outlined above. Also, reliant behavior can include a situation wherein the person relying is unaware of any risk involved to himself, such as that of a smaller child ignorantly following his unthinking brother across an expressway. In fact, an observer of a person who exhibits trusting behavior must recognize that the behavior observed may be the result of cognitions or cathects other than those of an attitude of trust; these may include imitation of others, conformity with others, or personal habits—all with no cognition of risk in the situation. Behavior which appears to be based upon an attitude of trust may in reality be based upon impulse, caprice, masochism, hopeless despair, or "virtue"—belief that it is immoral to act distrustful of a revered person, for example, a bishop.

Only the person who appears to be relying can indicate (1) the extent to which he is *aware of any personal risk,* and (2) whether or not he is *attempting to achieve some specified goal.* In some situations it may appear to be perfectly obvious that such a person is aware of a personal risk and is attempting to achieve some specified goal—but such data are inferential, even if they appear to be "perfectly obvious."

There are two major drawbacks to the practice of inferring from observed behavior that an *attitude* of trust exists: (1) the inference may be erroneous, and (2) to *measure* the degree (positive or negative) of an attitude from such inferential data is extremely difficult. Deutsch (1958) argued in favor of the validity of such an inference regarding the existence of trust (an attitude) under very carefully observed conditions of trusting behavior as identified above. He argued such an inference on the grounds that under such conditions, if trust were not present, such behavior would be *irrational*, and that no reasonable individual would engage in such behavior unless he had an attitude of trust; without trust, "such behavior would make no sense" (p. 270).

There is now evidence that in situations studied by Deutsch (gaming experiments), observed behavior does not necessarily reflect an attitude which "makes sense." People do not always behave in a rational way; that is, they do not always attempt to achieve that goal which would provide them with maximum utility values (cf. Messick and Thorngate, 1967). Sometimes people will repeatedly risk the loss of great amounts of utility values, for example, money, on the outside chance that they will be a winner once. The motivation to win over another person at almost any cost may be higher than the motivation to gain ultimate utility value by letting the other person also be a winner. Such is the "unreasonable" behavior of some people at some times.

The Measurement of Trust

The assumption that an attitude is present when certain behaviors occur is just as tenuous as the assumption that certain behaviors occur when a specified attitude is present. The two are opposite sides of the same coin, and both must be measured for the coin to be properly identified. Attitude scales must be validated against relevant behavior and assumptions about the attitudinal basis of observed behavior must be verified by the use of attitude scales.

Measurement of trusting behavior as defined above has been explored by Deutsch (1958), Rapoport (1962), and Roby and Carterette (1965). Measurement of the attitude of interpersonal trust has been pioneered by Giffin and Wilson (1968) and by Giffin (1968). It is important that research efforts of these two types be integrated if maximum value is to be achieved for they represent different levels of abstraction in an interpersonal encounter.

REFERENCES

Deutsch, Morton A., "Trust and Suspicion," *Journal of Conflict Resolution* (1958) 2, 265-279.

Edwards, Allen L., *Techniques of Attitude Scale Construction*, New York: Appleton-Century-Crofts, 1957.

Giffin, Kim, "An Experimental Evaluation of the Trust Differential," *Research Monograph R/19*, Lawrence, Kansas: The Communication Research Center, The University of Kansas, 1968.

―――――, and Susan Vance Wilson, "The Development of a Summated Ratings Scale of Interpersonal Trust," a paper presented to the Annual Convention of the Speech Association of America, Chicago, 1968.

Mellinson, J. R., *Principles of Behavioral Analysis*, New York: Macmillan, 1967.

Messick, David M., and Warren B. Thorngate, "Relative Gain Maximization in Experimental Games," *Journal of Experimental Social Psychology* (1967) 3, 85-101.

Newcomb, Theodore M., "An Approach to the Study of Communicative Acts," *Psychological Review* (1953) 60, 393-404.

Rapoport, Anatol, "Formal Games as Probing Tools for Investigating Behavior Motivated by Trust and Suspicion," *Preprint 98*, Ann Arbor, Michigan: Mental Health Research Institute, University of Michigan, 1962.

Roby, Thornton B., and Teresa Carterette, "The Measurement of Confidence and Trust," *Tech. Reprt. No. 8*, ONR Contract Nonr-494 (15), Meadford, Mass.: Institute for Psychological Research, Tufts University, 1965.

Thurstone, L. L., "Comment," *American Journal of Sociology* (1946) 52, 39-70, 1946.

Triandis, Harry C., 1964a, "Exploratory Factor Analyses of the Behavioral Component of Social Attitudes," *Readings in Attitude Theory and Measurement*, New York: John Wiley and Sons, Inc. (1967), 208-219.

―――――, 1964b, "Introduction," in H. C. Triandis, *et al.* (1964), *The Behavioral Differential: An Instrument for the Study of the Behavioral Component of Social Attitudes* (*unpublished manuscript*), 1-11.

THE SITUATIONAL ANALYSIS OF URBAN COMMUNICATION: AN EXTENDED-CASE STUDY OF RACIAL TENSION

RUSSELL W. JENNINGS
and
THOMAS J. PACE, JR.
Southern Illinois University
and
DENNIS E. WINTERS
Humboldt State College, Arcata, California

The problematic aspects of performing *in situ* social research, whether on an individual or group basis, are well-known to the social scientist. Many of these problems, particularly those associated with situation delimitation, seem, under normal conditions, to pose serious research difficulties. However, when they become cast into the "open" social environment and are focused on critical social-political questions, the problems sometimes pose nearly insurmountable barriers to the performance of research. Thus frequently, social researchers are forced to adopt methods that lack the control of the more strict laboratory approaches, but nevertheless do facilitate social-political examination, as does the case study approach.

The purpose of this paper, then, is to describe a methodology that is applicable to a case study approach. While the method may be sufficiently general to be applied to other case study conditions, it was adapted in these studies for the functional examination of dissident, extra-institutional community-action groups in the metropolitan Chicago area. This approach, referred to as the extended-case method (see Van Velsen, 1967), focuses on the juxtapositioning of cases in order that between-case comparison may be made, as well as to permit the construction of a composite of a single case.

Although individual, isolated cases are considered to be informative, when a number of such cases are placed in juxtaposition to each other, in a situational field, the prospects of obtaining more generalizable information tends to increase, by virtue of the comparative focus. Thus, such comparison tends to "quickly draw the observer's attention to [the] many similarities and differences . . . [which] contribute to the generation of theoretical categories, to their full range of types and continua, their dimensions, the conditions under which they exist . . . and their major consequences. The observed differences and similarities speedily generate generalized relations among the theoretical categories, which, in turn . . . become the hypotheses soon integrated into . . . theory." (Glaser and Strauus, 1965.)

As employed in the studies reported here, the extended-case approach permitted the examination of the same cases in a number of different situations[1] as well as allowed each situation to be latitudinally defined by juxtapositioning cases relative to each other in the same situation.[2] Whereas the situation within which data collection occurred differed from case study to case study, the question persisted: How do leaders of dissident community-action groups define, assess, interpret, and act on the particular tension situations faced by their groups in the urban society? Since the principal purpose of this paper is to explicate a methodolgy applicable to the case study approach, the substantive results of these studies will not be reported here. The remainder of this paper, then, deals with the rationale for this approach and brief descriptions of each situation in which the case studies were carried out.

---

[1] *Situation* is defined here as referring to a particular interact field within which relevant self-other patterns arise as dynamic relationships in response to interpersonal tension. [Fearing, F., 1968, "Toward a Psychological Theory of Human Communication," in *Interpersonal Communication: Surveys and Studies,* Boston: Houghton-Mifflin Co., pp. 32-34.] It is a unique constellation of events and processes which is unduplicable when once passed. [Murphy, Gardner, 1950, *Studies in Leadership,* New York: Harper and Bros., p. 37.]

[2] *Definition of situation,* as used here, means the system of expected "other" responses aroused in a given personality by a given situation. [Cottrell, L. S. Jr., 1968, "The Analysis of Situational Fields in Social Psychology," in *Interpersonal Communication: Surveys and Studies,* p. 387.]

The rationale for this methodolgy as applicable to the extended-case study approach is founded on three assumptions. First, the methodology recognizes the validity of contemporary "decision theory" based on the foundations of symbolic interactionism.[3] The theory assumes that the leaders in the institutionalized framework of the community-action groups are "fully interacting" with rather than "merely conforming" to the constituent demands of the group. While each community-action group has a normative framework that sets forth roles and divisions of labor, the actual role transactions "generate a more or less coherent and stable working agreement between the ideal set prescriptions and a flexible role-making process, between the structural demands of others and the requirements of one's own purposes and sentiments . . ."[4] The "leader's definitions of the situation" are not exclusively what he believes the situation to be, nor what he believes the group's assessment to be, but definitions that are isomorphic to the dynamics of the "fully interactive" community-action group.[5] In deriving these "leader's definitions of the situation" there is no attempt made to evaluate the "correctness" of particular statements of the leader. Often, the statements are empirically false, but they are the bases upon which ensuing behavior is founded. This type of investigation is principally interested in the "definitions" which are the symbolic world of the "fully interactive" community-action group.

The second assumption is that by altering the form of situations, the leader must redefine his interactive group in a new situational context. This allows the case data gathered from the new situation to be analyzed for changes, persistence, dissolution, etc. It is possible

---

[3]*Decision theory* is concerned with the rational choices, within human organizations, based upon examination of a given situation and its possible outcomes. [Von Bertalanffy, L. "General Systems Theory: A Critical Review," in *Modern System Research for the Behavioral Scientist*, Chicago: Aldine Publishing, p. 13, and Buckley, W., "Society as a Complex Adaptive System," *Ibid.*, pp. 497-98.]
[4]*Ibid.*, 504.
[5]Situational definitions, as elicited by a leader, contain (1) the group's perception of the situational demands, (2) the leader's perception of the situational demands, and (3) the product of the transactionally mediated interaction of 1 and 2. Thus, each situational definition manifests the dynamics of those transactional mediations between leader and followers and functional field in a fully interactive relationship.

that the "process level" as manifested in the symbolic language of the "leader's definition of a fully interactive group" may become so transformed that it is not identifiable when compared to the definitions of the previous case situation. Careful analysis, however, can reveal certain "invariant themes under transformation," which are important to any thorough examination of functional groups in a social-political field.

This methodology is not based on purely abstract theory nor exclusively bound to a collection of empirical facts, but rather is functionally founded on relevant empirical content with an adequate explanatory theory. Although many contemporary general semanticists are prone to criticize methodology that is not consistent with a "positivistic-behavioristic" "sensory perception-observation" bias, it does not appear consistent with Korzybski's basic approach to deny this type of cognitive theorizing as long as it is not devoid of empirical support. Therefore, the third assumption of this methodology in utilizing the extended-case study method, is that data collected from each leader in each situation is analyzable and open to authoritative interpretation. Unlike more "intuitional" approaches, inferential interpretations of the leader's definitions of dissident community-action groups and their social-political situation can be consensually validated and meaningfully interpreted by social scientists who are familiar with the substantive issues of the particular situational social-political field; who are grounded in relevant theoretical explanations; and most important, who are conscious of their abstractings and of the self-reflexivity of language. This last assumption is only now being explored for its maximal procedural application. It would be misleading to imply that the case studies, about to be discussed, grew out of this theoretical framework, or that this methodology emerged out of the case studies. Rather, the practical demands of doing field research in communication and the theoretical and philosophical biases of the researchers, particularly consistent with symbolic interactionism, converged to simultaneously produce both the theoretical bases and the appropriate case study methods. Both emerged out of the research situation.

Initial interest in developing a theory of social systems, through communication research, was launched in the form of two seminal field case studies in urban tension during 1967-1968. Under the direction of Tom Pace, two Ph.D. candidates (See Jennings, 1968, and Winters, 1968) moved to Chicago with the initial intent of performing an historical analysis of the now famous "1968 March into Cicero." During the course of initially interviewing community leaders involved in this event, it became apparent that more fruitful information might be obtained by focusing on two community-action groups[6] involved in a critical contemporary urban problem-area. Prior to this realization, a situational analysis had been planned (Cottrell, 1968, pp. 379-92). This essentially involved concentrating on a relatively narrow field—Cicero, Illinois, 1966, relating to Martin Luther King's threat to march into Cicero, his decision not to, Robert Lucas' leadership of the actual march, and the subsequent intra-community reactions to the event—and those salient instrumental factors—individuals and groups—which were functional preceding, during, and following the march, with each phase being examined principally through their public communication behavior.

With the decision to analyze two distinctive groups, however, it became necessary to employ case method techniques. This decision not only required the expansion of the initially defined situation to include the metropolitan Chicago area focusing on civil rights activities during 1967-1968, it also added another consideration to the analysis—that of dissident groups. These changes were not incongruent with the principles of situational analysis, since the two organizations[7] selected for examination were voluntary, grass-roots level community-action groups, principally concerned with *de facto* segregation (or integration, depending on your perspective) in the Chicago metropolitan area during 1967-1968. Most important, both groups were instrumental political forces situationally, and each was

---

[6] In these studies, *community-action groups* refer to those which, in the context of a particular community, concern themselves with only a narrow range of policies, those related to the peculiar interests of the group membership which they perceive to be of significance to the best interests of the community. *Ibid.,* 6.

[7] These groups were (1) the Concerned Citizens of Cicero and Berwyn (C.C.C.B.), an all-white anti-integration, community-level backlash organization led by John Pellegrini; and (2) Operation Breadbasket, a Negro economic self-help group, sponsored by the Southern Christian Leadership Conference, and led by Rev. Jesse Jackson, Director of Northern Operations.

overtly retaliated against periodically for their respective programs. Thus, they were essentially closed groups—groups to which access could be gained only by "trustworthy" individuals who could contribute to their operations. Trustworthiness involved receiving a complete security clearance by the group's intelligence network, while adequate contribution to the operation was determined by what you could do that they couldn't afford to do, either financially, politically, and sometimes legally. In this stance, payment was in the form of transcribing recorded tapes, providing copies of these tapes (all *gratis*), periodic library research, organization analysis, special types of informant tasks, as well as financial contributions. Even upon receiving "clearance" and having paid the ransom, access was given only on a restricted basis.

The tasks, then, encountered in carrying out these studies, involved (1) surveying the available demographic and ecological data, which was nearly non-existent since the groups operated on a socially marginal basis and had not been in existence long enough to permit collection of such data; (2) surveying all available mass media sources for reports of the groups' historical operations as well as to gain some insight into the general dimensions of the problem field and to acquire potential "leads"—persons either supportive or antagonistic to the groups or their leaders; (3) undertaking frequent interviews with selected individuals considered to be instrumentally related to the groups and their operations—this included frequent meetings with the leaders themselves as well as with their assistants and principal opponents; and finally, (4) developing an analytic technique which, when applied to the public communication of the leaders—the speaking done at open meetings, conferences, discussions, and interviews—would yield thematic propositions upon which could be built a core definition of their respective situation, as well as provide a perspectival definition of the transactionally mediated role of each leader as he attempted to relate his group to the situational demands and contingencies.

The "closedness" of the groups, the virtual absence of demographic and ecological data, and the unreliability of mass media reports, forced the researchers to rely principally upon the recorded speeches, discussions, conferences, and interviews as primary, directly observed data, while the mass media materials and available governmental statistics were treated only as supplementary, for the elaboration of already well-founded data derived from the primary sources. The principal application of mass media materials, however, was to provide a description of the general historical social-political context in which these two groups could be inserted for interpretation. The mass media sources were surveyed covering April, 1966, through May, 1968. Recorded speeches were used covering from January, 1967, through May, 1968. No pertinent demographic or ecological data was found to generally encompass this period.

Once the primary data was collected, a method of analysis developed jointly by Drs. Winters and Jennings permitted the extraction of propositional themes upon which the situational definition would be based. The method of analysis, based on the principles of symbolic interactionism, and decision theory, primarily focusing on the concept of role, was composed of five theme categories and procedurally involved four steps: Step 1.—An analysis was made of the speeches of the selected leaders to discover their identification of the situational crisis. Themes were distinguished by their frequency in the speeches. In this context, *disequilibrium* was defined as the social structure concretely opposing the group he represented. Step 2.—A thematic analysis of the leader's speeches concerning the appropriate counteraction was developed. In this context, the *counteraction* was defined as the explicit calls-to-action made by the leader to confront the opposing social structure. Step 3.—A thematic analysis was made of the speeches to determine the leader-perceived predispositions which, if internalized by the target audience, would develop an efficient response to the counteraction. This is the *target assumptive* theme. Step 4.—An analysis of the speeches was conducted to determine the resident and coping assumptive sets. The *coping assumptive set* was composed of those themes the leader utilized to facilitate the internalization of the situational target assumptive set. The assumptions on the part of the audience, which occasioned the repetition of these coping themes, were then interpreted to define the *resident assumptive set*.

By way of demonstration, consider the following brief example of themes extracted from the speeches (Jennings, 1968):

Step 1.—The central disequilibrium theme for the C.C.C.B. was "forced racial integration relates to the establishment of racial integration through the application of severe social-political pressures by institutional force" (p. 104). In developing this central theme, a sub-theme explicitly stressed that "the integration efforts are being forced by individuals and interests from outside the community who are not acting in the best interests of Cicero and Berwyn" (p. 104).

Step 2.—The counteraction deemed appropriate to this disequilibrium was focused on the churches as composed of individuals (their clergy) and having interests outside of their respective Cicero and Berwyn parishes, thereby justifying the withholding of money, withdrawing of children from parochial schools, and boycotting the churches, as well as sending written protests about church involvement in civil rights to the churches and the archdiocese offices (pp. 115-117).

In order to develop the necessary efficient response for the group members to engage in these activities and believe that disequilibrium theme, Step 3—the target assumptive theme—was that "people deserving of trust and support and who best serve the interests of the community are those who have invested concretely in the community" (p. 125). Obviously, the church falls outside of this group since the priests and ministers are transient, do not own real estate, and therefore are not to be trusted, much less supported.

Step 4.—Involves the delineation of the themes appropriate to the last two categories. The coping theme appropriate to this example was that "the church, directly and indirectly, is no longer functioning in behalf of its members or in the best interests of the community" (p. 134). As a complementary facet of this step, the appropriate resident assumptive theme was that "the church continually functions for the ultimate best interests of its membership and the community in which it exists" (p. 138).

The five thematic categories, as explicated in this example, delineate the group's held perspective, the leader's held perspective, and the manifested mediation of these perspectives in the form of coping behavior. When such themes are merged into a composite, it is viewed as a functional definition of a situation.

During the terminal phase of the two field case studies in Chicago, and in response to a growing awareness of the dimensions and severity of the racial problem there, especially in the first half of 1968, a seminar initiated and supervised by Drs. Winters, Pace, and Jennings was undertaken at Southern Illinois University to explore further the community-action group's definitions of the racial problem. It was at this juncture that the extended-case study was initiated. Again, the social-political situation—the interact framework from which the individual cases would be drawn and relative to which the results of the case studies could be interpreted—was expanded. Rather than concentrating on only two of the many groups potentially available within this situational context, leaders of eleven grassroots level community-action groups were enlisted for participation.

Among these groups were not only instrumental organizations, fully at the center of the racial crisis, both pro- and anti-integration, but groups which were marginal yet directly related to the issue, such as Latin Americans Defense Organization, Jobs or Income Now, and Students for a Democratic Society, were examined as well. Inclusion of marginal groups as cases in the situational field provided some indication as to the functional dimensions of the situation—whether groups periodically promoting or opposing racial questions were committed to the issue or only using it as a vehicle for the achievement of other goals.

The second dimension was that of examining the initial cases studied in a new situational context—thus extending the cases along a longitudinal continuum. In these cases, leaders of the C.C.C.B. and Operation Breadbasket were examined in a dialogistic situation—following a seminar format. The objectives of the seminar were (1) to compare the elicited definitions of the situation from the two previous case studies with those from the new situation in an effort to identify the similarities and differences between the situations; (2) to examine the definitions of the situation elicited by the new cases studied in an effort to identify the similarities and differences between the cases in the new situation; and (3) to examine the differences of the definitions of the situation as elicited by the marginal groups with the intention of establishing a criterion for the situational defining of group marginality.

The seminar was structured so that each community-action group leader would participate for a one day period, during which time they would testify as "expert witnesses" of the racial situation in Chicago. They interacted with interested graduate students and faculty from a variety of disciplines—sociology, speech, economics, political science, philosophy, and community development. The seminar focused on the perspectives from which these grass-roots activists, both black and white, defined their respective problems, solutions, and positions regarding the racial issue as they were manifested in their respective situational definitions; however, a secondary objective was to bring those scholars professing an interest in functional urban racial problems into contact with activists who could authoritatively describe the fundamental social-political tension in their situational environment.

At this time, analysis of the data has not been completed because of unanticipated logistic problems. However, based on cursory examination of the 56 hours of recorded interviews, a number of core themes have been identified as persisting in their original form throughout the seminar—from case to case. Meaningful interpretation of these themes, at this time, however, has not been undertaken.

Based on the completed results obtained from the two *in situ* field case studies, as well as the preliminary examination of the seminar materials, a third phase project is now being proposed as the next logical progression in these extended-case studies in urban racial tension. This involves interacting in a confrontation situation with individuals supposedly representing the identified disequilibrium. In this situation, the selected community-action leaders who participated in the seminar, as well as an equal number of leaders from institutional agencies—churches, law enforcement agencies, welfare agencies, schools, city government, and federal agencies, such as urban renewal—will live together in an isolated, closed environment for a ten-day period. During this time, they will room together, take common meals, participate in common recreation activities, and engage in a series of debates, discussions, and small group interpersonal experiences, all focused on the racial issue in Chicago. Only the leaders and the project staff will be permitted to participate.

All activities—meals, discussions, recreation, etc.—will be both audio and video recorded, with the exception, of course, of private functions. The primary emphasis during the entire session will be on maximum interpersonal confrontation, restricted only to avoid physical violence, or to refocus on the central issue.

Again, the objectives of this project are to make extended-case and between-case comparisons. This time, however, the comparisons will be made within the confines of a confrontational situation in which a leader not only articulates the situational definition espoused by his group, or the situational definition relevant to a particular line of questioning, but also must defend these definitions and the underlying ideology in a variety of contexts—open debate, discussions, at meals, etc. Although this situational format is expected to present unique logistic problems, the anticipated mass of information is considered vital to the further explication of the emerging theory of social action.

REFERENCES

Cottrell, L. S., Jr., 1968, "The Analysis of Situational Fields in Social Psychology," in *Interpersonal Communication: Surveys and Studies*, Boston: Houghton-Mifflin Co.

Glaser, Barney, and A. L. Strauss, 1965, *Awareness of Dying*, Chicago: Aldine Publishing, 290.

Jennings, R. W., 1968, "A Community-action Group's Definition of Urban Tension: A Situational Analysis Through Public Address in Cicero, Illinois, in 1967-1968," Unpublished doctoral dissertation, Speech Department, Southern Illinois University.

Van Velsen, J., 1967, "The Extended-case Method and Situational Analysis," in *The Craft of Social Anthropology*, London: Tavistock Publications.

Winters, D. E., 1968, "A Community-action Group's Definition of Urban Tension: A Situational Analysis Through Public Address in Chicago, Illinois, in 1967-1968," Unpublished doctoral dissertation, Speech Department, Southern Illinois University.

# HUMANISTIC APPROACHES

CONSCIOUSNESS OF ABSTRACTING IN LITERARY RESEARCH

DONALD E. WASHBURN
Edinboro State College, Pennsylvania

Nowhere is consciousness of abstracting more important than in literary research. The "fact territory" of the critic is only indirectly the world of events. He is concerned with words: with what somebody has written about what somebody else might have said about what he might have experienced (including what other people might have said about what he said, etc.). In a sophisticated work of literature the complexities are staggering. And, of course, the critic himself is making statements at even higher orders of abstracting. To avoid oversimplifications, allnesses, and other forms of misevaluation in such a hall of mirrors is difficult. It is the purpose of this paper to show how a knowledge of general semantics may be of assistance in various kinds of literary research and analysis.

One of the first applications is based on the awareness that the term "research" is multiordinal. Its meaning changes according to the level of abstracting at which it is being used. And this, in turn, depends on what aspects of the work the critic decides to pay attention to. Words may be studied in at least four basic ways. They may be viewed as objects insofar as they are held fixed in a medium that communicates their structure as language. They may be viewed as systems insofar as they generate hierarchies of complex interrelationships and patterns. They may be viewed as meanings insofar as they evoke semantic reactions and influence behavior. And they may be viewed as models or metaphors insofar as they allude to the universe itself, including human experience. In each of these perspectives "research" has a different meaning and presupposes somewhat different kinds of methods.

The first task of literary research is to discover and authenticate the text. At this stage the work exists as an artifact to be placed in its proper historical context. There may be problems of decipherment. Or there may be more than one version. Or the manuscript may be incomplete. When the record is slightly impaired, the researcher may bring his knowledge to bear in reconstructing the text, much as deteriorated paintings are restored by specialists in museums. Also, he may have to make inferences about authorship, date of composition, editorial corruptions, and other matters bearing on the fate of the text as object. The techniques are not much different from those applied in archaeology or history. And since the enterprise depends to a large extent on conjecture, it must be carried on with a sophisticated awareness both of the relevant data and of the abstracting process itself.

But there is also another sense in which a literary work may be studied as an object. It is possible to attend merely to measurable aspects of the text: the distribution of graphemes or phonemes, the incidence of a particular syntactic pattern, or the statistical profile of any stylistic feature. In other words, the text may be approached as a linguistic structure rather than an act of communication. The field of reference is thereby limited to characteristics about which nearly total agreement is possible. Although this may seem to be a handicap, such observations frequently bring to light information that is useful at the level of interpretation.

Take, for example, the following short poem:

> The roller rink whirrs with their pass-
> es. They skirr like gadgets in a gallery-
> y, their girlish flirtations fatuous and brass-
> y, bull's-eyes for some smoking gunner.
>
> Everywhere arms are cocked. The or-
> gan booms tunefully. Reeling, they giggle or
> grope at their skirts. The banging boys
> trophy them away like kewpies.

A phoneme count would reveal a higher than usual incidence of /r/ in the first stanza. It can be found in the words "rolle*r*," "*r*ink," "whi*rr*s," "ski*rr*," "galle*r*y," "gi*r*lish," "fli*r*tations," "b*r*assy," and "gunne*r*." This information in itself is not particularly interesting. But when it is brought into relationship with the rest of the poem, its place in a larger structure of onomatopoeia becomes apparent. The /r/ phoneme "fits" in that it is strongly suggestive of the roar that skates make on a wooden floor. It is not just an accidental feature, but rather contributes to the sense of scene which the poem evokes. The same could be said of the clause "The organ booms tunefully." And another formal feature, the frequency of hyphenated enjambments, is suggestive of the circular motion of the skaters.

The tie-in between form and sense is just one of the ways that structures at one level are coordinated with structures at another level. Actually, this principle is fundamental to the organization of the poem as a whole. A poem is non-elementalistic in the sense that if the artistic purpose is fully realized, every feature has its place in a hierarchy of patterns and relations that, taken together, are more than the sum of its parts. Change one atom in a molecule and the chemical properties of that molecule may be significantly altered. Change one word in a poem and the results may also be non-additive. Poems, in other words, are systems and must be approached by methods appropriate to the study of systems.

Since symbol systems are multi-dimensional, only a multi-dimensional awareness can do them justice. General semantics is most useful in this respect. It stresses the importance of multiordinality and indexing for differences. These insights can be applied both to the variables in the work of literature itself and to the critic's own abstractings. Since general semantics is based on a language of structure and relations, it provides a measure of protection against additive thinking and over-simplification. An "allness" attitude which reduces wholes to parts and hypostatizes functions is as pernicious in art as it is in life. Without consciousness of abstracting an interpretation may be narrowing the reader's response to the poem rather than amplifying it.

Literary research in one sense is a search for relations and principles of organization. It is an attempt to discover how each of the parts of a work may be assimilated to higher order strategies of insight and attitude. One short poem, for example, will be confusing until the reader understands that it is based upon the analogy between what happens at the roller rink and what happens at a shooting gallery. The two situations are held in a state of bisociation by means of a series of puns. "Passes," for instance, can mean either flirtatious advances or repeated motions. "Brassy" can refer to a noisy and ostentatious manner or to the metal part of a gadget. Other words appropriate to both contexts are "smoking," "arms," "cocked," "organ," "banging," "reeling," and, metaphorically, "bull's-eyes," "trophy," and "kewpie." Altogether, there are at least a dozen points of convergence.

What's more, an analysis of these pivotal terms reveals a third frame of reference not explicit in the girls-gadgets theme. This is the theme of sexual conquest, which is part of a hidden agenda that makes the roller rink more than just a place of fun and exercise. The triple pun on the word "banging" applies to all three situations: skating, shooting, and copulating. There are other Freudian possibilities in constructions like "bull's-eyes," "arms are cocked," and "organ booms."

The interpenetration of frames of reference calls attention to similarities that might not otherwise be noticed. Moreover, attitudes appropriate to one situation may be applied to another, and what is explicit in one context may manifest what is implicit in another. These strategies are a powerful means for revealing structure since both the invariance and the transformation are simultaneously before our eyes. Although we know the skating rink is not a shooting gallery, the poem forces us to become aware of numerous isomorphisms and axiological parallels. These are revealed in the vocabulary of the poem, which consists of variables that must be indexed for patterns of interrelatedness and relevance. The formulation of dimensions of relevance is one of the most important tasks of literary research.

Of course, relevance is a function of the relationship between parts and wholes. Not all associations are amplified by the rest of the poem. Although wings make a whirring sound, it would be a mistake to hear the sound of wings in the first line. Similarly, the possible allusion to fishing which might be heard in the word "reeling" finds no support at any other point in the poem. Paradoxically, while the whole is grasped by means of the parts, the parts cannot be understood fully until the overall strategy and purpose is clear. Some misreadings occur because the reader is unable to generate useful higher order abstractions. But others occur because his abstractions are not firmly established by lower order details.

Just as research in the physical sciences is aimed at testing hypotheses, so literary research is partly a matter of measuring generalizations about meaning and purpose against what the words will allow. This is not usually a simple matter, since most texts generate a range of possibilities. And even the sum of all interpretations is never equivalent to the meaning, just as a set of abstractions is never the same as the "ground" from which it is derived. The Korzybskian principle of non-identity can be seen here in the critic's insistence that no paraphrase can be completely adequate to the text.

On the other hand, one of the basic organizing principles of a literary work is that one thing may be understood or evaluated in terms of another. This is done through a network of symbolic equivalences. For example, the girls at the roller rink are equated with targets, the boys with marksmen competing for trophies. Such equations are possible because language selects, connects, and frames the irreducibles of experience. And in so doing, it provides for one kind of response rather than another. Metaphor, synechdoche, metonymy, paradox, and irony are names for structures that control the way the reader abstracts and provides the connotative cues that predispose one kind of evaluation instead of another. These structures in turn are determined by the rhetorical strategy that expresses the writer's own relationship to the experience he is writing about.

To visualize this, consider how the reader's responses are controlled in the poem about the girls at the roller rink. Since they are represented as "gadgets in a gallery" we see them in an ironically diminished perspective. Their motives and actions have been sufficiently restricted as to give them the appearance of machine-like regularity or inflexibility. (It is a stock device of comedy to account for behavior in relatively simplistic terms.) Our attitude is thereby disposed to be one of condescension. And this is reinforced elsewhere in the implications of words like "fatuous," "brassy," "giggle," and above all, "kewpies."

In literature there is seldom any separation between information and attitude. The poet makes no attempt to distinguish what he has experienced from how he has experienced it. To paraphrase Zola's words, literature shows us a corner of the world seen through a temperament. And since it is a total response, literary research must shun terminologies implying that distinctions such as "cognitive" and "emotive" or "subjective" and "objective" are more than convenient simplifications. Korzybski's preference for organism-as-a-whole terms such as "semantic reaction," "evaluation," and "orientation" is rooted in his reluctance to establish verbal discontinuities where there are none in nature. The same care must be taken in deference to the unities implicit in a successful work of literature.

To emphasize the sense of total involvement, the critic Kenneth Burke has proposed that literature is a form of symbolic action and that a dramatic rather than an epistemological scheme is most appropriate for analysis. The difference can best be summed up in the contrast between "reaction" and "act." The latter stresses not only knowledge but participation. It makes values and motives part of a strategy for encompassing reality rather than embarrassments beclouding one's judgment and objectivity. A successful poem, in this sense, represents a total symbolic solution to some problem of attitude or choice.

But the central difficulty remains that although we speak of meaning as though it were something that can be studied more or less objectively, the fact is that meaning is always somebody's meaning. It is true that the critic, like the scientist, has his methodology to protect him against the worst sorts of misreadings, but literary history is full of cases where even the experts were wrong. And it is no help to resort to the author or to a consensus of readers. Neither may be the final appeal, since neither may see deeply enough into the structure of the work. (The role of the unconscious in creation or re-creation should not be underestimated.) Therefore, research into meaning usually takes the form of an explication, the object of which is to show how the verbal structure of the work can be amplified paraphrastically, that is to say, placed in a fuller, more explicit context.

Korzybski's notion of function is useful here. Works of literature are made up of propositional functions, statements that are, strictly speaking, neither true nor false. But depending on what associations they evoke, they may be more or less convincing. Out of his own experience the reader provides the values that are missing and responds accordingly. Propositional functions are organized by system functions, which in turn take their character from higher order doctrinal functions. In a work of art these higher order functions are usually implicit and, if they are to become conscious at all, come to light as a result of a great deal of critical labor. Perhaps it is fair to say that one of the most important tasks of literary research is to make explicit whatever in a work of literature is implicit.

Even our poem about the roller rink, brief as it is, participates in a recognizable orientation. Surely familiar values and doctrines are discernible in the particular angle of vision that the speaker assumes. His stylistic choices vulgarize the motives and manners of the skaters, making them appear both exploiters and victims of the ritual taking place. It is not only that a courtship so public and venereal is an offence against propriety (i.e., class prejudices), but in a broader sense each sex is immersed in an illusion, which the poem proposes to penetrate. Anyone who could assume the standpoint of the poet is presumably immunized against the kinds of misevaluation that the poem is about.

Since a work of literature alludes to a semantic environment, everything in that environment is potentially relevant to the act of interpretation. There is nothing that the critic may not use if it helps him in his task. The traditional compartmentalizations of knowledge are a hindrance where literature is concerned. Anything that can be talked about—biography, psychology, mythology, religion, sociology, folklore, history—is grist for the critic's mill. Research, therefore, which in this sense is an attempt to establish valid relationships, must be wide-ranging and inclusive. The critic must be prepared to learn whatever the work of literature requires him to know.

He must be conscious of the medium as well as the message.

There is a sense in which literature is, to alter Aristotle's dictum, the imitation of communication. It is, at bottom, what somebody might have said. But the question of who is saying what about whom can lead to some tantalizing ambiguities, especially when the reader does not know whom to believe. And in a complex work the critic must do some fancy indexing to distinguish one line of testimony from another. Nowhere is consciousness of abstracting more vital than in sorting through the polyphony of voices that define the communication-world of the work. And there is the additional complication of the self-reflexiveness of language, which permits statements about statements (even one's own) ad infinitum.

It should be clear from these observations that a critic who is unsophisticated about language and human evaluations is at a great disadvantage. Perhaps it is fair to say that only the critic who has achieved consciousness of abstracting, either intuitively or in the systematic way provided by general semantics, is able consistently to be helpful in literary interpretation. But, by and large, general semantics has not had a great deal of influence among literary critics. The exception is Kenneth Burke (several references), who seems, based on his discussion of Korzybski's work in his own books, to have made use of *Science and Sanity*. But even Burke has doubts about the sufficiency of general semantics for literary analysis. In *A Grammar of Motives* (p. 240) he wrote,

> There is not to this day, nor is there likely to be, a Korzybskian analysis of poetic forms. Nor could a satisfactory one possibly be made without engrafting upon his doctrines a new and alien set of terms and methods. For "semantics" is essentially *scientist,* an approach to language in terms of *knowledge,* whereas poetic forms are kinds of *action.* However, the very incompleteness of his terminology readily allows for the addition of dramatist elements, should any disciple care to pick them up elsewhere and henceforth proclaim them in the name of Korzybskian "semantics."

It should be added, however, that in spite of Burke's reservations, in his own approach to the problems of literary research and criticism he seems to be applying many of the lessons that general semantics proposes to teach. One cannot read very much of Burke without noticing parallels, both in content and method.

Granted that general semantics is not specifically concerned with literary analysis. But it provides a systematic orientation that is helpful in monitoring the abstracting process, no matter what the subject. Research, even in literature, is conducted within the framework of an epistemology, usually implicit. Consciousness of abstracting is important because it is a kind of knowing about knowing. And it offers a way of dealing with the fundamental confusions that lie behind misinterpretations, misreadings, and misevaluations, whether they occur in response to the chain reactions of nuclear physics or the chains of metaphor and analogy in a poem.

REFERENCES

Burke, Kenneth, 1954, *Permanence and Change, An Anatomy of Purpose,* Los Altos, California: Herms Publications.

─────, 1955, *A Grammar of Motives,* New York: George Braziller, Inc.

─────, 1955, *A Rhetoric of Motives,* New York: George Braziller, Inc.

─────, 1957, *Counter-Statement,* Chicago: University of Chicago Press.

─────, 1957, *The Philosophy of Literary Form, Studies in Symbolic Action,* New York: Vintage Books.

─────, 1961, *Attitudes Toward History,* Boston: Beacon Press.

─────, 1961, *The Rhetoric of Religion, Studies in Logology,* Boston: Beacon Press.

─────, 1964, *Perspectives by Incongruity,* Bloomington: Indiana University Press.

─────, 1966, *Language as Symbolic Action,* Berkeley and Los Angeles: University of California Press.

Hockmuth, Marie, 1952, "Kenneth Burke and the New Rhetoric," *Quarterly Journal of Speech* (1952), XXXVIII, 133-143.

Korzybski, Alfred, 1933, *Science and Sanity: An Introduction to Non-Aristotelian Systems and General Semantics,* Lakeville, Conn.: International Non-Aristotelian Library Publishing Co., Fourth Edition 1958.

Rueckert, William H., 1963, *Kenneth Burke and the Drama of Human Relations,* Minneapolis: University of Minnesota Press.

THE CRITICAL APPROACH

A Research Design as used in a general semantic analysis of three of Arthur Miller's plays: *Death of a Salesman, The Crucible,* and *All My Sons*—1963.

ROBERT G. JOHNSON
Wayne State College

The chief problem which faces the critic is that of discovering order in the moving, changing, interdependent social and physical environment represented in a dramatic work. The critic's abstractions monitor the playwright's intention. If the playwright's intention is to direct attention to an incident of social disintegration, the critic would search for a causal relationship between the incident and the environmental factors which appear to have produced it.

Purposive writing is selective and it is the selective nature of playwrighting that unifies it as an abstracting process. So too, the critic must be selective in the ordering of abstractions he chooses to use in monitoring the intentions of a playwright.

It is in regard to the selectivity and patterning of abstractions that we find the systematized approaches of psychology and sociology helpful. Analogical patterns offer the critic clarity and accuracy, for when he finds similarities between two things, two operations, two relations, he may extend his knowledge of either or both by assuming that the similarity goes beyond what is already established. In developing his theory of general semantics, Korzybski found it necessary not only to use analogies borrowed from the natural and social sciences but even more, he discovered that his theory of evaluation in a non-elementalistic sense embodied these sciences. For this reason the critic, if he is to employ the principles of general semantics, must consider methodology in this inclusive context. In short, he must be aware that he is employing a system embracing a relational formulation that is non-elementalistic. Although our present language system enables us to break this formulation into fragmented parts represented by the labels "psychology," "physics," "chemistry," "biology," etc., such isolation appears to be contrary to the natural order of things.

By applying the systematized approaches of Cabot (1949), Thelen (1954), Piaget (1930) and Gardner Murphy (1947, 1958), the author attempted to define significant processes and focus more directly on abstracting the meaning structured in dialogue form.

In the play, *Death of a Salesman* (1960), the basic premise appeared to be the effect of Willy Loman's personality on the other characters and on the action of the drama. For this reason a systematized pattern suggested by Murphy in his *Personality, A Biosocial Approach* was used to structure the semantic analysis. Since Murphy's formulations appear to be fundamentally related to the communication process, and since his categorization provides structural guide to the understanding of a human being such as Willy Loman, the use of such a pattern appears justified.

In *The Crucible*, the events Miller represented affected not just the few people crystallized as specific characters for dramatic facility, but the entire community of Salem. For this reason "group behavior" appears to be an important factor in defining and monitoring the play's meaning. Hence, the systematized approaches of Richard C. Cabot, Herbert Thelen, Kurt Lang and Jean Piaget were used as a means of clarifying and defining sociological communicative elements. The use of such systematized approaches not only serves as a means of arranging the separate elements or events within a play, but also helps the critic focus more accurately on the intended meaning of the playwright. The developmental approach used by the critic must be determined by the nature of the play being analyzed. Because playwrighting is a selective process, there are as many developmental approaches as there are patterns discoverable in the world of people and things. The critic must choose that principle of organization which best suits his subject matter and his purpose.

To facilitate evaluating the "causal" aspects of the interrelation of character, action, and words, the 1963 study suggests structuring the analysis so as to separate the attributes of significant characters and events from the more broadly defined action generally manifest in the final resolution of a play. As conceived in this study, certain processes described by the dialogue affect other processes and precipitate future events. In the play *Death of a Salesman,* Loman's "allness" defined as a characteristic attribute and coupled with the "is" of identification leads to "absolutism," "dogmatism," and other semantic disturbances. Self-reflexive processes lead to distortion in his evaluations, and inner conflicts and tensions emanating from Loman's abstractions of himself lead to social conflict and determine the resultant action and final denouement of the play. Because a play appears to be an "artistic" representation (abstraction) of life and not "reality," events are condensed in time, magnified and otherwise altered so as to make a separation practicable. Characteristic attributes identified in this manner must be thought of as dynamic processes affecting and being affected by other processes. Although characters and events are singled out as a convenience to analytical treatment, they must be conceived of relationally as they affect and are affected by other characters and events.

Since the premise of a play is developed through dialogue, functional identification of characteristic attributes may be accomplished by applying such semantic principles as identification, allness, self-reflexiveness, and infinite-valued flexibility and degree orientations as well as other precepts which appear to describe such processes manifest in the dialogue of a play. Character motivation, intra-personal and inter-personal conflict and tension may then be identified as aspects of these same functional processes. Careful attention to the abstracting of the premise should determine which attributes the critic chooses to specify as "significant."

By adopting an actional, behavioristic, functional language, and by applying his knowledge of the scientific world outside him, the critic is able to define the characteristic attributes of significant characters and events as they are manifest in the dialogue of a play. He is able to identify them as dynamic processes which affect other dynamic processes, as "causal" aspects of a complex series of events involving "character-action-dialogue." The resultant action and final resolution of plot which follows as "effect" must also be conceived of relationally as part of the same complex series; it is a continuation of the process of "character-action-dialogue" and is treated separately only to facilitate the structure of the analysis. By applying semantic principles as well as scientifically derived precepts which appear to describe the processes affected in the final resolution of the plot, it is possible to detect contrived structures which are not in accord with "reality" from a semantic point of view. It is also possible to justify the resolution of a premise by evidence substantiating the playwright's invention, and to evaluate the force of the play's message in terms of development-survival.

The Critical Approach 1970

In 1970, we find the problems facing the critic not too different from those he faced in 1963. His primary concern is that of discovering order in the moving, changing, interdependent social and physical environment represented in a dramatic work. Although we find a rather drastic change in what is accepted as "theatre" in 1970, as compared to 1963, if we examine our general semantic method carefully we find that it suits the "new theatre" as appropriately as it did the "theatre of 1963" if not better. For in 1970 it is apparent that dramatists are using the machines used by scientists to record the life process. The theatre of mixed media of 1970 uses the electromicroscopic camera, random analogue projectors, multiple films and tapes, polarized light, chemically treated slides, the oscilloscope, the telescopic camera, and other scientific instruments. The symbolic game structures of 1963 are out of date. The creative performance of 1970 is a new combination of communicative symbols. It has developed an awareness of the infinitely changing electrical network outside and apart from the imprinted categories. If its critics are to understand it, they must of necessity turn to the scientific method. Korzybski's general theory of sanity can lead to a better understanding of the creative logic of discovery common to scientific advances in all fields. It is vital as well to artistic insight and offers a pragmatic method of evaluating the new point of view.

One of the basic tenants of gentral semantics suggests that the world is such that it is impossible to entirely isolate an event. Only a language of relations would have a similar structure to the world around us. For this reason the general semantic analyst must be aware of advances in science which are important to the understanding of his subject. He must be aware that in many instances scientific instruments are able to record what he ordinarily cannot see or hear. The human organism has a capacity to collect experiences of different individuals through a process known as "time binding." Such a capacity increases enormously the number of observations a single individual can handle and so our acquaintance with the world around and in us becomes much more refined and exact. In developing his system, Korzybski used mathematics to show that all verbalism should be, ultimately, similar to mathematics in structure. He used physiology, psychology, neurology, sociology, and anthropology to elucidate and amplify other precepts. Used in this manner, science becomes an extra-neural extension of the analyst's nervous system. The critic's consciousness is expanded.

REFERENCES

Cabot, Richard C., 1949, *The Meaning of Right and Wrong,* New York: The Macmillan Company.

Johnson, Robert G., 1963, *A General Semantic Analysis of Three of Arthur Miller's Plays: Death of a Salesman, The Crucible and All My Sons.* Dissertation, University of Denver. Ann Arbor: University Microfilms.

Miller, Arthur, 1957, *Collected Plays With an Introduction,* New York: Viking Press.

—————, 1947, *All My Sons,* New York: Dramatists Play Service, Inc.

—————, 1954, *The Crucible,* New York: Dramatists Play Service, Inc.

—————, 1960, *Death of a Salesman,* New York: Viking Press.

Murphy, Gardner, 1947, *Personality: A Biosocial Approach,* New York and London: Harper Bros.

Piaget, Jean, 1930, *The Child's Conception Physical Causality,* New York and London: Harcourt, Brace and Company, Inc.

Thelen, Herbert A., 1954, *Dynamics of Groups at Work,* Chicago: The University of Chicago Press.

GENERAL SEMANTICS AS A CRITICAL TOOL IN LITERARY RESEARCH

(A Critical Path)

PAUL HUNSINGER
University of Denver

Most literary critics believe that the assumptions, inferences and pronouncements they make about literature are intelligent and true. They have attained a top position of influence in our culture because of the tremendous volume of literature that has poured from the presses in recent years. Furthermore, since we are busy and evaluation is difficult, we are often prone to take the advice of a critic regarding a literary object and are grateful for an "expert opinion."

The person who uses the tools of general semantics is, in his own way, a critic. He has a method of evaluation which, if properly used, will enable him to make judgments regarding the communication process. What happens then when the general semanticist becomes the critic of the critic? Would critics become better critics if they had a sound background and training in general semantics? Is general semantics a useful tool for literary research and criticism?

Obviously, since there are many methods and modes of criticism, it is impossible to answer these questions affirmatively or negatively, but an in-depth investigation of the techniques employed by some literary researchers and critics reveals a sound and intelligent use of principles and practices of what we call general semantics.

General semantics provides an outline and procedure for literary research that can be of great help to the literary critic. And the semanticist can gain new insights by using the techniques of the literary critics. One major contribution that the semanticist can make

126 Paul Hunsinger

to the critic is that of providing a clearer outline of the communication process. The major contribution of the literary researcher and the critic to the general semanticist is in the area of values and aesthetics. The semanticist is generally more concerned with the scientific aspects of language and human behavior than with aesthetic aspects.

To focus on at least one critical tool used by general semanticists in literary research, I would like to trace a path followed in making critical judgments. The pre-literary experience of poet and critic will be examined first, then the literary expression and, finally, the critical response. For simplicity I will use one poem by e. e. cummings (1944) as the central illustration for this paper. The poem is as follows :

pity this busy monster, manunkind,

not. Progress is a comfortable disease :
your victim (death and life safely beyond)

plays with the bigness of his littleness
—electrons deify one razorblade
into a mountainrange; lenses extend

unwish through curving wherewhen till unwish
returns on its unself.

           A world of made
is not a world of born—pity poor flesh

and trees, poor stars and stones, but never this
fine specimen of hypermagical

ultraomnipotence. We doctors know

a hopeless case if—listen : there's a hell
of a good universe next door; let's go

The Pre-literary Process

We start with the assumption that good literature is not a mere description of something encountered by the writer. The author is not like a camera which merely records what it sees but is a person who makes a dynamic creative response to what he encounters. The composite of what makes up a creative experience that triggers off the writing is infinite in nature. Gilbert Nieman (1949) wrote in *Poetry Magazine,* "The poet has forgotten what Blake knew well. It's a supreme presumption to be a poet. A poet, while he writes, is god." The poet in the pre-literary experience has contact with infinite possibilities in terms of what he can experience and is limited only when he begins to write. The poetic feeling, even when only vaguely expressed, is akin to mystical experiences.

To describe the various elements that may enter into the pre-literary experience, we will use the idea of disteological surds (the smallest possible element of an event that has no known causation) and cepts (the smallest distinctive individual elements that combined can lead to a concept). We begin with the smallest possible element of an event or experience and the smallest possible element that can be the source of both feelings and ideas or concepts. These two sources, one outside the poet and one within, combine to form the pre-literary experience. Poetry is not what is primarily outside or primarily inside the poet, but a combination of these factors, blended and recorded by the poet. Archibald MacLeish (1938) wrote "In Challenge, Not Defense,"

> For only poetry, of all those proud and clumsy instruments by which men explore the planet and themselves, creates the thing it sees. Only poetry, moving among living men on the living earth, is capable of discovering that common world to which the minds of men do, inwardly, not knowing it assent.

The poet does not create a world that is, but a world that should be.

Let us assume that a surd and a cept both enter into the experience of the poet from among a group of cepts and surds. Other elements may have had some influence on the formulation but did not, even though they could be related. The two elements now combine in such a way that they form a gestalt and become a new element in the process.

Since the terms cept and surd are not commonly used in communication theory, it is necessary to provide a more complete definition. A cept is the smallest convenient unit of knowledge. It is facetiously defined as "half a concept." (*Time Magazine*, March 26, 1965, p. 44). For our purposes it is stipulatively defined as "the smallest distinguishable part of an idea, thought or concept."

A surd, according to Oxford English Dictionary (Vol. X, p. 225), is "that which is silent, mute, indistinct and not endowed with sense or perception, and conveying no sense." It is the part of an event which in itself is meaningless, but capable of generating meaning when connected to a meaningful event.

Let your imagination roam freely for a few seconds and review the poem by Cummings. Perhaps the two elements that flowed together were events related to the scientific triumphs of man and thoughts concerning the inability of man to deal with hopeless cases from the medical point of view. Or perhaps it was a happy combination of words that led to the phrase "Progress is a comfortable disease." It might have been a play of words such as "manunkind." At least, there was something in the pre-literary experience that started the poet working along lines that eventually led to the poem.

It is important to consider not only what entered into the poem but what is within the possible range of relationship that another person may sense or experience. Many elements within the poet's experience were not used, but could possibly be used in expressing an idea or feeling. Another person given the same elements might perceive a relation to other elements and come up with a quite different expression.

Remember that the author may not immediately use the elements that start the literary process to create the literature. The time interval between the formulation and the writing may be years and time does have an effect upon the process. Furthermore, the perception of each person will differ. Each sense organ has a signal detection threshold which may be increased or decreased by the individual's mental activity or by a process intrinsic to that organ. There is controversy over whether or not the sense organ relays to the brain all the information it detects, but it is assumed that this is not possible without overloading the circuit. The signal received by the senses organ may be blocked, inhibited, modified, amplified, distorted and changed in a variety of ways so that the signal received by the brain is not isomorphic with the signal that impinges upon the sense organ (Rosenblith, 1961).

The Literary Process

Poetry is experienced by the poet before it is formulated in words. At this level we are all capable of being poets since it is primarily a matter of insight and feeling. It is when we attempt to express our insights and feelings with words that many of us fail. Most of us go around, assuming we have poetic insights and aesthetic attitudes, with "great poetry" rolling around with us, but only blank sheets or piddling little verses as the evidence of what we thought and felt.

When the poet begins to put the experience in words, he encounters limitations that frustrate and inhibit his expression. The possible combinations of cepts and surds that enter into the process are organized into more formal expressions of thoughts and feelings, into words, before they are written. Note that their basic forms are changed in each step of the process.

The poem is first written in a sketchy or rough form, then goes through a series of revisions and editings. Other versions of the poem might be created and then rejected as the artist tries to select the best form.

In the final manuscript form submitted for publication the original combination of thoughts and feelings still appear but in a form that makes them the joint effort of author and editor. The literary process is regarded as terminated with the publication of the literature and the critical process begins at this point.

When the poem is published in book form, it is in the public domain as far as the communication model is concerned, but not in terms of copyright laws. Now it becomes a part of a much larger and infinitely more complicated aspect of the communication process, since now it is subject to public view. It can be studied, enjoyed, analyzed and appreciated by a wide variety of people. It is subject to criticism and compared to all other similar literature.

What started as a personal expression is now made public; words scrawled in pencil on lined yellow sheets of paper often look quite different when printed on a white page. The way the poem is printed and the position of the poem in the book are important. In the printing of E. E. Cummings' (1958) poems this is particularly true. Charles Norman in his biography of Cummings describes some of the problems encountered in the publication of Cummings' poetry and the battle between the author and the typographers who often insisted in correcting what they thought were mistakes. For instance, in the poem "pity this busy monster . . . ," which is more orthodox than many other poems by Cummings, printers might be tempted to separate words and change the punctuation. This style is a part of the poet's intention and purpose and adds to, rather than detracts from, the poem.

The arrangement of the poem in the book is also a matter of concern to the poet. Cummings gave the following instructions to Catherine Carver of the Harcourt, Brace staff regarding the placement of poems in the book and on the page:

> In general—I want as
> much space (empty) as
> possible BETWEEN poems;
> when two poems, or one poem
> and a part of another poem,
> occur on the same page : but it
> is an interesting fact
> that some poems, when juxta-

> posed, tend to intermingle
> more than do others; hence
> I can make no rule, &
> "lift" or "lower" poems
> as seems best (visually)
> —(Norman, 1958, p. 379).

We are now at the point in the communication process where the author has completed the expression of his thoughts and feelings. The poem (message and medium) stands alone waiting for an audience to complete the communication intended by the poet when he offered his literature to the public. The reader, the interpreter, and the critic should now try to complete the communication process by establishing a dialogue with the poet. Walt Whitman wrote, "To have great poetry you must have great audiences" and it is the function of the critic and interpreter to introduce the poet to the audience and provide for a creative dialogue.

The Critical Response

The principles of general semantics should be an inherent part of the overall critical response. First, the critic should be as semantically aware as possible to enable him to recognize his prejudices. "All criticism is prejudice since all is opinion" according to Phillip Hope-Wallace (See Fry, 1953, p. 47).

The critic who recognizes not only his prejudices, but his other semantic reactions can function better as a critic.

Secondly, the critical act involves research and insight gained through knowledge of principles which should enable the critic to better understand the author and the literature.

The literary object must be regarded as a part of a total experience in criticism and evaluation. The message and the medium are united. (It is not important to get into a McLuhan-type analysis at this point, since, it is obvious that the medium is in part the message and vice versa.) The critic brings to the message-medium his past experience and his aesthetic attitude. His response to message-medium may be negative and, if he does not appreciate or understand the literature, he may choose to disregard it. Or he may reject the literature for a number of personal reasons. If however he has a positive response, he engages in "feed forward" and approaches the critical act in a manner that may eventuate in some critical treatment of the literary object.

The literary critic may find that his response to the literature is so highly personal and subjective that he cannot make an "objective" analysis of the literary object. If he attempts an "objective" literary criticism, he must consider the various methods and modes of criticism. There is an accepted form and procedure for each type and, while there is considerable overlapping of one form with another, the method or mode of criticism determines to some extent how the critic can best proceed.

Figure 1 illustrates this process of decision making regarding the critical act and the use of the various methods and modes.

Methods and Modes of Literary Criticism
    Dialectic/Comparative
    Rhetorical/Form
    Literary/Scholarly
    Scientific/Technical
    Historical/Social
    Poetic/Aesthetic

Semantic Principles
    Indexing
    Dating
    Ever present *etc*.
    Consciousness of Abstracting
    Dangers of Self-reflexiveness
    Map/Territory Analogy
    Use of Hyphen
    Use of Quotation Marks
    Multiordinality

Figure 1

Dialectic/comparative criticism begins with the assumption that the particular literary object is a good piece of literature and the critic advances his reasons for his assumption of value or worth. The critic may compare this poem with others by the same poet to establish reasons for the excellence of this particular poem. The rhetoric/formal mode of criticism deals with the traditionally accepted methods of analysis applying a formal or rhetorical criteria. The critic looks for internal evidence to support his judgment. The literary/scholarly method may involve an examination of minute details in the literature but may also be a general philosophical and highly abstract aesthetic analysis. In making a scientific/technical approach to the literature, the critic can use a range of literary methods extending from linguistic analysis to examination of prosodic innovations.

Historical/social analysis and criticism is a method of making an evaluation of the implications the literature might have in the immediate present or on a developmental basis. The last of the list, (and this list is not all-inclusive by any means), is the poetic/aesthetic mode in which the literature is evaluated on the basis of the effect and feeling that may be stimulated by the literary object.

The critic, when he writes a criticism, is in a similar position to the original author of the literature he is criticizing. The literary object has become a part of his experience and he has brought to it certain attitudes and concepts. In a way, the entire process is self-reflexive since now the critic is the author and is subjected to criticism of his criticism.

It is at this juncture in the process that the principles of general semantics become most important in the critical path. The critic should remind himself that words do not mean, only words as used by people have meaning. He should attempt to get at the meaning of the poet as intended by the author and expressed in the poem. He should differentiate between what the poet may have meant and what the poem means to him (the reader or critic).

The words of the poet are a visual representation of sound and the sound of the words when read aloud have a very definite effect upon the message. (This is especially true of this particular poem.)

134 Paul Hunsinger

The way he reads the poem aloud or hears it read by another person will include nuances that may change his perception of the literature.

The principles of general semantics that are most applicable to literary research and criticism are indexing, dating, the ever-present etc., ordering of "levels" of abstracting, the dangerous aspects of self-reflexiveness, map-territory relationships, the use of the hyphen, the use of quotes, and multiordinality. There are other principles that could be cited, but these are the ones that are most applicable to literary criticism.

The literary critic must be specific in indexing the particular poem he is dealing with in the evaluation (E. E. Cummings' poem$_{89}$ is not E. E. Cummings' poem$_{81}$). It is difficult to deal with specific poems by Cummings since he usually did not title them and the researcher must often rely on the first line of the poem to indicate a particular poem. By careful indexing the critic can avoid generalizations such as "I like all of E. E. Cummings' poems," unless he is familiar with *all* of them and truly does like *all* of them.

Applying the technique of dating the poem gives the critic more freedom to admit that at a certain time he had a response to the poem and that his response may change at a later date. As a personal sidelight, my son is in junior high and he says he likes this particular poem by Cummings because it is an interesting verbal puzzle. I hope he dates his response and at a later date he may like the poem for a better reason. (E. E. Cummings' poem$_{89}$, 3/27/69 will probably be quite different in my perception in 3/27/79.)

No one, not even the poets, can say everything that can be said about anything. Cummings understood this and wrote:[1]

>   my sweet old etcetera
>   aunt lucy during the recent
>
>   war could and what
>   is more did tell you just
>   what everybody was fighting

---

[1] E.E. Cummings, 100 Selected Poems, p. 32.

for,
my sister

isabel created hundreds
(and
Hundreds) of socks not to
mention shirts fleaproof earwarmers

etcetera wristers, etcetera, my
mother hoped that

i would die etcetera
bravely of course my father used
to become hoarse talking about how it was
a privilege and if only he
could meanwhile my

self etcetera lay quietly
in the deep mud et

cetera
(dreaming,
et

    cetera, of
Your smile
eyes knees and of your Etcetera)

What better illustration of the use of the ever present "etc." could be found?

The critic must be aware of the "levels" of abstraction in dealing with literature. Appreciation of literature is often limited because the reader does not move to higher orders of abstraction and does not catch the inferences and implications implicit in the literature. However, it is dangerous to allow the level of abstraction to move so high that there is not a clear correlation between what the poet has written and what the reader abstracts from the poem. Some critics have been guilty of moving to too high orders of abstraction in evaluating literature and reading meanings and implications that were not intended by the author.

Over evaluation of levels of abstraction is a part of the problem of self-reflexiveness. The critic must distinguish between his own reaction to the literature and the reaction of the author to the content material about which he writes. For instance, in the poem by Cummings used as the central example here, I have a very strong reaction to the line "Progress is a comfortable disease." I regard it as one of the greatest lines of poetry I have ever read and have been guilty of using this one line as a basis for lectures on the decline of our over-mechanized culture and the great dangers of pre-occupation with gadgetry and new inventions. (The road to hell is paved with good inventions.) The critic must be able to control his self-reflexiveness so that he does not equate his response with the response intended by the author of the literature.

In applying the principle of map-territory relationships, the critic must realize that the poet creates a world that does not exist, except in his mind. Prose and especially scientific descriptive literature can be evaluated by checking the words against the "facts" to determine the degree of isomorphism, but this is much more difficult in creative literature.

Another way in which the map-territory analogy can be used by literary researchers is to separate what critics have written about literature and the literature itself. In this sense, the critics' "map" is a guide to help a person discover the "territory"—the literature itself.

Language enables us to make dichotomies on the verbal level that do not exist in "reality." The hyphen provides a way of healing these verbal splits. The critic must not only be aware of this in his literary research, but in his writing of criticism.

Certain words should be placed in quotes to indicate that these words are dangerous and not "true," or not used in a conventional way. The critic needs to be aware of the dangers implicit in the misuse of words as he reads and as he writes. The quotation mark, as used by general semanticists, calls attention to words that should be set off in this special way.

Multiordinality is of unique significance in the use of semantics in the critical process. Alfred Korzybski in *Science and Sanity* (1951) wrote:

> Human beings are quite accustomed to the fact that words have different meanings, and by making use of that fact have produced some detrimental speculations, but, to the best of my knowledge, the structural discovery of the multiordinality of terms and of the psycho-physiological importance of the treatment of orders of abstractions resulting from the rejection of the "is" of identity—as formulated in the present system—is novel.

The words used by the creative artist in the poem under analysis have many levels of meaning and the creative critic should endeavor to raise the level of understanding on the part of the reader.

Multiordinality, as Korzybski pointed out, is one of the novelties of language, especially when used in poetic form.

These principles of general semantics can help the literary researcher gain a clearer understanding of the process of communication and provide a good set of tools for writing criticism.

The critical path is not completed after the criticism has been made and the principles of general semantics have been applied. The critic should trace back through the literature and his own response to it to see if his organization, cognition, perception and experience is similar to that of the author. This checking back the "life facts" to determine the degree to which the words used to describe the events, experiences and feelings adequately reflect these "life facts" is a fundamental principle of general semantics.

REFERENCES

Cummings, E. E., 1944, *1 x 1,* New York: Harcourt, Brace and World, Inc.

Fry, Christopher, 1953, *An Experience of Critics,* New York: Oxford Press.

Korzybski, Alfred, 1958, *Science and Sanity,* Fourth Edition, Lakeville, Conn.: International Non-Aristotelian Library Company.

MacLeish, Archibald, 1938, "In Challenge, Not Defense", *Poetry Magazine* (1938) (July), 39.
Nieman, Gilbert, 1949, "To Write Poetry Now You Have to Have One Foot in the Grave," *Poetry Magazine* (1949) 74 (1), 34.
Norman, Charles, 1958, *The Magic Maker,* New York: Macmillan Company.
Rosenblith, Walter, 1961, *Sensory Communication,* Boston, Mass.: M.I T. Press.

RHETORIC, GENERAL SEMANTICS, AND IDEOLOGY

LAWRENCE W. ROSENFIELD
Queens College, C.U.N.Y.

I take as my goal today to assess the pertinence of general semantics to humanistic investigations. The discipline's logical foundations are adequately critiqued elsewhere (Black, 1949), and I shall not repeat them here. I wish instead to maintain that general semantics is fundamentally inimical to humanistic studies. My argument depends upon a distinction between the concepts of "theory" and "ideology." It strikes me that general semantics bears little resemblance to a theory in the sense that classical rhetorical theories do, but is rather one of a number of competing "communication ideologies" crowding in upon modern scholars. If my contention can be supported, I believe it renders suspect the general semanticist's claims to unique contributions to historico-literary thought; one might even speculate upon the melancholy prospect that our discipline constitutes a pernicious influence upon fruitful humanistic scholarship.

It is sometimes productive to ransack the archives of antiquity in order to illuminate contemporary thought. Such a method appears helpful in understanding those two terms, "theory" and "ideology" which hound modern thinking. In its original Greek sense, "theory" (theorain) meant "seeing" of a special sort, the kind of onlooking characteristic of a spectator at a festival (Snell, 1960). This notion of theory as a beholding or apprehension of objective phenomena was distinct from either the certainty of science (episteime) or confirming wonder (thaumazein); yet it still conceived of human communication as susceptible to objective theoretical analysis (see Aristotle, 1954; Stigen, 1966; Else, 1957; Barrett, 1962).

The intriguing element in this conception of a theory is its treatment of objectivity. The stress lies on the ordered manner in which the mind contemplates phenomena. There is implicit in such a theoretical stance, a tranquility, a distancing, quite different from disinterest and irrelevant to modern perception theory emphases on sheer organic sensation.[1] This form of objectivity, which pervades rhetorical theory, depends not upon vain efforts to avoid normative statements, but on the sense of impartiality afforded the dispassionate spectator (Germino, 1967, p. 13; Bergmann, 1951, pp. 205-218). It is in these terms that Aristotle (1940) conceives of the ultimate form of happiness consisting in the contemplative activities associated with the theorist's life. It was this conception of conceptual knowledge as serene recognition that sustained rhetorical analysis from antiquity down through the Enlightenment. And it is, I believe, in similar form that whatever humanistic thinking remains with us in our own day continues to thrive (Hexter, 1967; Rosenfield, 1968).

It is obvious, however, that at least in England and America, the conditions necessary to foster theoretical inquiry no longer hold. Theology and political theory, for example, are in disrepute in the academic world, passed on from teacher to student under the drumfire of behaviorism in a manner reminiscent of Christians transmitting the faith in the Roman catacombs. Philosophy has for the most part reduced itself to two alarming alternatives: the history of metaphysics and linguistic analysis. My own particular concern (rhetoric) has given way to assorted Byzantine successors: psycholinguistics, group dynamics, attitude change research, general semantics, and that queerest of all topics, communication theory. Theoretical investigation is generally dismissed with the *ad hominum* label, "armchair speculation."

I mean no invidious comparison when I claim that theoretical

---

[1] We may single out Aristotle, 1940, *Nichomachian Ethics,* Trans. W. D. Ross, Cambridge: Harvard University Press, 1139^{b}18-1141^{b}20 for one of several discussions of the varieties of objective knowledge understood by the Ancients. Also of value in this matter is R. Price, 1968, "Some Antistrophes to the Rhetoric," *Philosophy and Rhetoric* (1968) I (Summer), 145-164.

inquiry has been supplanted in our own day by ideological commitment to the dogma of behaviorism. Coined by the French philosopher Destutt de Tracy in 1801, the term "ideology" originally denoted that form of radical subjectivism which echoed John Locke in its assertion that sensation is the virtual origin of all thought. Coupled with this faith in the reality of sense perception (and its consequent aversion to any hint of innate ideas) was a peculiar distrust of language as a legitimate vehicle of thought (Aiken, 1956 and 1964). So far as I can ascertain, this anti-language attitude was first promulgated by a thoroughly non-ideological man, the father of modern science, Francis Bacon (1963). Professor Karl Wallace (1967), in his excellent study of Bacon, has pinpointed the issue—those disciplines which distrust verbal transactions eventually develop an urge to quantify:

> The old methods [of discovery] were methods of invention developed by dialectic, logic, grammar, and rhetoric. They were, therefore, tied inevitably and permanently to men's language . . . If man were to uncover nature's secrets . . . he must abandon old ways of search and inquiry and must devise new ways of querying nature directly.

* * * * * *

How did the "new" induction differ from the old invention? The new method was a way of controlling observation and abstraction by setting up two contradictions. First, the understanding was to be tied directly to the senses and thus to increase the chances that a concept would emerge . . . Second, the understanding was to be governed by an order and procedure designed to delay and control abstraction (pp. 157-158).

From these dual assumptions (faith in sense perception, lack of faith in language), it was an easy step to a third postulate—the positivism of Auguste Comte and Karl Marx, who held that human nature is largely determined by man's material existence, that one's inner life is a direct function of one's environment (see Barzun, 1968; Germino, 1967 Aiken, 1956).

A fourth and final strand to the notion of ideology needs consideration. That is the special brand of messianic humanism contributed by English Utilitarians such as Bentham (1948). If social institutions determined man's nature, it followed that systematic reform of institutions would lead directly to the uplift of mankind. Hence the unbounded faith of classical utilitarianism in advocating legislative reform in order to help people, to do some good, to reduce suffering in the world, based always on the principle of the "greatest good for the greatest number" (Briggs, 1959; Bentham, 1948; Mills, 1961), a posture smacking at its root of psychological egoism, and in any event quite unverifiable by any procedure (scientific or otherwise).

It is in this four-fold sense that ideological thinking has come down to us: faith in sense perception, faith in the reality of material existence, faith in man's capability to manipulate his social environment, distrust of verbal instruments. On its face, general semantics accepts these philosophical parameters. I believe it can further be argued that the popularity of such thinking (as typified in accounts of human communication such as general semantics) has annihilated theoretical analysis of the classical sort. From Korzybski and I. A. Richards to George Miller and Charles Osgood, the effort of modern communication specialists has been to specify human discourse in scientific terms.

The unfortunate consequences of the radical shift from theory to ideology fill our lives; I wish to mention only two. First, where the theorist, acting in his capacity as onlooker, eschews involvement in the public arena, the ideologist-behaviorist welcomes it. He thus commits himself to passionate support of social causes, despite his efforts at neutrality. It should not be surprising then that the past two centuries have seen the increase of the intellectual as publicist for a cause or point of view, and his correlative neglect of the philosophical domain. Witness John C. Calhoun, an admirable defender of his form of government, and hence a suspect political thinker; or the psychotherapist, a professional humanitarian, incapable of serious ethical speculation. A theorist is seldom messianic; an ideologist, if he is a good one, often is.

It should thus come as no surprise to find so many social scientists enlisted in programs of Urban Renewal, Mental Health, the Alliance for Progress, and Operation Headstart. These programs, all motivated by what I earlier called messianic humanism, faith that personal and social reality can be molded by administrative fiat to conform to the manipulator's will, have at best had no significant impact on society, and at worst have had unexpected evil results. Much as early industrialists did not deliberately pollute our air and water or erode our soil, so behaviorists set out with good faith and a premature vision of the outcome of their tinkering. That general semantics has not yet polluted our communication may be largely due to the happy accident that few among us have yet achieved the positions of public influence of some of our empiricist colleagues.

A second, related problem involves the relative capacity of theorist and ideologist to assess personal and social goals with some rigor. The theorist, because he was occupied with perennial (if abstract) issues such as justice, beauty, and happiness, was ordinarily alert to the intricate relation of means to ends. The ideologist, in contrast, denies the efficacy of values; and in so cutting himself off from metaphysics he does nothing more than admit unexamined the whole gamut of Enlightenment political objectives (Weaver, 1953). Thus, for instance, we naïvely accept the melioristic impact of education and dutifully set thousands of behavioral technicians to work establishing mechanisms to confirm our expectations. This failure to fully question the normative foundations of our disciplines threatens us, as John Stuart Mill recognized, with the most thoroughgoing spiritual despotism yet known to man. It is frightening precisely because it does compel belief commitments about the foundations of our knowledge of a sort completely foreign to ancient thought (Snell, 1960, pp. 23-27). I offer as evidence for this point the intolerance of virtually any behavioral scientist whom you wish to engage in a Euthyphro-like dialogue concerning piety to the scientific method.

I hope that I have not been misunderstood in what I have said. As a student of human communication, I have made no effort to single out general semantics for indictment. I merely suggest that to the extent that it strives to enhance itself with empirical trappings will it likely continue on a par with comparable ideologies and continue to impede those philosophically viable theories of communication whose current refuge is the historical-literary-critical disciplines. Part of the charm of general semantics has always been its congruence with the life of our times, its lack of intercourse with the wisdom of the past. I am, however, not quite comfortable with the prospect that behavioral notions of language will so thoroughly dominate our intellects that philosophical theorizing may disappear entirely. I leave it to you to judge the implications of such a triumph of ideology for the enrichment of humanity.

REFERENCES

Aiken, H. D., 1956, *The Age of Ideology,* New York: New American Library.
——————, 1964, "The Revolt Against Idealogy," *Commentary* (1964) (April).
Aristotle, 1947, *Nichomachian Ethics,* Trans. W. D. Ross, Cambridge: Harvard University Press, 1176^{a}30-1181^{b}25.
——————, 1954, *Rhetoric,* Trans. R. Roberts, New York: Modern Library, 1355^{b}26-37.
Bacon, F., 1963, *Novum Organum,* New York.
Barrett, W., 1962, "Phenomenology and Existentialism," in *Philosophy in the Twentieth Century,* 4 Vols, New York: Random House, III, 130-131.
Barzun, J., 1968, *Darwin, Marx, Wagner,* Garden City, N.Y.
Bentham, J., 1948, *The Principles of Morals and Legislation,* 1832, New York.
Bergmann, Gustoff, 1951, "Ideology," *Ethics* (1951) LXI (April) 205-218.
Black, Max, 1949, *Language and Philosophy,* Ithaca, N.Y.: Cornell University Press.
Briggs, Asa, 1959, *The Making of Modern England,* New York.
Else, G. F., 1957, *Aristotle's Poetics: The Argument,* Cambridge: Harvard University Press.
Germino, D., 1967, *Beyond Ideology,* New York.
Hexter, J. H., 1967, "The Rhetoric of History," *History and Theory* (1967) *VI* (1), 3-13.
Mill, J. S., 1951, *Utilitarianism,* 1861, New York: Longmans, Green, & Co.

Rosenfield, L. W., 1968, "The Anatomy of Critical Discourse," *Speech Monographs* (1968) *XXXV* (March).
Snell, B., 1953, *The Discovery of the Mind*, Trans. T. G. Rosenmeyer, Cambridge: Harvard University Press.
Stigen, A., 1966, *The Structure of Aristotle's Thought*, Oslo.
Wallace, Karl, 1943, *Francis Bacon On Communication and Rhetoric*, Chapel Hill: The University of North Carolina Press.
──────, 1967, *Francis Bacon on the Nature of Man*, Urbana, Ill.: University of Illinois Press.
Weaver, R., 1948, *The Ethics of Rhetoric*, Chicago: H. Regnery Co.

PHENOMENOLOGICAL APPROACHES

INTRODUCTION TO THE OG PRINCIPLE OF RESEARCH

(Being a Hostile Snarl at Academic Upward Mobility With a Modest Plea to Shape Up)

GERALD M. PHILLIPS,
Professor of Speech, the Pennsylvania State University and Director, Oral Communications Program PACE (E & S E A), Area J of Pennsylvania*

The investigator of human interaction frequently approaches his task in a non-human way. Those who participate in the act he studies approach each other looking for some human gain. The researcher, on the other hand, asserts that he seeks "wisdom," "truth," "beauty," and, hopefully, a publishable article. Since his primary goal is "not to perish," he necessarily finds himself fettered by the requirements of a scholarly establishment dedicated to the proposition that the "medium is the method." The researcher, thus, becomes more a media technician than a student of humanity. He serves an apprenticeship (baccalaureate), and becomes a journeyman (graduate student). When he demonstrates sufficient skill in the use of tools (a doctoral dissertation), he is admitted into the fellowship of "master scholars." Thus, what was once a personal transaction between a man and his curiosity has become an exercise in ritual methodology designed to achieve economic gain and social status.

The flagrant rejection of a human approach by students of human

---

*Who says we have a democracy? No British nobleman could tack a more impressive trailer or ethos builder after his name. But considering that I do not intend to one-up the reader with footnotes, no one would publish this thing, if I merely signed it "Fat Jer."

behavior has come about because of their desire to be "scientists." Since humanists are generally not sophisticated enough to appreciate the poetry of small particle physics or the lyric quality of topology, they perceive science as method or form rather than as a style of asking and answering questions. They emulate the technique of the scientist as they see it, without being able to imitate his style of asking questions. Science, as they see it, is method and so method becomes the preoccupation of their own craft. A good look at the recent literature of interaction behavior will demonstrate how fruitless this imitation has been.

Part of the reason for the application of pseudo-science is the restrictions imposed by academic institutions. Promotions and raises are based on publication. Publication depends on acceptance by editors who are often impressed by neat tables, graphs, and charts. Furthermore, productivity of articles increases quantitatively once a researcher discovers how to design neat, clean, and quick experiments. Certainly, every scholar knows that there is no longer any payoff for contemplative activity. Technique, then, is applied to the generation of lines in print. If the research also answers a question worth asking, it is a matter of accident, and there is really no way even to adjudicate the worth of what is written except by evaluating methodology, since humanistic studies somehow bypassed the deep thought which was preliminary to most work in the "hard sciences."

The search for method is, thus, superimposed over the search for "truth." Scholars seek methods which they can adapt and become expert in, and then proceed to apply them to all kinds of questions. Wherever the method fits, scholars will be working, and where no method fits, the matter is left to the novelists and poets and deemed not fit for attention by the human mind. Medium and method become one!

Those who call themselves "general semanticists" are particularly guilty of this latter-day methodolatry. When we ask ourselves "how can general semantics be used in research?" we are merely offering the world another method for it to fit into some research project or other. Why do we assume we have a system? What tests have we made of our own propositions? Do we have anything more than theoretical support, for example, for the assertion that there *is* an "intensional" and "extensional" orientation? What started as a man's attempt to understand the universe of communication has now become a system and a creed, complete with its own house organs, its own jargon, its own system of incantation, a body of faithful worshippers; it offers young scholars many opportunities to present papers and publish screed for their own professional advancement.

It would seem eminently more sensible to use the works of Korzybski as we use any other body of theoretical material: to apply it when its fits and reject it when it does not. Furthermore, it would be highly productive for us to ask how valid the whole theoretical construction is by attempting to test its propositions and to ascertain the effects of their application to human interaction problems which we presume, on good authority, its propositions can solve. If we wish to maintain academic viability, it is necessary for us now to escape from the binds of our methodology and turn our attention to real problems worthy of the attention of intelligent and rational men.

The OG Principle

Since it is apparently impossible to deal with a phenomenon in academia these days until we have given it a name, the process of research characteristic of interpersonal studies these days can be identified as the "OG Principle." In *Finian's Rainbow,* OG the Leprauchan sings, "If I'm not with the girl I love, I love the girl I'm with." Today's researcher into social phenomena intones, "If I don't have a method to answer my question, I'll ask the question I have a method to answer." Second-hand tools dictate the work. We borrow from soil agronomists, nuclear physicists, election pollsters and others, and we make our questions look as much like their questions as we can, so that we can "satisfy the assumptions of the method." We rarely ask whether the humans we purport to study look at all like wheat seeds or molecules. We have forgotten that the human is the only object we study that can change its mind and thus beat the test. The result has been a body of fragments which tell us little about humans, though it displays the fact that many of our associates have achieved virtuoso skill in the use of methods.

Even our theoretical models have been borrowed. Many of us still assume that human communication behavior is sufficiently similar to the transmission of signals on a telephone wire, that we can use the vocabulary and constructs of "information theory" to describe what happens when humans talk with each other. Furthermore, we assume that our samples, usually drawn from a college undergraduate population, are sufficiently like humanity to warrant the conclusions we draw. What we produce, however, tells us little or nothing about what people do to people when they talk. The constituents of the interpersonal act are holistic. Measurement of any part tells us nothing about the whole. We can measure stomach acid and skin sweat and demonstrate the existence of a reaction, but the cause or meaning of that reaction is still obscure. We do not know whether disturbance of the viscera distorts the message, or whether distortion of the message disturbs the viscera. The measurement of brain waves tells us that the brain is involved in an act, but our graphs are only a sign that activity is going on; they do not define its nature. They cannot tell us what the person graphed was thinking and why and what he is likely to do about it.

We have tools: Chi Square, analysis of variance, "t", taxonomies, historiographic methods, psychogalvanometers—but they cannot measure satisfaction, warmth, affinity, hostility, suspicion, attraction, curiosity, hate, love, or any of the other multiordinalities that give us the only vocabulary we have for the interpersonal transaction. "Love" may be what it is all about—and we do not have an "Amorometer;" we do not have a "transactional model" which divides "love" into its components; we don't even necessarily know when we are in "it." But who among us would deny its existence and its influence? It "makes the world go 'round" you know.

We are able to measure the flow of gastric juice, the electrical resistance of skin sweat, the number of vocalized pauses in a unit of speech, the ratio of nouns to verbs in an utterance. We can identify some of the details of overt past history, that is, we can see the history of actions, but we lose the history of feelings. We can measure "intelligence" but we have to define it to be whatever we are measuring. We

Introduction to the OG Principle of Research   153

can define "social adjustment" any way we like and measure it, without ever discovering whether our words refer to anything real.

As scholars, we learn the rules. We can make our tables conform to the requirements of the statistical text, and we can make our writings conform to the requirements of the style manuals and we can make sure that our conclusions are sufficiently hedged so that they cause no one damage and we can allege that we have found "truth." But the calling of it does not make it so!

Take Clyde and Sally, for example, in the midst of an interpersonal transaction in the front seat of that car over there. What we see is Clyde with his arm around Sally, and Sally with her head on Clyde's shoulder. Now if we intervened to do a little measurement we could find out the respective I.Q.'s, identify temporary emotional derangements, measure skin resistance, make charts of brain waves and heart action. We could conclude, from our measurements, that both Clyde and Sally deviate from the mean a certain number of "sigmas." Of course, Clyde and Sally knew that they were "shook up" anyway, and they have a somewhat better idea of what that means (to them) than we do.

As we indulge our voyeur urge (a prime motivation for interpersonal research) we can watch Clyde "hustle" Sally; we can observe intensive body contact and we can watch as they "consummate the act." (Isn't it odd that with all our jargon we have no intelligent taxonomy for this most human of all processes?) We can now check our charts and graphs and come up with some hypotheses. We can, for example, assert an association between a particular skin sweat pattern and a specific rating of emotional disturbance and since our association is at the "one per cent level" we can declare that any time this pattern appears, the person displaying it is "in love." Now we need empirical validation. What we have to do is find some people that we know are "in love" and take independent measurements; then we have to find some people who are not "in love" and adjust their ratings and then find out what they are "in" and then we will "know" something.

Of course. we will not know about Clyde's lust and Sally's guilt. We will not know about poetic passion or sensuous pleasure; or about the feeling of warmth that followed and the feeling of terror that preceded. We will not feel Sally's sense of security or Clyde's sense of triumph. We can never know these things with the tools we have, and it appears that we cannot get tools—ever—to help us find out about these things, for they are not "things" in the sense that livers and gonads are "things." They are constructs, metaphors, poetic phrases, hypostatizations, designed to communicate about the noncommunicable and there you have it! The source of the OG principle! We cannot measure what we want to measure so we want to measure what we can measure.

Since it is necessary that we all publish, lest we perish, we must use our tools, borrowed from the scientists, hope that we do not ruin them before we return them and produce what we can. After all, who will care? We might even find something out. And who reads the journals anyway? It's all a game!

IF I CAN'T ANSWER THE QUESTION I ASK, I ASK THE QUESTION I CAN ANSWER!

Is this any kind of life for an honest man?

My friends in the physical sciences who are enthralled by the music of the Heisenberg Principle pity those of us who are still trapped in Snedecor's Soil Searching. But the man who can manipulate a matrix can move the world—at least the part of it that deals with academic advancement and raises in pay.

Is that what it's all about, Alfie?

Some Proposals for a New Way

I have some friends who are also called "students." They have no academic credential, as yet. Nonetheless, they are experts on interpersonal transactions, since this is the way they spend most of their time. They offer some interesting questions motivated out of their life experience.

1. When a white man supports black causes, how much of that support is motivated by a feeling of guilt; how much from a feeling of desire to fill a power vacuum; how much by sincere feeling of concern? And what other reasons might there be?

2. When I "fall in love" is it a random occurrence? If I lived in

Chillicothe would I still find someone to love? If so, why is it so necessary to think about "one and only" or to legalize fidelity? By the way, how will I know when I am "in love"?

3. How come I seem to like more people than like me? What can I do to get people to like me? What does "like" mean? What happens when people "like" each other? What is a friend? What would a person have to do so that I would know he is a "friend"? Is there a difference between "friend" and "friendly"?

4. How can I get people to do what I want them to? How come people can get me to do what they want, but I can't seem to get anyone to do what I want? What makes people angry?

5. What did you mean by that last question? And how can I find out? Anything! About how people *are* when they talk to each other.

6. And so on . . .

Of course, there are no methods to answer these. And I, also, can look into my own folk beliefs and ask a few questions that bother me.

1. Why is it that so many people I know that are "experts" in interpersonal relations have such a hard time carrying them on? Or am I not seeing the world correctly?

2. How come so many general semanticists who allege they have the "extensional orientation" are really neurotic? What happened to Hayakawa anyway?

3. Why is it that liberals who claim to love people find it so difficult to relate to individual humans, while conservatives who don't like people seem to relate so well?

4. Why does my wife get mad at me sometimes? Why do I get mad at her? Why doesn't my boss appreciate my wisdom? Why do I sometimes confuse my students? Why can't everyone understand that I love them? Why don't they pay attention to me?

5. And so on . . .

And, of course, there are no methods available for these, either.

Those of us who give a damn about what humans do when they come together (and don't give a damn about how many lines we publish) must take a new and different look at what we are studying and how we go about it. People are not wheat seeds, and if our methods of getting information make people look like they can be manipulated into something sub-human, then we are doing humanity a disservice. Yet, our captivation with the positivism of behavioral technique makes it look like what we are seeking is a method of conditioning humanity into subservience—and we do not know, even, to what. Even if "conditioning" did work on humans, and there is considerable doubt that it can with any certainty, to develop more and better ways of conditioning implies our willingness to sacrifice our human condition. What we really need is applied research in how to resist conditioning, and thus in becoming more human.

Our young students recognize this. They function like the lad in Copenhagen who knew the emperor wasn't wearing clothes. They see right through us. They know that what we are doing is rank imitation, and that we really know little about the natural life of humanity. Most of us sacrifice our human passion when we become scholars anyway. We don't want to be involved. We want to be "objective." And the people around us know that the answer to the plight of man lies in involvement and subjectivity. They are pushing us for new ideas and new ways. They are, for example, demanding "sensitivity training," even with as little as we know about it, and in so doing, they are expressing their concern about the reality of human behavior.

If we resist the demands of our constituency, we are fools. We really need not be bound to borrowed tools and outmoded methods. Even if we cannot think up our own ways, there are enough original thinkers to offer us a variety of methods to bring to our work. Following is a summary of some of them.[1]

---

[1] Note that this is the only footnote in this "non-scholarly" piece. It will give you very little information. If you are interested in the works of any of the men I list here, you can find them in the library, the same way I did, or you can drop me a line. I refuse to be party to the licensed plagiarism implicit in our footnote syndrome. If this is terribly confusing to you, it merely means that you are so locked into the system that this piece will have no impact on you. Feel free to attack. Your attack may stimulate some young rebel to read it. For those of you who demand that I prove up and submit my "credentials," if you will tear off the title page of your last published article and mail it to me with 14 cents in stamp or coin to cover handling and mailing, I will send you by return mail all of the footnotes I left out of this article, together with several other excellent footnotes I have prepared for articles I do not intend to write. If you act fast, I will also supply some of the finest Chi Squares that have been computed in the last five years and a quick guide to some of the more exciting tables of random numbers. *Pace!*

1. In their book, *Individual Behavior,* Combs and Snygg assert a basic dictum for understanding human interaction: *"all behavior is rational to the behaver at the time of behavior."* (Italics supplied by me.) One of the problems we face in research is capturing the act of the moment. We always seem to be working through hindsight, and this is misleading for we can never get to the "why?" of the response. When we ask our subjects to reconstruct for us, their answers are fogged over with social exigency, rationalization and a desire to please or fool the investigator. They cannot be accepted as trustworthy guides to why a behavior was done, for they are little more than recollections appropriately distorted to meet a perceived social demand.

If we can develop a research technique based on empathy, so that we can use our inference capacity to fill in reasons why a person acted as he did, we might get to a more substantive understanding of why people communicate as they do. We might also have reinforced in our minds the uniqueness of the human, and thus be pushed gently from our tendency to generalize about motivations.

2. We ought to be studying more about how humans behave in the natural state, even though we cannot record our observations in neat little tables. We might well take our cue from the ethologists and the work they have been doing studying animals. Dart, Carpenter and Lorenz have contributed more to our understanding of animal behavior than all of the Zukermans and Skinners together, for they look at the real and whole animal, not the rigidly controlled animal in a fascist, laboratory setting.

Ernest Becker in *Birth and Death of Meaning* stresses that communication is a totally human act—"all that is specifically human." It is as much our "human thing" as the long neck is a "giraffe thing." It is what makes us human. It cannot be isolated for separate analysis, for the isolation of it deprives us of our humanity. Or, saying it another way, if we seek to study humans through communication there is no escape from studying the whole human.

But we can examine the human in ethological terms and try to discover how he communicates to satisfy his basic animal requirements for survival, territory, homeostasis and stimulation. Transactions between people could be critiqued against the standards for satisfaction of both parties, and new ways of interacting could be devised so that people could mutually gain instead of remaining forever in a jungle-like, behavioristic paradigm of win or lose.

3. We ought to understand and take into account that we react to what we have in our heads and not what is the "real" world; thus "objectivity" in measurement is not possible. It is quite possible for numbers to behave with regularity, but things that the numbers represent need not be quite so regular. To impose the conclusions from regular numbers on non-regular people is to design a map purposely that does not fit the territory. We might then finally realize that the similarities our statistical findings offer us are superficial and egregious differences may exist between the people they attempt to describe. This, in turn, might help us to be a little more open in our acceptance of differences between people. We also might not get so frustrated and disappointed when our predictions about human behavior do not come true.

4. We ought to be able to do something to curb our very human tendency to look at things vertically, that is, on a hierarchical scale. We are, all of us, moralists. We tend to evaluate anything that is different as "inferior" or "superior" and there seems to be the latent assumption lurking among scholars that once we have discovered a difference we ought to do something about it. (Hence the proliferation of various remediation specialists.) Who was it, anyway, that first decided that a lisp was a "bad behavior" and that it was to be "remedied." (Or is it "remediated"?)

If we could dispel this tendency to evaluate, it might be possible for us to learn something about our neighbors without starting offensive and demeaning "head-start" or "upward bound" programs. We might be able, in fact, to accept some cultural changes into our own regular behavior, and we might spare whole generations of school children the insult of being defined as candidates for special education.

5. It might be wise to learn something about the fiction of the "mean" and "the standard deviation." We should know that they are reifications, but so many of us take them seriously. But, really, we know that there is no average man. The concept of average tells us little about individual behavior. And collectively, even if we know that in a large group of humans, the majority of people will

Introduction to the OG Principle of Research   159

be more likely to behave one way than another, we still don't know who will behave in what way, or why, or what we can do about it.

Those who have to deal with humans directly, like psychiatrists, have found that nominal and modal designations do not work. They may use words like "disturbed," "alienated" or "bizarre," and then they will add "characterized by," and they will proceed to give a description of what the human was doing. They understand that their multiordinal terms resist measurement, and if they succeed in measuring, they measure only a hypostatization, not a reality. Their quest is to reflect human uniqueness first, and let the generalizations emerge when they are clear, rather than attempt to force humans into a mode of generalized behavior.

It is impossible to make sensible predictions of what people will do by examining what they say they will do or by predictions of what they are likely to do. In matters that don't count, some measurement devices are quite accurate. When people don't care much about an election, it can be predicted with considerable reliability. But when they care, the predictions go awry. The citizens of Los Angeles and Minneapolis in the summer of 1969 knew all about that.

When we ask people what they believe, we seek to confirm our own prejudices and expectations. However, if each of us examined the way we behave when others have asked questions of us, we might find something out about why our information from attitude scales and questionnaires is so fragile and tenuous.

The choices a person will make can only be known for sure when he makes them. If your house was on fire, would you save your manuscript, your dog, or your insurance policy? You might be surprised to find yourself saving your wife. The only way to get at what people really believe is to observe behavior under life conditions and then try to deduce the values, rather than the reverse. After all, what is more important; the way people behave or the way they talk about the way they think they will behave?

In research, we tend to seek:
1. Understanding of what we see or experience.
2. Relevance of our understandings to ourselves and others.
3. More productive questions for us all to try to answer.

Everything that we study demands a method specifically suited to the task of discovery. There are some scholars that have come up with such methods, and used them well. The work of Raymond Dark, C. R. Carpenter, Konrad Lorenz, and Jules Masserman seems to demonstrate, for example, that it is possible to study natural state behavior unobtrusively and draw intelligent conclusions from the observation. Gardner and Thompson found that they could "anchor" subjectivity and do a consistent job of measuring and evaluating changes in behavior. Hans Eysenck effectively applied critical techniques to a quasi-art-form like psychiatry. The new journalistic "muckraker" types like Jonathan Kozol or William Herndon have told us more about children in schools than whole reams of "scholarly" studies. Field studies, clinical case histories, and pure speculation as in the case of Rollo May and Edwin Hall show us that speculation about phenomena can be even more productive of conclusions and ideas than manipulation of them.

In addition, a number of exciting studies have been done attempting to objectivize some subjective perceptions and values. Walter Kassoway and Dennis Klinzing, for example, are trying to assess the use of public utterance as a projective device. Ronald Applebaum has produced a scalar method for using subjective criteria in making objective judgments about improvement in speech behavior. In each of these, numerical procedures were used to serve the ends of the investigation. They were not used as ends in themselves.

There is no "tested and true" method for studying the human transaction, any more than there is an anatomical guide to the location of the human soul. But we know that the "wisdom" we have produced under the influence of the OG Principle has given us nothing new, nothing we can use, and we know that people are crying out in pain looking for ways to improve the way they deal with one another. If we wish to be able to claim the title of "scholar" with any degree of probity, it is imperative that we cast away our rusty and outmoded tools, and turn our heads to the production of what is useful to us in the task we must do.

A PERCEPTUAL APPROACH TO RHETORICAL STUDY

RICHARD B. GREGG
The Pennsylvania State University

In the past few years we have begun to witness a growing number of new approaches to the analysis of public rhetoric. The innovative spirit seems to me to reflect two things. First it indicates an increasing dissatisfaction with the results of the critical methodology which is labelled "Neo-Aristotelian." While Neo-Aristotelian methodology is the most thoroughly explicated critical approach we have to date, it appears to be overly rigid in its scheme of classification, arbitrary in its description of human communication behavior, and unable to account for more than a portion of the total universe of rhetorical discourse. (For a thorough critique of Neo-Aristetolian Methodology see Black, 1965.) Second, our society is witnessing new forms of rhetorical appeal, e.g. a rhetoric of confrontation in which inflexible demands replace the milder entreaties of negotiation, slogans and epithets take the place of more detailed argumentation, and physical commitment in scenes of action substitutes for ritualistic verbal identification and brotherhood (see Scott and Smith, 1969). At the very least, these new rhetorical forms require a re-evaluation of our analytical procedures in order to assure realistic assessment.

The development of controlled, empirical communications research has caused the rhetorical analyst more dissonance than comfort. A number of studies in several areas have clearly revealed the inadequacies of certain neo-Aristotelian assumptions. For example: experimental studies of the effects of various message structures on listener comprehension and attitude are inconclusive (Bettinghaus, 1968); results of studies on the relative effectiveness of evidence in argument question the usual assumptions made about the role of evidence (McCroskey, 1967); and research reveals that the typical distinction between logical and emotional appeals is not realistic in terms of listener's response (Becker, 1963). But for the most part, behavioral studies have failed to provide new assumptions which might be used as points of departure for the analyst. The feeling persists that we are still not accounting for some of the most crucial dynamics of the rhetorical transaction.

Several years ago, George Gerbner (1966) discussed the "tactical approach" employed in most communication research. The "tactical approach" as Gerbner describes it is an analytical method which concentrates on short-run effects of messages with primary attention being given to the "tactics" of persuasion. In Gerbner's view, the preoccupation with tactics obscured both the concept of communication as a special type of social interaction and the meaning of effect. According to Gerbner, "the production and perception of message systems cultivating stable structures of generalized images . . . rather than any tactic calculated to result in 'desirable' (or any other) response . . . is at the heart of the communications transaction" (pp. 102-103).

Gerbner's statements contain some interesting implications for the study of public rhetoric. According to his view, public messages create certain perceptual images which will interact with perceptual patterns already formulated in a listener's mind. The "news" of a rhetorical transaction lies in the nature of the interaction among the various image patterns and the resulting behavior.

The primary assumption underlying Gerbner's remarks is the same assumption made by so-called phenomenological psychologists in their research on human behavior. The assumption is that human behavior is a function of human perception; that is to say, our behavior is always influenced and limited by our perceptions of reality at the moment of behavior (Combs and Snygg, 1959, pp. 16-36). The human organism receives and is affected by a large number of incoming stimuli. Spoken messages certainly constitute one kind of data. However, the starting point for understanding behavior is not the data itself, but the perception of it, for human perception will interpret the meaning of the data. This assumption may provide a fruitful orientation for rhetorical analysis. We need more than an orientation, however. We must attempt to develop a methodology from the orientation. It seems to me there are several areas of behavioral research which will help in the construction of such a methodology. We will look at these and then mention the kind of analysis which may increase our understanding of rhetorical transaction and effect.

The first area of investigation has to do with the relationship between language and perception. A good many studies in psychology, sociology, anthropology and linguistics have been spun from the Whorf-Sapir hypothesis, sometimes called the Sapir-Whorf-Korzbski hypothesis. A number of studies involving short-term exposure to linguistic labels support the hypothesis that words do affect perception. When presented with an ambiguous series of stimuli, for instance, subjects tend to see what the labels suggest they should see (Berelson and Steiner, 1964, pp. 178-192). Studies undertaken from a cultural point of view indicate that there is a positive correlation between cultural experience, motivation, and perception. The most acceptable position in this regard seems to be that the codability potential of a cultural linguistic system determines the perceptions most accessible to members of that culture, though perceptions are in no sense unalterably bound by language (Brown, 1956).

A recent study in the psychology of language by Robert Terwilliger (1968) undertakes a thorough review of research data concerning the relationships of language, perception and behavior. Terwilliger concludes that most of the data supporting the Whorf-Sapir hypothesis has the air of triviality about it and is, at best, ambiguous. Even the hypothesis about codability or availability of linguistic concepts can ultimately be reduced to the principle of familiarity, a principle which tells us very little about the influence of language on perception (pp. 258-292).

Terwilliger proceeds to examine the hypothesis from another perspective. He defines linguistic meaning as a set of readinesses to respond which have been associated with a word or utterance. His definition of perception is similar; a perception is a set of readinesses to respond which have been associated with a particular stimulus array (pp. 163-193). These definitions, formulated on the basis of data we have about the development of language in children, assume that both linguistic meaning and perception are developed from the same behavioral tendency.

Next, operating from the viewpoint that language is a weapon used by humans to influence and control each other, and starting with an analysis of a simple command situation, Terwilliger constructs the way in which manipulation of the external situation, an individual's motives, and a system of rewards can cause the meaning of a command to translate the potential for action into actual behavior. One of his vivid examples concerns the inculcation of proper responses in military trainees. Noting that meaning exists only amidst possibilities for ambiguity, Terwilliger points out that a part of military training consists of reducing the ambiguity of certain command utterances until there is literally no meaning left and human behavior becomes unconscious response to sign rather than conscious response to symbol. The situation achieved is one in which there is one stimulus and one response with all other possible responses having been extinguished. Terwilliger suggests that "Nothing can break this cycle once it has been established, save some radical change in the stimulus situation or context. Put an individual in a truly new world and he may reacquire meaning. But to the extent that command is exercised in wider and wider spheres of life, to that extent escape from its influences becomes increasingly remote" (p. 306).

The dramatic process of brainwashing provides Terwilliger the final link in his chain of reasoning. The usual procedure calls for a prisoner to be isolated from the social contacts which reinforce his already acquired perceptions and meanings. The system of reinforcement is controlled completely by the captors who begin the substitution of a new set of meanings for the old by extracting a "confession" from the prisoner. The statement of confession is a repudiation of everything the prisoner has always believed. The confession is rewritten many times and the prisoner is called upon to discuss and defend it with his captors. The prisoner is put through rote practicing of ideological statements and some uses of terminology are punished while others are rewarded. The interrogation situation, which remains the same throughout the process, begins to evoke a constant response and soon becomes meaningless. But the language of the exchange between prisoner and captors remains significant. The outcome of the process is not the elimination of meaning but the transposition of one set of ambiguities for another; in other words, there is a change in meaning and an accompanying modification of behavior indicating perceptual change as well (pp. 296-325). Terwilliger suggests that, dramatic and exaggerated though his examples are, they contain the "germs of most other contemporary examples of verbal influence" (p. 306). He asserts that all language learning is a kind of brainwashing and concludes that, when viewed from this perspective, the Whorf-Sapir hypothesis becomes a tenable explanation.

What are the implications here for the study of public rhetoric? Let me start microscopically. The rhetorical analyst will begin his investigation of rhetorical situations by focusing on the language of the transaction. If it is the case, as I believe it is, that language reflects the perception underlying behavior, a fruitful line of investigation might proceed from the question: what are the linguistic stimuli that can be examined as clues to perception? I have in mind here more than the rather obvious choices of noun, pronoun and verb. Rather, taking a cue from the process of foreign language translation, it seems reasonable that clumps of words, whole phrases, perhaps whole paragraphs exhibiting specific language characteristics need to be treated as perceptual units.

Because a large percentage of our language is metaphorical, the metaphor suggests itself as a prime candidate for investigation. The number of studies dealing with metaphor as a literary or stylistic device are legion (for listing see Adolph, 1968) and Osborn (1967) states that until recently rhetorical theorists also consigned metaphor to the canon of style which "spotlighted its linguistic attachments and threw into shadow its basic mental components." Some contemporary studies, however, have begun to treat the metaphorical process as symbolic of basic mental response. There have been attempts to explain the peculiar nature of metaphorical thinking (see Black, 1962; Osborn, 1967; Osborn and Ehninger, 1962) and to discover the impact and influence of certain metaphors when they appear in discourse (Bowers and Osborn, 1966). Though our data is yet sparse, it appears to evidence a positive correlation between linguistic metaphor and perception. Roland and Maryanne Force (1961), both cultural anthropologists, broaden the scope of linguistic analysis when they remark that figures of speech act as the models which help people define their universe and render the abstract concrete.

If we extend the principle of metaphor, we can see that verbal sentences of comparison and contrast also function to structure images, though perhaps in a different fashion. To compare Communist aggression in Vietnam with various acts and actions of aggression preceding World War II is to cast forth a whole series of evocative images. To say that the current United States posture in Vietnam does not parallel earlier French involvement is to attempt to reject a series of images, even if it does not succeed in structuring any new ones.

Single words or brief combinations of words will operate as image builders, particularly if they condense a large amount of information and feeling into a pattern or formulation which forces value judgments. The impact of such symbols is derived from their tendency to complete the imagery with a judgment of "good" or "bad," "friend" or "foe," "favorable" or "unfavorable," "for me" or "against me."

"Militant," "reactionary," "radical," "un-American," "aggression," "Yippie," "Black Power," "middle class," "Establishment," "the System," "Participatory Democracy," are all terms, titles, or slogans which imply value judgments in some direction and enjoy peculiar force from the implication. In some cases they are traditional symbols whose connotations have become encrusted through long traditional usage; others are newly coined symbols which gain their force through association with extant controversial and emotional ideas and happenings. In yet other cases they are ordinary words whose emotive or image-casting force is to be found mostly within the lexical setting and existential environment in which they are used. An example of the latter type was discussed by Hermann Stelzner (1966) in his excellent analysis of Franklin Roosevelt's "War Message" delivered to Congress and the nation on December 8, 1941. Stelzner explicates the way in which Roosevelt's phrase, "Japanese air squadrons," drew upon both public imagination of the previous day's Pearl Harbor attack and a certain formality of style which, in combination with other lexical patterns, cast forth an image of well-planned and executed Japanese duplicity. Stelzner's example indicates that nearly any word or combination of words may be "fair game" in perceptual analysis, depending upon its contextual surroundings. I suggest that we need to undertake renewed analysis of linguistic style from a perceptual point of view.

A second line of enquiry must concern itself with the validation of critical methodology. Suppose that a rhetorical scholar builds his analysis around certain linguistic clues to perception found in a discourse. Can he interpret the perceptions correctly? Can he somehow correctly gauge the perceptual worlds of those who may receive the communication?

Walter Kassoway (1967) conducted a study here at Penn State which attempted to determine whether or not Kassoway, the analyst, could accurately determine and describe the perceptual world of Carl Oglesby as projected in a speech Oglesby delivered in Washington, D. C., November 27, 1965. The occasion of the speech was an anti-Vietnam war march on Washington, attended by an estimated 20 to 30 thousand marchers who congregated at the Washington Monument for some five hours of speech-making.

Kassoway's procedure was interesting. Starting with the text of the speech, he first described the political world as he thought Oglesby saw it, with particular reference to the war situation. Within this framework, Kassoway next defined and delineated what appeared to be specialized meanings and images evoked by certain key terms. Then, largely by inferential contrast, the ideal world, or world Oglesby thought "ought to be" was constructed. Finally, Oglesby's value judgments and assumptions were closely scrutinized and interpreted to complete the picture.

With the rhetorical analysis completed, Kassoway, with the help of several psychologists, constructed three different psychological tests which were used to attempt to validate the analytical procedure. First, in order to uncover values specific to the speech, Oglesby was asked to generate and rank thirty self-values in numerical order according to his recollection of their relevance at the time he gave the speech. Second, a personal values Q-sort was used to reveal general information about Oglesby's value structure. Third, an attempt was made to measure the specific meaning-value of key words and concepts in the Oglesby speech. A semantic differential, based on fifteen semantic concepts which were thought to be dominant in the Oglesby speech, was constructed and administered to Oglesby.

At the same time Oglesby was taking the three psychological tests, Kassoway took them; first as he thought Oglesby would take them, based solely upon what Kassoway inferred about Oglesby from the speech analysis; second as Kassoway himself, based on his own perceptions; third as Kassoway thought a "liberal" might take them. Finally, to check the possibility that anyone with a sufficient grasp of the English language could do as well as Kassoway, a third individual with political beliefs similar to Kassoway's was asked to take the same three tests, but without having attempted the speech analysis.

I do not have time to relate all of the procedures of correlation or all the results, but generally speaking, Kassoway's success in describing Oglesby's perceptual world was moderate to good, in some cases excellent, and much better than that of the third individual. Further, Kassoway discovered that he could successfully depart from his own perceptual world to define the world of another. This study is only a beginning but in my opinion a very important beginning and it uncovered several fruitful lines for further research. The work of William Stephenson (1967), who authored Q-sort methodology, indicates that the perceptions of listeners may reasonably be investigated and described as are those of the communicator. Obviously much more work needs to be done in this area.

Let me conclude now by talking macroscopically for a moment. Our contemporary "mass media" world presents a complex situation for those of us interested in understanding the role of public rhetoric. It seems unlikely that the measurement of message effect in terms of immediate or short-range impact will provide any realistic appraisal. The full public dialogue on such matters as the racial problem, the urban situation, and United States foreign policy is made available to the public via television. To further complicate matters, images projected and evoked by the dialogue are both verbal and visual; thus a public statement by the Secretary of State asserting that our

Vietnam posture is helping to secure the well-being of the South Vietnamese may be juxtaposed with television footage which shows weeping peasants observing United States marines destroy their village to save their village.

The Vietnam debate is a perfect illustration of the analyst's problem. No one message or part of the dialogue can be isolated for examination without distorting the holistic impact the dialogue will have. And any one message or series of messages, such as the Senate Foreign Relations Committee Hearings, occurs amidst a full panoply of televised events and other rhetorical messages. How do we get a grasp on the possible influence of the hearings? Perhaps Terwilliger's brainwashing example gives us a clue.

The public debate over Vietnam presents us with two sets of ambiguities in conflict. One set of ambiguities, promulgated by John Foster Dulles via Dean Rusk, depicts the threat of monolithic Communism, with the domino imagery and all the rest. The challenging set of ambiguities, verbalized by William Fulbright and others, speaks of a great diversity of nations, motivated more by nationalistic than by ideological considerations. The background for the debate is composed of a multitude of shifting images projected by various media, many of which are inconsistent with official governmental proclamations. A disturbed public through interpersonal conversation reinforces the sense of unease. Sometime during the course of the dialogue, the situation may be just right for popular acceptance of the second set of ambiguities over the first. When will it happen? What forces will work to make it happen? Are the trends of change already visible? What form will the perceptual changes take? The total picture needs to be observed and synthesized by a series of rhetorical studies.

The potential for perceptual change is present on a number of social and political fronts in contemporary society. It will be impossible for any one individual to delineate them completely. But the formation of a number of research task forces, analyzing the influence of public rhetoric on public perceptions, should be able to provide a meaningful contribution to our understanding of public controversy and conflict.

REFERENCES

Adolph, Robert, 1968, *The Rise of Modern Prose Style,* Cambridge, Massachusetts: M.I.T. Press.
Becker, Samuel L., 1963, "Research on Emotional and Logical Proofs," *Southern Speech Journal* (1963) XXVIII (3), 198-207.
Berelson, Bernard A. and Gary A. Steiner, 1964, *Human Behavior,* New York: Harcourt, Brace & World, Inc.
Bettinghaus, Erwin P., 1968, *Persuasive Communications,* New York: Holt, Reinhart and Winston.
Black, Edwin, 1965, *Rhetorical Criticism: A Study in Method,* New York: Macmillan.
Black, Max, 1962, *Models and Metaphors, Ithaca,* New York: Cornell University Press.
Bowers, John Waite and Michael M. Osborn, 1966, "Attitudinal Effects of Selected Types of Concluding Metaphors in Persuasive Speeches," *Speech Monographs* (1966) XXXIII (2), 147-155.
Brown, Roger W., 1956, "Language and Categories", in *A Study of Thinking,* New York: John Wiley & Sons, Co.
Combs, Arthur W. and Donald Snygg, 1959, *Individual Behavior,* New York: Harper.
Force, Roland W. and Maryanne Force, 1961, "Keys to Cultural Understanding," *Science* (1961) 133 (3459), 1203.
Gerbner, George, 1966, "On Defining Communication: Still Another View," *Journal of Communication* (1966) XVI (2), 99-103.
Kassoway, Walter, 1967, "A Perceptually Oriented Approach to Speech Criticism," unpublished Master's thesis (The Pennsylvania State University).
McCroskey, James C., 1967, *Studies of the Effects of Evidence in Persuasive Communication,* East Lansing: Michigan State University Speech Communication Research Laboratory.
Osborn, Michael, 1967, "Archetypal Metaphor in Rhetoric: The Light-Dark Family," *The Quarterly Journal of Speech* (1967) LII (2), 115-126.
Osborn, Michael M., 1967, "The Evolution of the Theory of Metaphor in Rhetoric," *Western Speech* (1967) XXXI (2), 126.
—————, and Douglas Ehninger, 1962, "The Metaphor in Public Address," *Speech Monographs* (1962) (3), 223-234.
Scott, Robert L. and Donald K. Smith, 1969, "The Rhetoric of Confrontation," *The Quarterly Journal of Speech* (1969) LV (February), 1-8.

Stelzner, Hermann G., 1966, " 'War Message,' December 8, 1941: An Approach to Language," *Speech Monographs* (1966) XXXIII (4), 425-426.

Stephenson, William, 1967, *The Play Theory of Mass Communication*, Chicago, Illinois: University of Chicago Press.

Terwilliger, Robert F., 1968, *Meaning and Mind*, London: Oxford University Press.

INTERDISCIPLINARY APPROACHES

INTEGRATION OF THE INTEGRATIVE DISCIPLINES*

GLYNN HARMON
University of Denver

General semantics might be viewed as one of several studies directed towards approximately the same problem or constellation of problems. Using the analogy of the blind men studying the elephant, general semantics, as well as general systems theory, information science and similar fields, appears to be studying the same massive elephant. As blind men can assist each other in forming a helpful gestalt of their elephant, so can the interdisciplinary studies assist each other. Konrad Lorenz (1962) states, "In the systematic unity of all cognitive achievements, the perception of complex gestalten plays a scientifically legitimate and *completely indispensable* part."

The extremely wide applicability of the general semantics model also invites a gestalt approach. "General semantics continues to develop, because there is no end to the study of the intricate relationships between language, thought and action" (Hayakawa, 1962). Recently, general semantics has been concerned with "the quest for structures, patterns and themes that undergird the corpus of the most important knowledges, as well as the communication process" (Murray and Hunsinger, 1968).

Emergence of Integrative Disciplines

Before examining the emergence of general semantics and similar integrative disciplines, one might first note the historical peculiarity of

---

*Work partially supported by U.S.O.E. Grant OEG-6-95-45-0620-0015, Case Western Reserve University.

independent, simultaneous discoveries. The frequent phenomenon of simultaneous discovery indicates that more than one party responds to the same problem at the same time. Consider the following examples (see Harvey-Gibson, 1931, and Struik, 1967):

Logarithms	Napier 1614	Burgi 1620
Calculus	Newton 1664	Leibniz 1673
Oxygen	Priestly 1774	Scheel 1777
Atomic Theory	Higgins 1789	Dalton 1814
Non-Euclidean geometry	Lobachevsky 1829	Bolvai 1832
Energy conservation	Meyer 1842	Joule 1847
Algebra of logic	Boole 1847	DeMorgan 1847
Evolution	Darwin 1858	Wallace 1858
Periodic Classification	Mendeleef 1869	Meyer1869

Such coincidental discoveries might be motivated by what Edward Boring (1950) calls the *zeitgeist,* or "spirit of the time." Or, in accordance with Goffman and Newill's theory (1964) that human susceptibility to ideas is analogous to human susceptibility to diseases, certain groups of investigators or entire disciplines can be "infected" with aspects of the same problem at the same time. One might reasonably hypothesize, then, that different disciplines could have a common origin in the same problem. The dimensions of the underlying problem might be more fully revealed by examining similar disciplines which emerged at the same time. The following discussion reviews the features of the unity of science movement, the behavioral sciences, information science, and general semantics as similar integrative fields which emerged in the 1930's.

Unity of Science

The unity of science movement, marked by the First International Congress for the Unity of Science in 1935, involves two major purposes, according to John Dewey (1955). First, it involves the coordination of a large, scattered body of specialized findings into a systematic whole. Second, it involves unification of those individuals willing to use scientific methods and attitudes in the conduct of their daily affairs—in spite of frequent opposition to the scientific attitude by nationalistic, class, commercial, racial, or religious interests.

Concurrent with the unity of science movement, several new fields of investigation emerged during the 1930's and particularly since

World War II. Since the early 1950's—as a result of joint efforts by the Ford Foundation and groups of scholars to deal synoptically with behavioral problems—these disciplines have been collectively referred to as the "behavioral sciences." A 1956 functional description of behavioral science is provided by the founding editors of the journal *Behavioral Science* (Alexander and others, 1956):

> If the fragments of multiple sciences were brought together in a unitary behavioral science. . . . The uniformities among disciplines could be recognized; better communication among them established; generality of findings magnified; additional benefits derived from comparing theories in diverse fields, explaining both similarities and differences; and the validity and applicability of empirical work increased by planning individual studies as components of an explicit mosaic of research strategy.

In 1963 and 1964 the Behavioral Research Council made a distinction between the "older fields" of behavioral inquiry (anthropology, sociology, history, economics, political science, psychology, education) and the "newer fields." The newer fields include those of communication theory (information theory, cybernetics, linguistics, sign-behavior) and those involving preferential behavior (game theory, decision-making theory, value inquiry and general systems theory). General features of the newer behavioral sciences are summarized in Table 1 (Handy and Kurtz, 1964).

In addition to the listed behavioral sciences, other fields have emerged recently. *Operations research,* considered in some quarters to be an applied component of general systems theory, developed as a scientific arm of the executive function during World War II. Operations research brings the systems approach and the intellectual resources of interdisciplinary teams to bear on organizational problems (Ackoff and Rivett, 1963). *Bionics,* defined as "the art of applying the knowledge of living systems to solving technical problems," has developed since it was publicly launched in 1960; Cybernetics and bionics "may be seen as two sides of a coin: while in bionics one

TABLE 1

THE BEHAVIORAL SCIENCES

Field	Locus of Inquiry	Chief Founders
Information Theory	Effective coding, transmission and reception of messages in communication systems, without regard to value or significance of information involved in the communication process.	Hartley 1928 Shannon, Weaver and Wiener 1948
Cybernetics	Regulative processes of physical, biological, and behavioral systems with special emphasis on feedback in machines and nervous systems	Wiener 1948
Linguistics	Language structures, principles underlying the organization of languages, historical changes and relations between languages or linguistic codes	Sapir 1921 Bloomfield 1914, 1933
Sign Behavior	Verbal and non-verbal naming, signalling and symbolizing. Critical analysis and clarification of language and cognitive behavior.	Korzybski 1933 Morris 1938
Game Theory	Cooperative and competitive behavior patterns involving alternative choices and outcomes.	Von Neumann and Morgenstern 1944
Decision Theory	Aspects of human behavior in which choices are made among alternatives. Descriptive and normative study of decision-making.	Wald 1939
Value Inquiry	Behavior indicating preferences among alternative choices available to individuals and groups; the set of preferences that influence selections.	Perry 1926 Reid 1938
General Systems Theory	Models, principles and laws applying to generalized physical, biological or behavioral systems, or their subclasses.	Lotka 1925 Von Bertalanffy 1939, 1950

studies . . . physical systems by analogy with living systems; in cybernetics living systems are studied by analogy with physical systems" (Gerardin, 1968, pp. 11, 22). The recent establishment of the World Future Society in Washington, D.C., and the Institute for the

Future in Middletown, Connecticut, suggest the beginnings of *futurology*.

> Multidisciplinary and integrative research will be applied to such questions as the cities of tomorrow, the future as related to communications, computers, education, food, population, developing nations' business and industry (Darling, 1968).

Another relatively new field of investigation is *information science,* which has been described as "parasitic upon, symbiotic with, and host to" all other disciplines and technologies.

> As a discipline, Information Science investigates the properties and behavior of information, the forces that govern the transfer process, and the technology required to process information for optimum accessibility and use. Its interests include information representations in both natural and artificial systems; the use of codes for efficient message transmission, storage, and recall, and the study of information processing devices and techniques such as computers and their programming systems.
>
> It is an interdisciplinary field derived from and related to mathematics, logic, linguistics, psychology, computer technology, operations, research, librarianship, and graphic arts, communications, management, and similar fields.[1]

A shorter definition of information science is the "investigation of communication phenomena and the properties of communication systems" Rees and Saracevic, 1968). Although the roots of information science extend back to such landmarks as the establishment of the International Institute of Bibliography in 1895, and the American Documentation Institute in 1937, the field's major development has occurred since the end of World War II.

---

[1] Announcement brochure of the American Society for Information Science, Washington, D.C., 1968.

Approach to Integrative Research

To the extent that investigators in general semantics, other behavioral sciences and information science share a common problem, some degree of rapprochement and dialogue between these fields seems desirable. Table 2 provides an approach to comparing two fields of study. Thematic comparisons may be drawn to locate research approaches and designs existing in one field and applicable in the other. For example, information science and general semantics are compared; topics are drawn from Korzybski (1958) and Cuadra (1968).

TABLE 2

COMPARISON OF INFORMATION SCIENCE AND GENERAL SEMANTICS

	Time Binding	Abstracting	Semantic Reactions	Modern Logic	Symbolism	Ordering	Isomorphism
Information Need and Use	1	2					
Information Generation							
Information Dissemination							
Information Collection							
Information Storage							
Information Retrieval			3				
Information Systems							

The three numbers in the above matrix designate examples of areas wherein useful formulations, findings and approaches could be exchanged:

1. Time binding (the unique human capacity to transmit infor-

mation from one generation to the next, so that each generation or individual can resume inquiry where the other left off) can be studied from the standpoint of how individuals and groups develop and express their needs for information, and assimilate information during the conduct of inquiry. Some 130 information need and use studies are reviewed in *The Annual Review of Information Science and Technology,* Volumes I-III. For a discussion of relationships between general semantics and librarianship, see Shera (1965).

2. Weinberg (1967) has referred to Korzybski's structural differential as a possible guide for the reorganization of the scientific community in order to deal with the fragmentation and increasingly higher abstractions of scientific knowledge. Scientists would be hierarchically stratified according to the level of abstraction at which they worked. Though the philosopher at the top would know almost nothing about almost everything, such a hierarchy could serve to systematize induction. In addition, Weinberg discusses a "proliferation of the semantic environment," which results largely from the number of semantic contacts growing approximately in proportion to the square of the human population. Because the normal ability to absorb sensory impressions is relatively limited, an over-abundance of sensory data can confound normal cognition. The confrontation of this problem, particularly among information system users, would seem to require the acquisition of skills along the lines suggested by Korzybski—identification of key variables, consciousness of abstracting, the formation of higher order abstractions, and training in non-Aristotelian logic.

3. In the design and evaluation of information systems, several experimental studies have focused on the concept of relevance. A "good" information system supposedly provides its user with information or documents "relevant" to his information needs, assuming that his questions do accurately reflect his underlying information needs. The unresolved relevance problem has proved to be complex and formidable (see Cuadra and Katter, 1967; Rees and Schultz, 1967). Numerous other comparisons could be made in such common areas as automatic semantic analysis, communication content analysis, indexing, abstracting, vocabulary control, man-computer communi-

cation, or general information networks involving hook-ups with esoteric subsystems.

Conclusion

To summarize, general semantics has been viewed as one of several integrative disciplines which emerged during the last four decades. These disciplines include the behavioral sciences, information science and others. The hypothetical position of this paper is that these fields had their origins in a common problem, and developed as relatively simultaneous responses to that problem. Perhaps these integrative disciplines have arisen to perform the syntheses hitherto accomplished through the prodigious life-time efforts of single scientists, such as Newton or Darwin. Now, some degree of synthesis among the integrative disciplines appears to be essential to the formation of mutually helpful gestalts and adequate research designs.

The aims of these disciplines are similar, though their approaches vary. They seek optimal communication and interaction between and among men, machines and nature. Collectively the integrative disciplines appear to be involved in a unity and use of science movement. They focus on systematic intrapersonal and interpersonal communication, through variable space and time contexts, in order to promote adaptive behavior in the cooperative or competitive pursuit of valued ends.

REFERENCES

Ackoff, R. L., and P. Rivett, *A Managers Guide to Operations Research,* New York: Wiley, 1963.

Alexander, F. and others, "Behavioral Science, a New Journal," *Behavioral Science* (1956) 1, 2.

Boring, E. G., *A History of Experimental Psychology,* New York: Appleton-Century-Crofts, 737-745, 1950.

Cuadra, C. A. and R. V. Katter, "The Relevance of Relevance Assessment," *Proceedings of the 30th Annual Meeting of the American Documentation Institute,* Washington, D. C.: American Documentation Institute, 95-99, 1967.

Darling, C. M., "New Forecasting Facilities for Managing The Future," *The Conference Board Record* (1968) VII (July) 2.

Dewey, J., 1955, "Unity of Science as a Social Problem," *International Encyclopedia of Unified Science*, I: 32-33.

Gerardin, L., *Bionics*, New York: McGraw-Hill, 11, 22, 1968.

Goffman, W., and V. A. Newill, 1964, "Generalization of Epidemic Theory," *Nature* (1964) CCIV (October 17), 225-8.

Handy, R., and P. Kurtz, 1964, *A Current Appraisal of the Behavioral Sciences*, Great Barrington, Mass.: Behavioral Science Research Council. Originally published as supplements to *The American Behavioral Scientist*, VII (Sept., 1963 through March, 1964), Sections 1-7.

Hayakawa, S. I., 1962. *The Use and Misuse of Language*, Greenwich, Con.: Fawcett Publications.

Harvey-Gibson, R. J., 1931, *Two Thousand Years of Science*, New York: Macmillan.

Korzybski, A., 1958, *Science and Sanity*, 4th ed., Lakeville, Conn.: International Non-Aristotelian Library Publishing Company.

Lorenz, K., 1962, "Gestalt Perception as Fundamental to Scientific Knowledge," *General Systems*, Seventh Yearbook of The Society for General Systems Research, 68.

Murray, E. and P. Hunsinger, 1968, "The Interdisciplinary Analogue Laboratory on Structures, Patterns, and Themes", *Communication Spectrum '7*, Lawrence, Ka.: Allen Press, 1968, 322-329.

Rees, A., and D. G. Schultz, 1967, *A Field Experimental Approach to the Study of Relevance Assessments in Relation to Document Searching*, Final Report, Cleveland: Center for Documentation and Communication Research, Case Western Reserve Univ.

─────────, and T. Saracevic, 1968, "Education for Information Science and its Relationship to Librarianship" (unpublished paper), quoted in "Of Librarianship, Documentation and Information Science," *UNESCO Bulletin for Libraries*, 1968, XXII (March-April), 63.

Shera, J. H., 1965, "Social Epistemology, General Semantics and Librarianship," in *Libraries and The Organization of Knowledge*, Hamden, Conn.: Archon, pp. 12-17.

Struik, D. J., 1967, *A Concise History of Mathematics*, New York: Dover.

Weinberg, A. M., 1967, *Reflections on Big Science*, Cambridge. Mass.: M.I.T. Press, 4, 47.

LINGUISTICS AND GENERAL SEMANTICS: A REAPPRAISAL

JOSEPH A. DeVITO

Herbert H. Lehman College
The City University of New York

In 1952 Martin Maloney (1952) explored some of the similarities and differences between linguistics and general semantics. Utilizing the frame of reference supplied by Leonard Bloomfield for linguistics and that supplied by Alfred Korzybski for general semantics, Maloney elucidated some of the important points of contact and divergence.

While general semantics has remained, at least relatively so, Korzybskian, linguistics has not remained Bloomfieldian. M.I.T. linguist Noam Chomsky (several references, 1957-1969) has changed the direction and emphasis of linguistics to the point where a totally different orientation prevails today. Because of this it might be profitable to examine again some of the similarities and differences between linguistics and general semantics. Maloney's five generalizations will serve as the basis for this discussion.

I

1. Both linguistics and general semantics deal with similar basic subject-matter, i.e., the complex of speech-plus-"practical events."

While this is still true—in general—the emphasis is no longer valid. Linguistics is not primarily the science of speech plus practical events but rather of language, the abstract system of syntactic, semantic, and phonological rules. It would probably be more accurate to say that both disciplines are concerned with similar subject matters, namely language, but whereas the linguist is concerned with language-as-known, the general semanticist is concerned with language-as-used.

Whereas linguistics is the study of language competence, general semantics is the study of language performance, or at least of some subportion of this.

II

2. The linguist conventionally abstracts from this complex the speech signal for study, although theoretically at least, he does not deny the existence of the "practical" concomitants of speech. This is to say, his orientation is more or less toward "the science of language."

While this might have been a fair characterization of linguistics 1933 or even of linguistics 1952, it is not of linguistics 1969. The linguist is not concerned primarily with speech. He does recognize that speech (when compared with writing) is the primary system of communication and that writing is a system derived in imitation of the spoken signal. But his primary concern is not with this signal—spoken or written—but rather with language, the abstract system of rules. Put in terms of communication theory, the linguist is concerned primarily with the code rather than the message.

A distinction introduced by Chomsky, or more correctly reintroduced, will perhaps make this point clearer. The linguist is concerned primarily with competence—that is, with the native speaker's ability to produce and understand an infinite number of sentences. He is not primarily concerned with performance, that is, the actual speech utterances. His ultimate goal is to formulate a theory of competence, not performance. This distinction is an important one because performance is confounded by numerous extralinguistic variables, e.g., memory span, attention span, type of audience, mode of communication, etc. Competence, ideally at least, is the native speaker's uncontaminated linguistic knowledge. It is this "pure language" which is of primary concern to the contemporary linguist.

III

3. The "general semanticist," for his part, is less concerned with "the science of language" considered as the detailed analysis

of utterances—though he can never afford to ignore or even slight the utterances in any given situation—and is more concerned with the "semantic reactions," or *evaluations,* of speaker and listener.

The science of language should not be considered as the detailed analysis of utterances. This is not what it is in modern linguistic theory. Nor is it or should it be the primary concern of the general semanticist. It is perhaps more clearly the province of phonetics.

Both linguistics and general semantics, however, must be vitally concerned with all aspects of language—especially metalanguage since it is this aspect which enables one to analyze language regardless of the point of view taken. Thus, the general semanticist must be concerned with the nature of language and particularly metalanguages because it is through this means that persons become "general semanticists" or function in the way advocated by general semantics. The linguistic scientist must be concerned with this simply because it is through metalanguage that he is enabled to analyze object language. Advances in the description of language and in the prescriptions for adequate language usage will almost surely come from advances in metalanguage.

IV

· 4. The "general semanticist" uses mathematics as a kind of yardstick for evaluating the propriety or adequacy of linguistic forms, which the linguist does not, although linguists are quite well aware of mathematics as an "ideal" language. Indeed, linguists do not usually consider it their business to make value judgments about a language, but rather to make descriptive and analytical statements, which may be used by others: "The tasks of stating a situation in mathematical (usually, in numerical) terms, and of deciding what types of restatement are consistent (that is, lead to a correct response), are independent of linguistic features . . . It is not the linguist who can tell us that we shall get into trouble if we now act on the statement that *two plus two equals three.* All that linguistics can do is to reveal the verbal character of mathematics and save us from mystical aberrations on this score." [Leonard Bloomfield (1933), *Language,* New York: Holt, p. 507.]

The separation of grammar from semantics as advocated by Bloomfield and as restated by Maloney no longer exists. In generative grammar, grammar is conceived of as having three parts—syntax, semantics, and phonology. The linguist today is vitally concerned with semantics and would be very much interested in the sentence *two plus two equals three.* Ultimately, the semantic rules of the language would have to identify and describe such a statement as semantically meaningless. Meaninglessness as well as such phenomena as semantic ambiguity, which have long been a major concern to the general semanticist, are now also of major concern to the generative grammarian.

Furthermore, the linguist is also concerned with the human reactions to statements (grammatical or ungrammatical, meaningful or meaningless, ambiguous or unambiguous) since it is by examining such reactions that the psychological reality for linguistic constructs is established. For example, it has been shown that linguistic structure is a significant factor in determining where a subject will hear inserted clicks. That is, a subject listening to a sentence in which clicks have been inserted will not hear them where they objectively appear but rather will "hear" them at major syntactic breaks in the sentence. Evidence such as this illustrates that the divisions and analyses offered by contemporary linguistic theorists are not mere abstract conveniences but rather are psychologically real —they influence and in part determine behavior in predictable and clearly specified ways.[1] In this area of the psychological reality of linguistic constructs the general semanticist should feel much at home and should be encouraged and aided in his research by the numerous and ingenious methods for the study of such phenomena provided by linguists and psycholinguists. The general semanticist might well

---

[1] For excellent reviews of this research see Garrett, Merrill, and Jerry A. Fodor, 1968, "Psychological Theories and Linguistic Constructs," *Verbal Behavior and General Behavior Theory,* Englewood Cliffs, New Jersey, pp. 451-476, and Fodor and Merrill, 1966, "Some Reflections on Competence and Performance," *Psycholinguistic Papers,* Chicago: Aldine Publishing Co., pp. 133-154.

direct himself to the study of the behavioral correlates of metalanguage—as considered in general semantic theory—using those methods and procedures proving profitable in linguistics and psycholinguistics.

The generative grammarians' distinction between deep and surface structures likewise stresses the importance of semantics to a theory of grammar. All sentences are conceived of as having both a deep and a surface structure. The deep structure provides the input to the semantic component of a generative grammar and the surface structure the input to the phonological component. The semantic component yields a semantic interpretation and the phonological component a phonetic representation of the sentence. Semantic ambiguity can thus be viewed as occurring when there is more than one deep structure for a given sentence. For example, in the sentence "Flying planes can be dangerous," to use a popular example, there are at least two possible deep structures: "Flying planes is dangerous" and "Flying planes are dangerous." In generative grammar sentences are viewed as being understood on the basis of deep, rather than surface, structure.

The implication here should be clear. General semanticists, in analyzing language, have too often restricted their focus to the surface structure of sentences. They need now to look at the deep structure since it is this aspect of sentences which is more closely related to "semantic reactions."

V

5. The linguist concerns himself very little with the structure/language-structure/fact correspondence. His orientation, as we have noted, is toward the verbal utterance. Present-day linguists have indeed shown an increasing interest in the total *speech* situation (which includes non-linguistic behavior); but they have not concerned themselves with the adequacy of linguistic forms considered in relation to "the facts" (which they are used to represent).

As already observed, the linguist today is not concerned merely with the verbal utterance but rather with the totality of language. And in his consideration of semantics does consider the adequacy of language-fact relations. Moreover, he is concerned with this question not only in the abstract sense of how adequately does language reflect reality but also with the more practical and concrete questions of how an individual speaker utilizes language in describing reality.

The recent interest in language universals—grammatical, semantic, and phonological universals—likewise illustrates this broad concern with the totality of language.[2] Here is another area where the general semanticist will find significant hypotheses and questions. Language universals—those linguistic features common to all natural languages—are the aspects of language which probably influence behavior most significantly since they probably operate below the level of consciousness and are elements of deep, rather than surface, structure.

The point of all this is that the common conception of the linguist studying language apart from speakers is no longer true—if, indeed, it ever was. The linguist has redirected his focus to the speaker of the language and seeks to formulate a theory of language competence. Since language competence, however, cannot be observed directly the linguist focuses his energies on language behavior, *i.e.*, language performance. A theory of language competence puts the speaker of the language at the center of the linguist's concern where he has been for some time in general semantics.

Each field could profit greatly from the insights of the other. The linguist could learn a great deal about reactions and evaluations to language and the general semanticist could learn a great deal about the structure of language and the rigorous methods for examining language and language behavior.

If such a joint effort is made, the science of language will become a science of language behavior—a trend which is already in evidence in much of contemporary linguistic theory. And clearly it is to a science of language behavior which general semantics and linguistics are aiming, though each takes a different road in a different vehicle.

---

[2]See, for example, Greenberg, Joseph H., 1963, *Universals of Language*, Cambridge, Mass.: M.I.T. Press; Bach, Emmon, and Robert T. Harms, 1968, *Universals in Linguistic Theory*, New York: Holt; Chomsky, Noam, 1967, "The Formal Nature of Language," in *Biological Foundations of Language*, New York: Wiley, pp. 397-442.

REFERENCES

Chomsky, Noam, *Syntactic Structures,* The Hague: Mouton, 1957.
———, *Current Issues in Linguistic Theory,* The Hague: Mouton, 1964.
———, *Aspects of a Theory of Syntax,* Cambridge, Mass.: M.I.T. Press, 1965.
———, *Topics in the Theory of Generative Grammar,* The Hague: Mouton, 1966.
———, *Language and Mind,* New York: Harcourt, Brace & World, 1969.
Maloney, Martin, "General Semantics and Linguistics: Some Similarities and Differences," *General Semantics Bulletin* (1952) 8 & 9, 57-62, 70.

PSYCHOLINGUISTICS AND GENERAL SEMANTICS: SOME CONCEPTUAL "PROBLEMS" AND "RESOLUTIONS"

JOSEPH A. DeVITO
Herbert H. Lehman College
The City University of New York

The relationship between general semantics and psycholinguistics must be a strong one for John C. Condon, Jr. (1966, p. 3) to remark that "some day behavioral semantics will pass into another field, probably psycholinguistics, where today comparable and more sophisticated research is rapidly developing. In the meantime, semantics takes its place among the behavioral sciences as an approach leading to an attitude about what makes us behave as we do, be it wisely or foolishly, sanely or 'unsanely'."

In the general semantics literature, however, it is a very peculiar brand of psycholinguistics which is considered. Harry L. Weinberg (1966, p. 87), for example, offers two possible definitions. "First, we can view psycholinguistics as a metalanguage, a language for talking about the language of psychology: that is, a study of the linguistic patterns of psychological theories and therapies. Secondly, psycholinguistics can be described as a study of the effects of language usage —more precisely, the effects of linguistic patterns—upon people themselves." And Joost A. M. Meerloo (1964) notes that "the science of psycholinguistics is easily defined: namely, the study of the behavioral means man uses to bridge the gap between him and his fellow man."

It would, of course, be foolhardy to argue over the "real" meaning of psycholinguistics. It is important to note, however, that definitions such as these (aside from their being outside the mainstream of

194   Joseph A. DeVito

contemporary psycholinguistic theorizing) fail to specify any manageable and "researchable" area of investigation; they fail to encourage or direct any systematic attempt at theory construction and often lead to and in fact encourage research which is poorly conceived, ill-defined, and premature.

Admittedly, "psycholinguistics" is not an easy term to define. Sol Saporta (1961), in the introduction to his *Psycholinguistics: A Book of Readings,* wrote that "psycholinguistics is still an amorphous field." And Susan Ervin-Tripp and Dan Slobin (1966) observed that "psycholinguistics appears to be a field in search of a definition." Often psycholinguistics is only loosely defined as the study of the psychology of language or the psychology of speech; a psycholinguist, by such definitions, is a linguist interested in behavior or a psychologist interested in speech and language.[1] Clearly such conceptions are of little heuristic value.

Previously I noted that psycholinguistics is concerned with "(1) structured language; (2) how this language structure is learned; (3) how it is encoded or produced; and (4) how it is decoded or understood" (DeVito, 1967). More formally, psycholinguistics may be defined as the study of the psychological processes involved in the acquisition, encoding, and decoding of language.[2] Although this defi-

---

[1] The following works and those cited therein should provide a reasonably representative view of the varied approaches to the nature of psycholinguistics: Roger Brown, 1958, *Words and Things,* New York: Free Press; John B. Carroll, 1964, *Language and Thought,* Englewood Cliffs, New Jersey: Prentice-Hall; A. Richard Diebold, 1965, "A Survey of Psycholinguistics Research 1954-64," in *Psycholinguistics: A Survey of Theory and Research Problems,* Bloomington: Indiana University Press. pp. 205-291; George A. Miller, 1964, "The Psycholinguists: On the New Scientists of Language," *Encounter* (1964) 23, 29-37, reprinted in Osgood and Sebeok, *Psycholinguistics,* pp. 293-307; Charles E. Osgood, 1953, "Psycholinguistics," in *Psychology: A Study of a Science,* Vol. VI, New York: McGraw-Hill, pp. 244-316; Leon A. Jakobovitz and Murray S. Miron, eds., 1967, *Readings in the Psychology of Language,* Englewood Cliffs, New Jersey: Prentice-Hall.

In none of these works, it should be noted, is general semantics even considered. The only attempt to deal with general semantics within the framework of Psycholinguistics (as currently conceived) that I am aware of is my own, *The Psychology of Speech and Language: An Introduction to Psycholinguistics,* to be published by Random House this year.

[2] For a similar but more detailed argument for such a definition see Jerry A. Fodor, James J. Jenkins, and Sol Saporta, 1967, "Psycholinguistics and Communication Theory," in *Human Communication Theory: Original Essays,* New York: Holt, pp. 160-201.

nition may not be completely satisfying, it does have a distinct advantage over the previous loosely defined approaches. The advantage is simply that it clearly specifies the research questions to which the science of psycholinguistics must direct itself.

It appears that part of the problem with general semantics research is that the field itself has been too vaguely defined for any such research questions to be generated, too loosely defined for it to suggest any direction for theory building, and so abstractly defined that it encourages research which should never be undertaken. The very eclectic nature of *Etc.: A Review of General Semantics* and *General Semantics Bulletin* indicates that general semantics has not been clearly and specifically defined. The paucity of valid and reliable research in general semantics,[3] I think, is, at least in part, a function of the failure of the field to have defined itself in research-generating terms. To define general semantics as "the study of the relations between language, thought, and behavior: between *how we talk,* therefore *how we think,* and therefore *how we act,*" as has Hayakawa (1962, p. vii) or as the "Body of data and method leading to habits of adequate language-fact relationships," as has Lee (1941, p. 8), or as "an empirical natural science of non-elementalistic evalua-

---

[3]That little research has been done in general semantics is, of course, a familiar song. John B. Carroll, for example, notes that "in the nearly twenty years of its existence it has produced very little which can qualify as scientific research." (*The Study of Language: A Survey of Linguistics and Related Disciplines in America,* Cambridge Mass.: Harvard University Press, 1959, p. 166). On this same problem S. I. Hayakawa writes: "One of the constant complaints made about students in general semantics is that they do not have a sufficient body of experimental proof to establish their contention that semantics does people good. All that semanticists have are the glad cries and hosannas from people who only claim that the study of semantics is beneficial to them. You are familiar with his phenomenon I am sure." And, as a preface to his review of some attempts at research, Hayakawa says: "The results which I am going to recite to you are not very impressive because educational research of this kind is always a little difficult and no large scale attempt has been undertaken in this field. People unsystematically here and there try to do what they can within their own bailiwicks." ("Crucial Questions in Speech-Communication Research," in *The Frontiers in Experimental Speech-Communication Research,* Syracuse: Syracuse University Press, 1966, p. 5.)

Other examples of criticism because of the absence of any substantial body of research can easily be found in the numerous critical evaluations of general semantics. Cf., for example, Margaret Gorman, R. S. C. J., 1962, *General Semantics and Contemporary Thomism,* Lincoln: University of Nebraska Press and the references cited therein.

tion," as has Korzybski (1958, xxii), is to encourage wondering in theory and research.

I propose, therefore, to define general semantics in terms which will, first, specify a manageable and "researchable" area of investigation, and second, link it clearly and closely to psycholinguistics. I define general semantics as *the study of the psychological processes involved in the acquisition, encoding, and decoding of metalanguages, involving both descriptive and prescriptive concerns*. Whether or not one would agree with this definition is not important; probably it is inadequate from a number of different points of view. The only advantage I would claim (at this point at least) is that it clearly and unmistakably specifies an area which can be researched and in which attempts at theory construction can be undertaken with at least some direction.[4]

Descriptive general semantics, the logically prior area of investigation, has been sadly neglected by general semanticists. In fact, with the exception of Korzybski himself, I believe no one has provided any significant insight into this area. Descriptive general semantics, as viewed here, is a science of discovery, concerned with isolating and describing the relevant "facts" concerning the psychological processes involved in the acquisition, encoding, and decoding of metalanguage.

Prescriptive general semantics can only be built upon a firm descriptive foundation; applications can only be derived from sound descriptive data—a logical necessity which seems to have been ignored by too many "researchers." Although probably the more interesting area and the one to which most writers have addressed themselves, investigations here have, for the most part, been premature; therapies have been suggested without any understanding of the disorder. Prescriptive general semantics, as viewed here, is an applied science, concerned with how metalanguage can be taught

---

[4]It is not necessary to enter the controversy over whether general semantics deals only with linguistic behavior or whether it deals with all behavior. The definition proposed here refers only to that area of general semantics which is concerned with language and language behavior. Whether one views this as only part or as all of general semantics is not pertinent to the argument advanced here.

and how it can be most effectively utilized in the processes of encoding and decoding.

Metalanguage

Before attempting to consider the research questions suggested by this point of view, it is necessary to state explicitly what is meant by "metalanguage" and some of the underlying assumptions concerning metalanguage.

By "metalanguage" and "metalinguistic" I refer to language which is used to talk about language and not to the Sapir-Whorf-Korzybski hypothesis of linguistic relativity. Metalanguage is that aspect of language which refers to or talks about language-as-object.

Metalanguage may be either verbal or nonverbal. Verbal metalanguage would include, for example, the safety and working devices Korzybski proposed as well as language serving a glossing function. Any statement which makes reference to language, such as this one, is metalinguistic. Nonverbal metalanguage would include, for example, gestural movements which make reference to language, for example, the pounding of one's fist to emphasize a point or the winking of one's eye to indicate disbelief.

The following assumptions concerning metalanguage seem pertinent to the argument advanced here. All of these are testable, though perhaps as yet untested.

First, all natural languages have a metalanguage. All natural languages possess the design feature of self-reflexiveness: they can all be used to talk about language. All natural languages are, inherently, tools of language analysis.[5]

Second, all native speakers acquire certain metalinguistic competencies in the normal course of language acquisition. No special or direct tutoring is necessary or possible since most adult speakers cannot verbalize the principles of metalanguage. Other aspects of metalanguage, however, are only acquired by direct instruction. Most speakers not specially trained would probably say that "never say never" is self-contradictory, evidencing an untaught metalinguistic

---

[5]See, for example, Charles F. Hockett, 1963, "The Problem of Universals in Language," in *Universals of Language,* Cambridge, Mass.: M.I.T. Press. p. 10 *et passim.*

knowledge. They would fail to see that the first "never" is a metalanguage term whereas the second is an object-language term, evidencing that certain aspects of metalanguage are not acquired without special training.

This appears similar to the child's acquisition of vocabulary. Certain words are learned without any special instruction: function words (*i.e.,* words serving a grammatical rather than a semantic function) are probably the most obvious class. But other words, *e.g.,* the highly abstract terms such as *concept, system,* and *abstraction,* are probably learned only through direct and specific instruction.[6]

Third, natural languages differ in the specific ways they employ metalanguage. In Navaho, for instance, it is obligatory for a speaker to make discriminations which are only optional for English speakers. For example, "he uses one verb form if he himself is aware of the actual inception of the rain storm, another if he has reason to believe that rain has been falling for some time in his locality before the occurrence struck his attention. One form must be employed if rain is generally round about within the range of vision; another if, though it is raining round about, the storm is plainly on the move" (Kluckhohn and Leighton, 1967).

Naturally, there are many other assumptions which can be made about metalanguage. These few will suffice to suggest the general approach argued here and will provide the necessary preface for considering the research questions to which general semantics might profitably direct itself.

Although perhaps more in the province of metalinguistics, the general semanticist must be very much concerned with the nature of metalanguages, much as the psycholinguist must be concerned with the nature of languages. The questions to which research must direct itself are many and, for the most part, represent virgin territory:

What types of metalinguistic devices can be identified?
What aspects of metalanguage are obligatory?
What aspects of metalanguage are optional?

---

[6]See Roger Brown, 1958, "How Shall a Thing Be called?" *Psychological Review,* (1958) 65, 14-21 for an excellent discussion of the acquisition of naming behavior.

How do different languages treat metalanguage?
What aspects of metalanguage are overt?
What aspects of metalanguage are covert?
What are the universals of metalanguage?

Korzybski's safety and working devices represent only a beginning in this area. What is needed now is a full scale analysis of metalanguage, comparable to the analysis of directive language by rhetoric, referential language by semantics, emotive language by psychology, and so on (See DeVito, 1967).

Descriptive General Semantics

Once the nature of metalanguage has been identified, even if only partially and tentatively, general semanticists might direct themselves to those questions generated by our basic and preliminary definition of general semantics as the study of the psychological processes involved in the acquisition, encoding and decoding of metalanguage. Questions concerning description must be given priority.

First, *how does the child acquire metalinguistic competence?* Although the specific ways in which metalanguage is acquired will probably have to wait for considerable advances in developmental psycholinguistics, some tentative directions for thinking might be suggested.

It is probable that the child comes equipped with certain abilities for dealing with language and language analysis. The child, during his first few years, is essentially a language analyzing (*i.e.,* metalinguistic) organism.[7] This innate component enables him to induce the basic structure of object as well as metalanguage from the corpus with which he comes into contact. In other words, on the basis of the examples in his linguistic environment and his innate language

---

[7]For a provocative, but highly abstract, conception of this language analyzing organism see Jerry A. Fodor, 1966, "How to Learn to Talk: Some Simple Ways," in *The Genesis of Language: A Psycholinguistic Approach,* Cambridge, Mass.: M.I.T. Press. pp. 105-122.

Ruth Hirsch Weir has provided an excellent beginning for research on the child's acquisition of metalanguage. See her *Language in the Crib,* The Hague: Mouton, 1962, pp. 101-141.

acquisition device,[8] the child develops metalinguistic competence. Part of his metalinguistic abilities, however, are probably taught explicitly by the adult community, by his older siblings, parents, and teachers. Although currently not in favor among psycholinguists, one might consider that part of this metalinguistic ability (or, at least, metalinguistic performance) is developed by a process of conditioning.[9] If the child is positively reinforced, *e.g.*, is given candy or some verbal compliment, or is negatively reinforced, *e.g.*, some aversive stimulus is terminated, his metalanguage efforts will be learned and strengthened. If, on the other hand, his efforts are punished, his metalanguage will be unlearned or inhibited. The role of the listening audience in providing such reinforcement or punishment needs to be investigated as do differences among cultures, social classes, and even age groups.

Second, *what are the psychological correlates of metalinguistic encoding?* Here one is concerned with the psychological states of organisms encoding given metalinguistic statements.[10] Equally important, of course, are the psychological states of organisms not encoding metalinguistic statements. (Normative data on metalanguage encoding is particularly valuable here since it would provide some means for determining the distance any given individual is from the average.) The range of such psychological variables is extremely broad; the individual's degree of dogmatism, level of anxiety, need for social

---

[8] For a particularly insightful discussion of this "language acquisition device" see David McNeill, 1966, "Developmental Psycholinguistics," in *The Genesis of Language,* Cambridge, Mass.: M.I.T. Press; pp. 15-84 and "On Theories of Language Acquisition," *Verbal Behavior and General Behavior Theory,* Englewood Cliffs, New Jersey: Prentice-Hall, 1968, pp. 406-420.

[9] B. F. Skinner, 1957, *Verbal Behavior,* New York: Appleton-Century-Crofts. For criticisms of this approach see especially Charles E. Osgood, 1958, "A Question of Sufficiency, Review of B. F. Skinner's *Verbal Behavior,*" *Contemporary Psychology* (1958) 3, 209-212 and Noam Chomsky, 1959, "Review of B. F. Skinner's *Verbal Behavior,*" *Language* (1959) 35, 26-58.

One need not assume that all aspects of metalanguage are attributable to operant conditioning procedures. Rather, it is possible that conditioning only accounts for the frequency of metalanguage statements, for example. That is, one might argue that metalanguage is acquired by some process other than conditioning but that it is maintained, strengthened, or weakened on the basis of its contingencies. Of course, it is possible that operant conditioning has nothing to do with metalanguage in any sense.

[10] One of the best examples of such research, though not undertaken from a general semantics point of view nor limited to metalanguage, is Charles E. Osgood and Evelyn Walker, 1959, "Motivation and Language Behavior: A Content Analysis of Suicide Notes," *Journal of Abnormal and Social Psychology* (1959) 58-67.

approval, degree of impulsivity, need for order, need for achievement, degree of exhibitionism, and degree of ego-involvement are just a few which might be correlated with the presence or absence of given metalinguistic devices or statements.

Third, *what are the psychological correlates of metalinguistic decoding?* Here the concern is with the psychological effects of metalanguage both on oneself (as a receiver of one's own message) and on others. Again, equally important are the effects of an absence of metalanguage. Much activity in general semantics has addressed this question. Do persons who fail to differentiate between factual and inferential statements, for example, behave differently and if so in what way? Do those who fail to use the implicit *etc.* behave as if their statements say all that is to be said? Despite the amount of work in this area, however, general semanticists have not succeeded in establishing any lawful relations between the use of metalanguage and behavior. It is to the establishment of such laws or principles that future research needs to be directed.

Prescriptive General Semantics

The other half of the coin is prescriptive or applied general semantics. Although every general semanticist is a teacher, whether by profession or only by disposition, little substantial research has been done on the application of general semantics principles. Some attempt, of course, has been made to investigate the effects of general semantics training on the attitudes and the cognitive abilities of students[11] and the effects of general semantics principles in treating certain speech problems,[12] for example. This research is in the right

---

[11] See, for example, Alvin Goldberg, 1965, "The Effects of a Laboratory Course in General Semantics," *Etc.*, (1965) 22, 19-24; Luther F. Sies, 1955, "An Application of Semantic (extensional) Techniques to the Language Arts Activities of a Fifth Grade Class," *General Semantics Bulletin,* (1955-56) 18 and 19, 55-67; Rachel M. Lauer, 1963, "Effects of a General Semantics Course Upon Some Fifth Grade Children," *General Semantics Bulletin,* (1963-64) 30 and 31, 106-112.

[12] See, for example, Wendell Johnson, 1944, "The Indians Have No Word For It: I. Stuttering in Children; II. Stuttering in Adults," *Quarterly Journal of Speech* (1944) 30, 330-337, 456-465, reprinted in *Etc.*, 2 (1944-45), 65-81; Laura L. Lee, 1958, "Two Kinds of Disturbed Communication," *General Semantics Bulletin* (1958) 22 and 23, 47-50, and "Brain Damage and the Process of Abstracting: A Problem in Language and Learning," *Etc.*, (1959), 16, 154-162.

direction but, needless to say, indicates only a very small part of what needs to be done. Prescriptive general semantics spans all three major areas of research outlined in the discussion of descriptive general semantics.

First, *how and when can the child be most effectively taught metalanguage?* Here we are concerned with the methods and procedures for effectively teaching metalanguage. The work of Catherine Minteer (1965) and Rachel M. Lauer (1967) provides excellent guidelines for the researcher interested in this aspect of general semantics.

Second, *how can speakers be trained to effectively utilize metalanguage and what are the psychological correlates of such training?* Wendell Johnson (1946) has remarked that "if you destroy the terminology of maladjustment you destroy the maladjustment." And Harry L. Weinberg (1959) argues that *"theoretically,* if we could learn to introduce these devices [the index, date, and etc.] into all our evaluations and have the habit sink down to the feeling level, we could never become neurotic or psychotic; we would never indulge in the wrong kind of worry." These are particularly powerful statements but, while both authors provide compelling arguments for these assumptions, neither offers any substantial evidence. Yet, clearly these are testable hypotheses and are representative of the type of questions to which general semantics researchers should address themselves.

Third, *how can receivers be taught to deal with metalanguage and what are the effects of such training?* Here we are concerned with the problems of effective communication, with the problems of efficient utilization of information, with the problems of audience reactions to metalanguage. The concern here, then, encompasses all those activities in which metalanguage is or can be one of the variables in message reception.

Another way of putting this whole argument is to say that general semantics is concerned with those psychological processes involved in becoming, acting, and reacting as a general semanticist. That is, general semantics is the study of how one becomes a general semanticist. As a scientific discipline it includes descriptions of the psychological processes involved in the acquisition, encoding, and decoding of metalanguage and the prescriptions for effective inculcation and utilization of metalanguage.

In this brief discussion I started out with a redefinition of general semantics which at first may have seemed quite different from the popular and prevailing conceptions of the field. In actual fact, however, this redefinition neither adds to nor takes away any of the province normally considered general semantics. The only claims made for this approach are that it provides some guidelines for research, focuses attention on answerable questions, and concretizes some of the basic assumptions and hypotheses hinted at only vaguely in much of the general semantics literature.

REFERENCES

Condon, John C., Jr., 1966, *Semantics and Communication,* New York: Macmillan. By "behavioral semantics" I understand Condon to refer to general semantics, particularly as exemplified by the work of Chase, Hayakawa, Johnson, Lee and Rapoport.

DeVito, Joseph A., 1967, "The Meaning of Psycholinguistics," *Today's Speech* (1967) 15, 20.

——————, 1967, "Style and Stylistics: An Attempt at Definition," *Quarterly Journal of Speech* (1967) 53, 248-255.

Ervin-Tripp, Susan, and Dan Slobin, 1966, "Psycholinguistics," *Annual Review of Psychology* (1966) 17, 435.

Hayakawa, S. I., 1962, "Forward," *The Use and Misuse of Language,* Greenwich, Conn.: Fawcett Publications.

Johnson, Wendell, 1946, *People in Quandaries: The Semantics of Personal Adjustment,* New York: Harper.

Kluckhohn, Clyde and Dorothea Leighton, 1967, "Language and the Categorizing of Experience," in *The Language of Wisdom and Folly: Background Readings in Semantics,* San Francisco: International Society for General Semantics.

Korzybski, Alfred, 1958, *Science and Sanity: An Introduction to Non-Aristotelian Systems and General Semantics,* 4th ed., Lakeville, Conn., The International Non-Aristotelian Library Publishing Company.

Lauer, Rachel M., 1967, "General Semantics and the Future of Education," *Etc.* (1967) 24, 391-401.

Lee, Dorothy, 1944, "Linguistic Reflection of Wintu Thought," *International Journal of American Linguistics,* (1944) 10, 181-187.

Lee, Irving J., 1941, *Language Habits in Human Affairs: An Introduction to General Semantics*, New York: Harper.

Meerlo, Joost A. M., 1964, *Unobtrusive Communication: Essays in Psycholinguistics*, The Netherlands: Koninklijke Van Gorcum, 1960; "The Network of Communication (A Psycholinguistic Analysis of Speaking and Listening)," *General Semantics Bulletin* (1960) 26 & 27, 56-62.

Minteer, Catherine, 1965, *Words and What They Do To You: Beginning Lessons in General Semantics for Junior and Senior High School*, Lakeville, Conn.: Institute of General Semantics.

Saporta, Sol, 1961, *Psycholinguistics: A Book of Readings*, New York: Holt, 1961.

Weinberg, Harry L., 1966, "Psycholinguistics and Psychopathology," in *Approaches to Psychopathology*, Philadelphia: Temple University Publications.

──────, 1959, *Levels of Knowing and Existence: Studies in General Semantics*, New York: Harper.

POSSIBLE AREAS OF RESEARCH IN GENERAL SEMANTICS: AN INTERDISCIPLINARY APPROACH

GEORGE A. BORDEN
The Pennsylvania State University

The study of man's behavior, not as mere behavior but as behavior within a context, is at the same time the simplest and the most complex study one can engage in. The first question one should ask is: do we want man to be the dependent or the independent variable in this study? That is, do we want to see how man is manipulated by stimuli impinging upon his central nervous system, or do we want to see how man manipulates his environment? Ideally, I suppose, it would be better if we could develop the rigorous formulae to allow him to be switched from dependent to independent variable at the discretion of the investigator. However, this mathematical rigor is still in the future, so we must make do with what we have and press on toward the formulation of a rigorous description of man's inter-contextual behavior.

Since our interest is man's behavior in context, it seems pertinent to me to start our search for possible areas of research with man himself, i.e., what is there about a human being that enables him to behave the way he does? After coming to some understanding on this point, then, perhaps, we can put him into the proper context to see how these contexts affect his behavior. It seems, then, that we must first look at man as an independent variable, then as a dependent variable. Having done this we will have indicated a vast number of possible areas of research in general semantics and also the disciplines concerned with the primary research units in these areas. Most of what I have to say has been said in much greater detail in a book just published by Prentice-Hall called, *Speech Behavior and Human Interaction* (Borden, et al., 1969).

If we choose the individual as our unit of study and look at him as an independent variable, we may ask the question, "What does he possess that enables him to behave as he does?" We immediately think of the systems that a person possesses, such as his central nervous system, proprioceptive system, and digestive system. Do these systems play a part in man's behavior? The answer is obvious and needs only to be put into context. Thus we might conceive of an individual as a system of systems. This immediately indicates that the powerful discipline of systems theory is a possible avenue of research in general semantics.

By simple observation we detect that this multisystem system receives information and transmits information. Closer examination reveals that many times there is a significant relationship between these two events. We assume, therefore, that there are processes occurring within the individual which connect these two processes. As I sketched in my paper to the International Conference on General Semantics last summer (Borden, 1969) this internal process may be subdivided (verbally) into memory (both storage and recall), thinking, and learning. Neurologists, physiologists, psychologists, learning theorists, and philosophers are all involved in this area of research relevant to the general semanticist.

Furthermore, if we become aware of the interaction of some of the systems making up this individual, we find that cybernetics and computer simulation studies can play an important role in general semantic research. Questions about the role of feedback and decision making are taking on new perspectives since neurophysiology, cybernetics, systems theory and computer science (with its emphasis on artificial intelligence) have been found to coalesce on problems of man's behavior. However, I believe the most fundamental problem for those who would study the internal processing mechanism of man is that of memory—both storage and recall. Psychologists and neurologists both seem to be making considerable headway in the study of memory, but they will have to make major breakthroughs before we can really begin to understand man.

Closely related are the problems associated with the processes we call encoding and decoding. Can we find and examine the neurophysiological counterparts for these processes? Are they the same function with the information just moving in opposite directions? Or are they two distinct processes? Psycholinguists are working on this problem, and I suggest that the results of their research are of utmost importance to the general semanticist, for it is precisely at this point in the human-communication process that most of the communicative disruptions hypothesized by the general semanticist occur.

If we continue to expand our investigation into the individual's communication system, we arrive at two very important aspects of human behavior—namely, the physical acts of reception and transmission. These are significant areas of research for the general semanticist in only a peripheral way. If impairments occur in these phases, noise is introduced into the system and faulty communication may result. Speech pathologists, speech scientists, audiologists, physiologists and neurologists as well as acoustical engineers, computer scientists, physicists, and mathematicians are all working in these areas. The results of their research should help the general semanticist to recognize the "normal" range of human behavior.

Several other areas of research that have developed into full-fledged disciplines in the last few years are also supplying valuable information to the general semanticist. In most cases they represent a merging of two older disciplines to concentrate on a specific problem. Bioelectronics, bioengineering, biochemistry, and microbiology are all investigating areas of human behavior only touched upon by their parent disciplines. These developments in the biological sciences should help us understand the biological bases of human behavior.

Specific human behavior patterns are the subject for research in such disciplines as psychiatry and psychoanalysis. Researchers in these areas have increased considerably in the last few years though they generally draw on the results from other areas. Perhaps their most useful information is on deviant behaviors and the projected causes for these behaviors. One of the most exciting developments in this area of research is the new school of analysis proposed by Viktor Frankl (1965) called Logotherapy which emphasizes the central role of "meaning" in man's life. Its relationship to general semantics should be obvious.

Most of the work of psychiatrists and psychoanalysts is done through the medium of language. It is precisely this medium that forms the basis for research of another large body of investigators. Taken as a whole this area of study may be called Semiotics—the study of signs; broken up into its several parts it may be considered linguistics, psychology, psycholinguistics, anthropology, kinetics, speech behavior, or communication theory. In this area of human behavior we may consider our individual either an independent or a dependent variable. If he is the receiver of the signal, he may be classified as a dependent variable and the researcher will be interested in his resulting behavior. If he is the transmitter of the signal, he may be considered as the independent variable and the researcher may be interested in the behavior he engages in to transmit specific signals. Rhetoric has often treated the speaker as an independent variable, though he could just as well be treated as a dependent variable.

Language and language behavior are the primary targets of researchers in general semantics. However, Korzybski emphasized that general semantics deals with a general system of evaluation in which language is only one, though a crucial, aspect. Significant strides are being made to understand the connections between one's language and his cognitive structure by child psychologists, developmental psychologists, speech behaviorists, and linguists. They are all trying to find out how humans develop their linguistic competence. It seems to me that this is also a major area of research for the general semanticist.

When we consider an individual's behaviour as a dependent variable, then we usually consider the specifics of the situation this person is in as the independent variables. This being the case, we can return to our initial formulation of man as a system of systems and say that when two or more individuals are bound together by a commonality, they, in turn, create a new system in which each individual is an important element. The information we have accumulated about the individual through research in the aforementioned disciplines can now be used to help us understand why an individual acts as he does in a group situation. Interpersonal communication research is developing very rapidly and telling us a good deal about how the individual behaves as a dependent variable.

Social psychology, sociology, T-group training, group psychotherapy and group dynamics usually look at the individual as a dependent variable. The results of their research show rather clearly that we cannot study man's behavior in isolation and expect our results to agree with reality. We must, as Korzybski pointed out, be concerned with the organism-as-a-whole-in-an environment. Although research on the individual's behavior as outlined above is necessary to know how he works as an autonomous system of systems, it is not sufficient to allow one to predict how this individual will behave in the larger group system. We have a pretty good idea what unites the various systems within an individual to enable him to function as a human being; it is less clear what unites several individuals into a group and enables them to function as an autonomous system.

Our increasing complexity of systems does not stop with the group. We may consider society as a system of groups in which various individuals have commitments to one or more groups and also to the society as a whole. At the same time two or more societies may, through some common bond, form a more complex system which we might label a culture. Again, an individual may have commitments to two or more societies within this culture. The interactions of cultures may well be the most complex system we have. However, the individual who has a commitment to two or more cultures is becoming more and more prevalent. This makes the understanding of these more complex systems of vital importance to the understanding of man himself. Sociologists, cultural anthropologists, political scientists, historians, musicologists, philosophers, and all types of artists give us insights into the functioning of these very complex systems while at the same time making us realize that these systems are composed of human individuals. It should be evident, then, that when one is studying the behavior patterns of an individual he must be aware of the commitments of this individual to systems larger than himself.

In this conference we are discussing the possibilities for research in general semantics. It appears to me that research in any known discipline can in some way aid those who are working in the field of general semantics. There are many disciplines which I have not mentioned but I am sure a case can be made for the applicability of research in each of them to the understanding one needs to construct a rigorous theory of human behavior. When this is done Einstein's dream (1934) will have become a reality, and man will have become God.

REFERENCES

Borden, George A., Richard Gregg, and Theodore Grove, *Speech Behavior and Human Interaction,* Englewood Cliffs: Prentice-Hall, 1969.

Borden, George A., 1969, "Relevant Areas of Research in Human Communication," *Proceedings of the International Conference on General Semantics 1968* (In Press).

Einstein, Albert, *Essays in Science,* New York: The Philosophical Library, 1934.

Frankl, Viktor E., *The Doctor and The Soul,* New York: A Bantam Book, 1965.

RESEARCH ON STRUCTURAL DESIGN IN SCIENTIFIC DOCUMENTS

BESS SONDEL
Illinois Institute of Technology

First, let me define the term "information" as we understand it.

Information is considered to be patterned signals that are goal-directed. A "program" is an input of such signals with the objective of getting an answer to a question—of solving a problem. The human "animal" may and should use patterned signals to achieve his purposes. In the machine, the input-output continuum is monitored by "sensors." Man, unfortunately, is hell-bent on output without regard for possible input that would indicate deviation between the actual results and his intended results. In any case, the communication operation is one that can be controlled by *patterned* signals. In scientific writing—or speaking—the communicator can achieve his objective by using patterned signals.

I now teach science information in the Graduate School of the Illinois Institute of Technology, and I would like to tell you what I am trying to teach and the kind of research we are trying to do.

We are trying to discover patterned signals in documents that might be called scientific. We think we can establish a method by working in the pure sciences first. But some of what I have heard here leaves me with the feeling that we will go from the pure sciences, certainly to the biological sciences, particularly because of what has been done in medicine. In that field medical scientists are always looking for causes of something or other, and this is the formulation of order—*what causes what?* And they are looking for cures—what will cure this disease? They are looking for patterns and they do have evidence, certainly. Clinical evidence. Research evidence.

Then we will go on to the humanities, and we might talk about a play and what it is the author is trying to say. We believe we can penetrate to the order, the pattern of his thinking. If everyone would penetrate to the same basic structures, this would be sophisticated communication. In the humanities we sometimes think that these structures are strictly personal. I do not believe the humanities are strictly personal. And I believe, further, that we must structure an idea if we want to communicate it. *There is no other way to communicate.*

All my academic life I have been working communication structures on the practical level. And what little I know about the making of patterns I have learned from listening to people who are considering problems and methods of solving those problems. A can manufacturer was talking about spoilage of peas in cans, for example. He tried everything. He could not find the cause of the spoilage, until it was discovered that the cans were not being properly sealed. Then, what did he do? He invented a new lid and sealed the cans differently. No more spoilage. A cause and a disastrous effect. A means and an end. The scientist who has recourse to controllable data and to repeatable operations can give us a bonafide cause-to-effect relationship. Every researcher who looks for something different—something new—is looking for a new means to end hypothesis.

Take the affair of the laser beam. A laser beam was first used in medicine because of its effect on bloodflow in ophthalmology. Other researchers interested in hematology asked "Why can't we use that beam to correct blood clots?" They tried it and it worked. Then the dermatologists said, "That's easy; we'll use it for dermatology." Great. But a few months ago another laser beam hypothesis was developed. The laser beam was used in the reading of meters—an industrial use. And then I read not so long ago that the Defense Department was experimenting with the beam for underwater detection of one kind or another. I did not understand it, of course, but here we were, the means was the laser light and the ends, first, medical; second, industrial; and third, defense.

Patrick Meredith thinks of a pattern as a program-generating function. This is wonderful. This means that the pattern, the structure, is dynamic. I like this program-generating function idea because I say a pattern moves on its own steam. When you start with causes, you've got to go to effects. The two words hang together to make one idea—one pattern. Talk about means and everyone will ask: to what ends? A pattern is a program-generating function—and this is why, when we use a pattern, the parts hang together like glue and we communicate. We communicate because as the receiver you are way ahead of the speaker. If I talk about trouble, you will ask, "Why? What is going on?" You want to know the reason, the *cause*.

Charles Morris, Professor of Philosophy at the University of Chicago and later at Harvard, wrote the book *Signs, Language and Behavior* (1946). He defined four uses of language. The fourth and most important use was what he called "the systemic use in the formative mode." The only function of this use is to *systematize*. Morris explicated two kinds of patterns only and there he stopped. In working at the University of Chicago with executives and faculty I learned that as people think they make patterns and we isolated the kinds of patterns that they were making. I was not satisfied with only the conjunctive and disjunctive patterns of Morris. I wrote another book—*Humanity of Words* (1958)—and sent it to Prof. Morris asking him to read it and to tell me what he would like to have me change. Well, he accepted it. And since then I have been hammering home at the systemic use of language in the formative mode of Morris. The formative mode makes it possible for us to systematize. If I talk about causes to effects, that is in the formative mode. The form is cause/effect. If I talk about means to an end, that is in the formative mode.

It is interesting to find at IIT that the scientists are not using the strictly formative mode and yet we have to discover the pattern. What we are finding now is that the scientists are using what I call subformators. If a scientist says "Our objective is," the subformator is what? *Objective*. It is a synonym for end-in-view. Every scientific document is full of subformators, so you can't miss.

The head of our research institute at IIT is very much interested in this project, so she wrote up a request for funds from the National Science Foundation. She took five titles—scientific titles—and reduced them to structural design, to pattern, and guess what? Though you'd never believe it by looking at the titles, they all made the same pattern. Let's assume a researcher wants to find a scientific document —the causes, let's say, of leukemia. It would be filed under cause and effect. The researcher who wants to know if he can use the laser beam in a new way could look under "laser beams, means to an end" to see what had been done and what had not been done.

If you read the science journals regularly, as I must in my work, you will find that titles tell very little. Sometimes we have to go to the abstract and when we see the word "effect" three or four times in it, we know we are dealing with a cause-effect pattern.

Well, that's the story. The Computation Center of the Illinois Institute of Technology is now working to devise a program for an all-purpose machine using an all-purpose language and we have hopes—that is all.

REFERENCES

Morris, Charles, 1946, *Signs, Language and Behavior,* New York: Prentice Hall.
Sondel, Bess, 1958, *The Humanity of Words,* Cleveland: World Publishing Co.

CONCERNING RESEARCH

SEMANTIC FACTORS IN THE RESEARCH PROCESS

D. DAVID BOURLAND, Jr.
Information Research Associates, Inc.
McLean, Virginia

Introduction

For a number of years people active in the various experimental sciences have called attention to, and have had their attention called to, a variety of *linguistic* aspects of scientific research. A long time ago Poincaré (1913) wrote that:

> A well-made language is no indifferent thing; not to go beyond physics, the unknown man who invented the word *heat* devoted many generations to error. Heat has been treated as a substance, simply because it was designated by a substantive, and it has been thought indestructible.

Poincaré also asserted that:

> In sum, *all the scientist creates in a fact is the language in which he enunciates it.*

Korzybski generalized that kind of early twentieth century *linguistic* insight in developing the basis for a more extensive recognition of the role *semantic* factors play in our various evaluations. Our orientation at this conference focuses upon the factors affecting human semantic reactions which become involved whether or not we wish them to do so.

Naturally, I use the expression "semantic reaction" in Korzybski's psychophysiological sense of "the psycho-logical reaction of a given individual to words and language and events *in connection with their meanings,* and the psycho-logical reactions which *become meanings and relational configurations* the moment the given individual begins to analyse them or somebody else does that for him" (Korzybski, 1933, p. 24).

In this brief paper I shall invite your attention to various major problems which semantic factors generate in the research process.

General Comments on Semantic Factors

Occasionally we may seem to use certain expressions too glibly and, in the process, mystify and confuse some, while simultaneously convincing others that we may not understand adequately the very substance of our expositions. Lest this difficulty arise with the present paper, I should like to review in general terms the major semantic factors which may become involved in our orientations and evaluations.

The primary semantic factors include at least those having bearing upon: (i) structural considerations, (ii) evaluational considerations, and (iii) symbolic processes. We seem to have both conscious and unconscious (but conditional) assumptions which generate our personal techniques for dealing with or reacting semantically to those three sets of considerations.

The structural considerations include our assumptions and consequent reactions to our personal versions of the "outside worlds," which encompass our perceptions of physical, socio-logical, economic, political, etc., "realities," and our personal versions of the "inside worlds," which encompass our understandings of our own nervous systems and various attendant psychophysiological reactions.

The evaluational considerations consist at least of the following:

- Our conscious and unconscious (but, again, conditional) hierarchy of values as we order them.
- The relations that we perceive between interacting components of a situation, happening, etc.
- Our attitudes and approaches pertaining to the extensional/intensional balance.

From a non-Aristotelian point of view, the considerations just enumerated also may become knit together depending upon our degree of consciousness of abstracting.

Korzybski's creation of a non-Aristotelian system gave a basis for coming to grips with the semantic factors having to do with symbolic processes. Previously one would have to flounder about in terms of urging increasingly "precise" language, because as Korzybski (1933, p. 506) pointed out, the "unconscious" structural assumptions remain *"totally unknown and unsuspected,* unless uncovered after painful research."

Building upon Korzybski's demonstration of non-Aristotelian possibilities, we can recognize a variety of important semantic factors in the symbolic processes. In stating divergent Aristotelian and non-Aristotelian orientations, we do not simply set up dichotomies, but rather establish a group of spectra or continua along which we can (in effect) allocate evaluations.

The most fundamental spectrum concerns the "degree" to which our evaluations, as reflected in symbolic representations, involve the mechanism of identification. To a second continuum we may ascribe the degree to which allness considerations become involved in our evaluations and representations, or the degree to which we recognize the partiality (partialness, incompleteness) of our representations. We may ascribe to a third scale a measure of the degree of elementalism employed in the symbolic processes.

One could devise further representational spectra; the ones mentioned above seem to constitute the ones deserving primary attention. This treatment extends slightly Korzybski's investigation of function (1933, pp. 143-144).

Typical Research Process

I suspect that each of you has put together, for your own use or for the use and edification of your students, a description of "the research process." I shall give such a description that I have developed so that you may better understand what I mean by that expression, and just possibly for the use of subsequent speakers as a common frame of reference for us here.

In my experience, scientists all too often ignore the fact that the

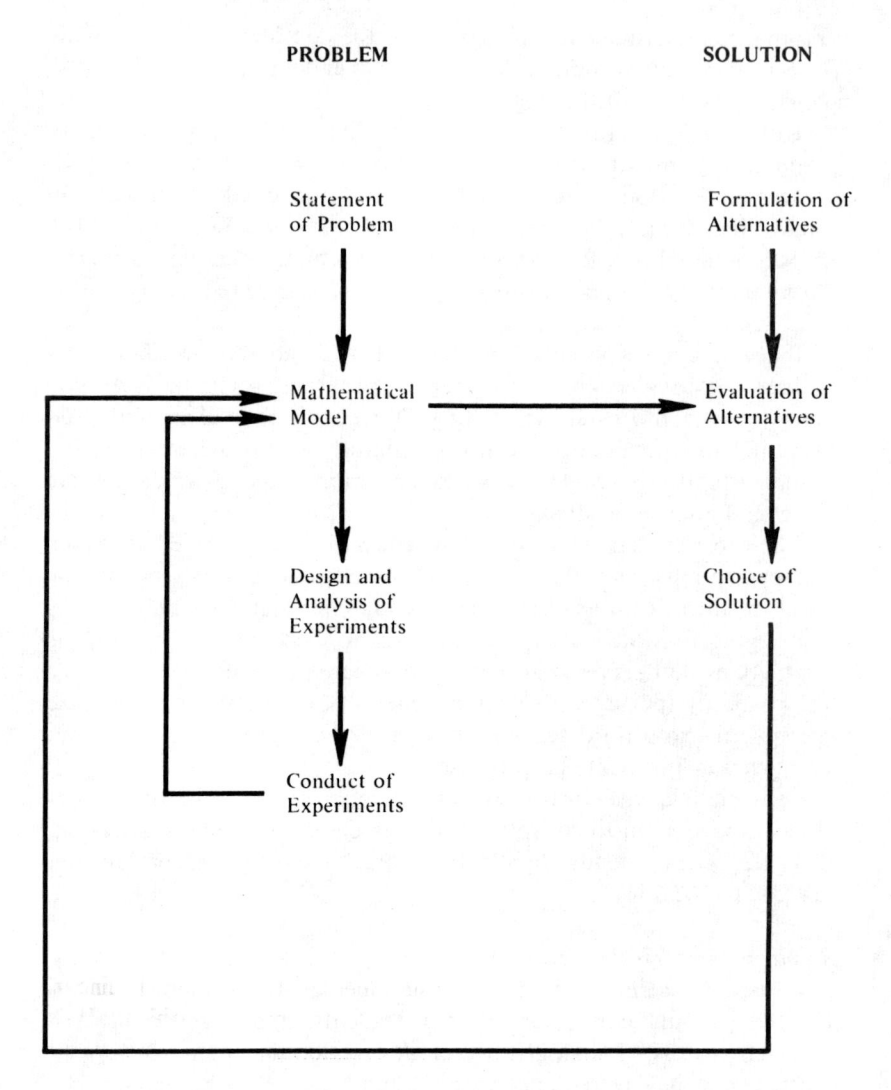

Figure 1
A Problem-Solution Statement (Goode)

research process depends intimately upon certain fundamental inputs. The goals, resources, unconscious assumptions, and (to put the matter generally) semantic reactions of the scientists themselves constitute the major fundamental inputs for any research effort. Those fundamental inputs play an enormous role in determining the quality and nature of the eventual research, as well as serving as an "information sink" or repository for the consequences of research carried on by oneself, one's colleagues, and those who went before.

Figure 1 shows a somewhat stylized statement of the research process, considered from a Problem-Solution orientation, developed by the late Dr. H. H. Goode (1957). A more detailed presentation of the significant stages in the research process which I have put together appears in Figure 2. That figure shows the stages and feedback loops that seem most important to me.

The potentially cyclic (or recurrent) paths in Figure 2 labeled A_1 to A_4 represent feed-back paths important when conducting some given research project. The path labeled B shows the relevance of one project to subsequent ones performed by the same individual or group, while path C represents the more formal process whereby one affects other research workers (and conversely).

The stages cited in Figure 2 call out nine major areas in which semantic factors affect the research process. While the semantic aspects of most of those areas appear obvious, discussion seems needed for Stage 4 and Stage 6.

Even in the seemingly astringent area of developing mathematical models, a lack of awareness of semantic factors can produce the "procedural fallacies" that Professor B. O. Koopman (1956) has called linearitis, maximitis, mechanitis, and authoritis. He described these maladies as follows:

> *Linearitis* is the assumption that every function is linear, and that simple proportion is the measure of all things. It is responsible for the over-emphasis on linear programming, and for the fabulous law of averages:
>
> average F(X, Y)=F(average X, average Y),
>
> by the magic power of which many of the most difficult

222 D. David Bourland, Jr.

Stage 0:
Fundamental Inputs: Goals,
Resources, Unconscious
Assumptions, Semantic
Reactions, etc.

↓

Stage 1:
Statement of
'The Problem'

↓

Stage 2:
Development of a
Research Program

A_1

↓

Stage 3:
Selection of the
Research Team

A_2 B   C

↓

Stage 4:
Development of
Math. Models

A_3

↓

Stage 5:
Design of
Experiments

↓

A_4 Stage 6:
Conduct of
Experiments

↓

Stage 7:
Interpretation
of Results

↓

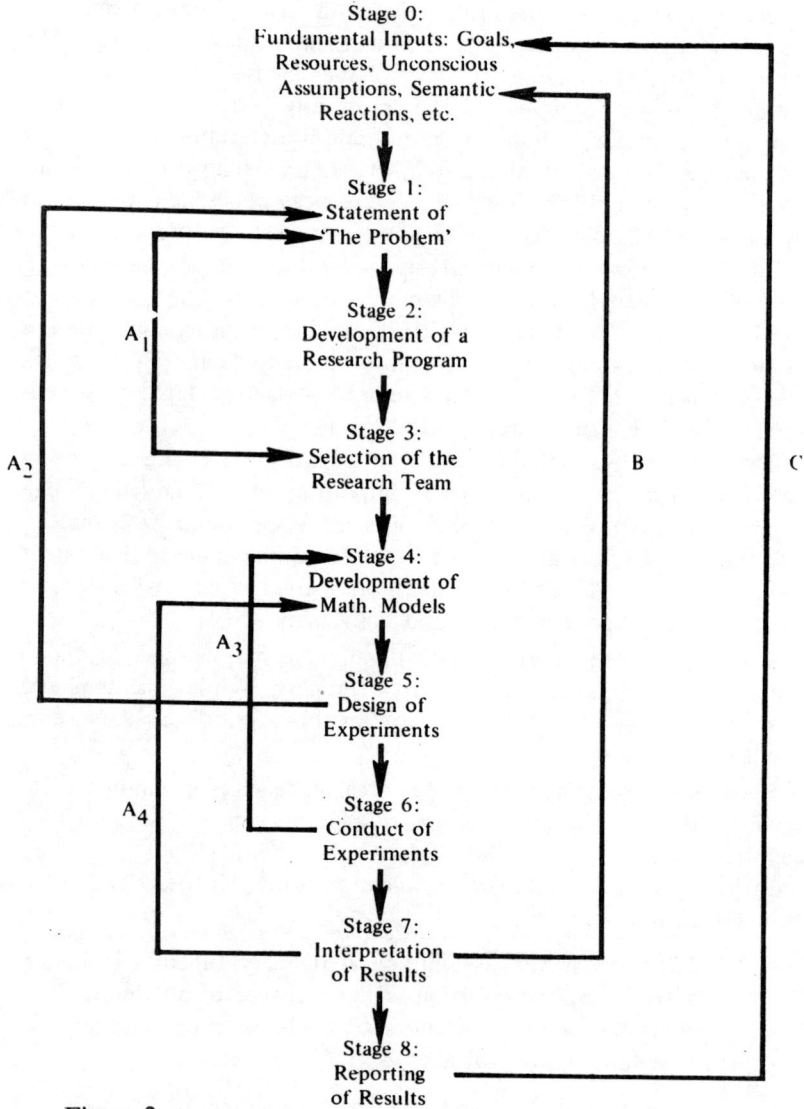

Stage 8:
Reporting
of Results

Figure 2
Nine Significant Stages in a Typical Research Process (0-8)

problems of analytic probability are given a two-minute solution.

Maximitis is the mental condition leading to the assumption that the most probable thing will happen; and, since the average is often the most probable value, the belief in its virtual certainty. Confronted with the administration of a research team, the victim will appoint the best member (the one most likely to solve the problem) as czar over the others, so that the quality of independent trials, which could build up the probability of success in a team of free men, is prevented from operating: the chance of the team is only the chance of the leader.

Mechanitis is the occupational disease of one who is so impressed with modern computing machinery that he believes that a mathematical problem, which he can neither solve nor even formulate, can readily be answered, once he has access to a sufficiently expensive machine. "Monte Carloism" is a special case; and so is the dangerous notion that a war game can serve as a means of computing probabilities of the results of various tactics. As Dr. L. H. Thomas of IBM has pointed out to (the Operations Research) Society,* any proof of the accuracy of such methods requires so much specific knowledge that a direct mathematical attack would be much easier.

Authorititis is that regression to logical infantilism which believes that the missing links in one's solution of a problem, as well as the missing common sense required for relating it to reality, can be readily supplied by the uniformed officer or the company executive who must eventually use the result. It leads indirectly to that feature of certain definitions of "operations research" which require that their results are for "executive decision." According to this, Hitler's astrologers did operations research, while Lanchester did not do it.

---

*See L. H. Thomas, "A Comparison of Stochastic and Direct Methods for the Solution of Some Special Problems," *Operations Research*, Volume 1, p. 181, 1953. (Koopman's footnote.)

Indeed, these definitions imply that there is one kind of truth for the scientist and another kind for the executive.

With reference to Stage 6, research activities which involve measurements and data acquisition more complex than the simple reading of a single digital dial tend to depend heavily upon semantic factors. In addition to work relating to this on the general theory of electrical signal detection developed by Middleton (1960), and Van Meter and Middleton (1954), Nash has recently explored the techniques, constraints, and criteria associated with the statistical decision processes involved in selecting the most appropriate inferential signals. Nash developed a model which explicitly treats "situations in which some action A_r related to the events E_n is chosen on the basis of the observed absence or presence of some signal S^q. In this information, two decisions must be made in sequence. The first decision t^q is a choice between the detector outputs V_1^q and V_0^q, the second being the choice of an action A from among the R possible actions." (Nash, 1969, p. 74). The structural and evaluational aspects of the situation seem apparent, and illustrate the semantic factors described earlier.

Metric Space and Semantic Space

I now wish to discuss an explicit application I have made of Korzybski's methodology in a research context. I have found it useful to draw distinctions between events and occurrences allocated to two abstract "spaces": those which occur in the "outside world" and which require geographical and temporal considerations, I allocate to "metric space," while those dependent primarily upon human evaluations and representations, I allocate to "semantic space." Problems of consequence then obviously arise pertaining to the ways certain aspects of metric space and semantic space interact.

In seeking the necessary degree of structural similarity between corresponding elements in metric and semantic spaces, we have a variety of landmarks and benchmarks available, as pointed out by Korzybski so long ago. Table 1 contains a summary of these guides.

I have found these notions helpful in coming to grips with the problem of the "quantity" of information, and more particularly

Table 1

LANDMARKS AND BENCHMARKS IN THE SEARCH FOR STRUCTURAL SIMILARITIES

Characteristics of Structures in Metric Space (The "Outside," "Real" World)	Corresponding Characteristics of Representations in Semantic Space (Linguistic Structures)
Uniqueness of each structure (individual, circumstance, event, etc.)	Basic assumptions of non-identity, non-allness; extensional orientations
Processes in various degrees of flux	Non-static, non-stationery, non-additive representations
Interactions and interfaces between structures may exert key determining influences	Non-elementalistic representations (e.g., "space-time")
Living organisms function as-a-whole, with environmental and time-varying effects	Non-elementalistic representations (e.g., "abstracting," "semantic reactions")

the *change* in quantity of information, in the study and analysis of Information Transfer Systems. Difficulties seem to proceed from confusions which can arise through inadequately distinguishing between semantic space considerations and metric space considerations. Fluctuations in the quantity of information within or available to Information Bases* result from the interplay between the generation of information and the process of information decay.

Processes leading to information decay with the passage of time result from a variety of factors, which may interact. The following illustrate the more significant factors which may become importantly involved in information decay:

- Semantic Factors (as in the change in importance with the passage of time).

---

*"A collection of representations, oriented towards the conduct of some operation, which occupies metric space-time and has weight and cube requirements." (Bourland and McManus, 1965).

- Psycho-logical Factors (as in a psycho-logical blockage resulting in information suppression).

- Linguistic Factors (as in the forgetting of a language or the unavailability of a code).

- Mechanical Factors (as in the accidental reset of detents).

We may define the "semantic rate" as that rate of arrival (or departure) of collections of symbolic structures which can stimulate semantic reactions within an Information Base, and thus affect the available quantity of information. The pertinent operations performed in *semantic space* consist of converting the symbolic structures into semantic reactions upon arrival, and conversely upon departure.

Subsequently, and in *metric space,* the Information Transfer System may apply the necessary redundancy and then initiate transfer operations. The quantity of symbolic structures which a specific portion of the system must handle per unit time constitutes the "information rate," while the quantity of the combined load of symbolic structures plus the applied redundancy handled per unit time constitutes the "data rate." In practical applications the given Information Transfer System must implement in terminal equipment, etc., the data rate requirements as just defined. These matters received further treatment in Bourland and McManus (1965).

Concluding Remarks

The fundamental elements of semantic space, as employed in the preceding section, consist of symbolic representations generated by and evocative of human semantic reactions. We cannot manipulate human semantic reactions directly. However, through abstraction, these semantic reactions may form the structural bases for symbolic structures (such as mathematical and other models) which in turn we *can* manipulate, aggregate, analyze, etc.

In these terms, then, the overall goal of the research process becomes to develop structures in semantic space that can provide some measure of predictability and control in metric *and* semantic space. My primary point consists of emphasizing that we can, and must, work toward making the manipulations just described a *conscious* process, lest we leave ourselves at the mercy of a largely archaic language structure and a heritage of automatic, animalistic semantic reactions.

REFERENCES

Bourland, Jr., D. D., and R. P. McManus, "A General Model for Information Transfer Systems," U.S. Navy Electronics Laboratory Technical Memorandum TM-804, 21 May 1965. Also printed in part in *General Semantics Bulletin* Numbers 32 & 33, 1965/1966.

Goode, H. H., "The Application of a High Speed Computer to the Definition and Solution of the Vehicular Traffic Problem," *Operations Research* (1957) 5 (6), 775-793.

Koopman, B. O., "Fallacies in Operations Research," *Operations Research* (1956) 4 (4), 422-426.

Korzybski, A., *Science and Sanity: An Introduction to Non-Aristotelian Systems and General Semantics,* Lakeville, Conn.: International Non-Aristotelian Library Publishing Co.; Fourth Edition, 1958, Institute of General Semantics, Distributor.

Middleton, D., *Introduction to Statistical Communication Theory,* New York: McGraw-Hill, 1960.

Nash, R. T., "Event Classification," *Operations Research,* (1969) 17 (1) 70-84.

Poincare, J. H., *The Foundations of Science,* New York: Science Press, 1913.

Van Meter, D. and D. Middleton, "Modern Statistical Approaches to Reception in Communication Theory," *I. R. E. Transactions on Information Theory,* (1954) 4, 119-145.

THE PROPER STUDY OF MANKIND IS MAN

Who knoweth the interpretation of a thing? Eccles. 8:1.

JAMES M. BROADUS
Transylvania College

The notoriously inadequate index to *Science and Sanity* has no *research* entry. Anyone familiar with Korzybskian methodology and general semantics would believe that *research* is a vital part of the discipline—at several levels of abstraction.

It seems to me that the very awareness of Korzybski's work—i.e., the practicing of general semantics—becomes an exercise in research. To the extent that general semantics furnishes some guidelines for evaluation, for decision making, the practitioner of Korzybskian methodology is *researching*. I view each human being, all human beings, for as long as we are alive, as creatures making decisions, evaluating, seeking answers, doing research.

Apart from the view of general semantics as operationally and inherently a practice of research, a continuing exercise in researching, as suggested above, Korzybski has suggested some extremely valuable guidelines for the improvement of research in any field, including general semantics itself.

The well-grounded, well-disciplined student of general semantics will certainly have "second thoughts," "additional insights," and new avenues for concern when he approaches some of the basic steps constituting research design. For example, when delineating areas for study, when asking questions about those areas, when collating data, when reaching conclusions, and when making recommendations, he will behave, I think, differently because he is aware of Alfred Korzybski and his work.

It seems to me that the extensional devices (Introduction to the 2nd Edition of *Science and Sanity*) furnish some helpful reminders toward the avoidance of pitfalls in research design.

For example, take the hyphen. How much time and energy are spent—wasted—in trying to deal with a problem whose "solution" resists categorization, but which can be treated in terms of a continuum? How much frustration grows out of the search for isolates where there are no isolates? How much wheel-spinning goes on in the name of "objectivity," of specificity, when these qualities exist only in the nervous system of the observer?

How much research is conducted with assumptions based on assumptions bearing silent quotes? How many levels of abstraction are reflected in 50 individuals' responses to a single question?

The usefulness of dating and indexing seem obvious. They can help yield much more operational statements of "conclusion." Here is what we find *at this time, under these circumstances, with these subjects.*

Perhaps most important is the *etc.* The recognition that not all can ever be said or known about even one thing becomes at once both a crutch supporting pessimism and procrastination; and at the same time the most heartening and encouraging challenge man might know. For now and forever there are new, interesting, and exciting experiences.

Korzybski reminds us of the implications of "undefined terms," and of the ubiquitousness of the temptation to "identify." He reminds us to search for differences among similar phenomena and for similarities among different ones.

Our awareness of Korzybski can help us relax—to be less self-demeaning because of the elusiveness of the "answer." He helps us escape the fetish of "objectivism."

> Linguistic and grammatical structures also have prevented our understanding of human reactions. For instance, we used and still use a terminology of "objective" and "subjective," both extremely confusing, as the so-called "objective" must be con-

sidered a construct made by our nervous system, and what we call "subjective" may also be considered "objective" for the same reason (Korzybski, 1921).

Korzybski would free us from the slavery of insistence on "causality." If one can deal with infinite-valued causality, the final causation hypothesis is not needed.

Korzybski encourages our escape from the chains of convention; from adherence to "that which has proved itself," from stagnation growing out of "the tried and true." Daniel Lerner (1958) in *Evidence and Inference* says that "research on the physical universe is compromised only by the human behavior of the experimenter" (p. 16).

> Under the rule of Social Science there are no external mysteries in human behavior, but only phenomena that have not yet been adequately observed. Nothing human is inscrutable; all behavior is amenable to inquiry (p. 11).

In the same volume, Erickson (1958) says:

> It is the very nature of man's intelligence that it can serve both the rational approaches to the facts of nature and also the rationalization and disguise of man's own nature. Therefore in dealing with the *sense of evidence* in clinical matters, we must accept irrational belief as well as irrational disbelief as part of an inescapable dilemma which calls for a new kind of disciplined self-awareness (pp. 90-91).

And Deutsch (1958) adds:

> Now it is clear that if one is too strongly attached to one's preconceived model, one will of necessity miss all radical discoveries. It is amazing to what degree one may fail to register mentally an observation which does not fit the initial image (p. 102).

Korzybski helps us gain the "new kind of disciplined self-awareness"; he opens up our receptivity to change in "the initial image."

So, man studies his environments, he studies himself studying his environments; he recognizes the mutual dependence of the two and knows that they are not two, but one.

Korzybski would, I think, applaud the following by Aron (1958):

> It is impossible to establish a rigorous distinction between data and inferences, between what we know as fact and what we infer from the facts (p. 27).
>
> Psychologically, I agree that one must discriminate at any moment between the data gathered by the scientist and the inferences made from them. Logically, however, in the development of a science the same propositions have taken turns as inferences and data. Are we to engage in a study of the psychology of the scientist or the logic of scientific procedure? (p. 20).

Perhaps all of this constitutes some kind of response to Edward L. Thorndike's contention: anything that exists, exists in some amount; anything that exists in some amount can be measured. Perhaps the researcher needs first to examine the extensionality of the object of his search. The researcher needs to know the degree of "reality"—the placement on the continuum of intensional-extensional—with which he is dealing. It seems to me that we engage in many futile exercises by attempting to measure "out there" that which exists only in our own nervous systems. This is not to say that our research must be limited to objects which can be weighed, to areas yielding only to tape measures and scales. It does seem important, however, to recognize the folly in assuming that all research must result in "numbers" which presumably describe some of the characteristics of something "out there."

Finally, it seems to me that the practicing general semanticist has this advantage. He recognizes that he is fulfilling his human role when he researches and when he puts his newly "structured structures," his "new facts and truths," in the best possible form for generalization and for transmission—that he is being most human when he is time binding.

REFERENCES

Aron, Raymond, *Evidence and Inference,* Daniel Lerner, Ed., Glencoe, Ill.: The Free Press, 1958.
Deutsch, Martin, *Evidence and Inference, op. cit.*
Erikson, Erik H., *Evidence and Inference, op. cit.*
Korzybski, Alfred, "What I Believe", *Manhood of Humanity,* International Non-Aristotelian Library Publishing Co. xli-lvii, 1921.
Lerner, Daniel, ed., *Evidence and Inference, op. cit.*

THE RESEARCHER AND THE THREE "LAWS OF THOUGHT"

ELWOOD MURRAY
Institute of General Semantics*

Utterly dependent upon language, the researcher at the same time demands the utmost of rigor and precision. The problem being investigated must be defined and limited to manageable proportions. The methodology of investigation must be described with accuracy. The results and conclusions must be free from ambiguity and held to a strict relevance. His chief difficulty is to avoid the elementalism which his language tends to project into his objects of study.

While the rigor required of language in research applies to all areas about which we would study, the demand is even more pronounced when general semantics itself becomes the subject of investigation. Here principles of general semantics must be applied to general semantics. Researchers in general semantics must bring general semantics to bear upon themselves. In this the investigator must distinguish another order of language functioning which brings uses of language about language. There must be a suitable talking about talking in others and in himself.

Herein lies a paradox and a challenge of which the researcher often becomes aware rather late and through "the hard way." Describing, summarizing, generalizing must overcome the hazards of falsification through the chopping off of relationships. Difficult to avoid is the freezing into static language that which exists only in operations and

---

*Director, Institute of General Semantics, 1967 to 1969. This paper is a modification of a paper originally delivered at the convention of the Speech Association of America in Denver, Cola., August 18 to 21, 1963.

relationships of the "fact" phenomena. The very use of words (including, in lesser degree, the languages of mathematics) tends to atomization and elementalizing that which exists in various levels of process, with order, and succession in their accompanying functionings, and in the deeper levels, the patterning of structure.

There is no existence, no significance, no meaning of the object of investigation except in its relationships within and without itself. "Reality," as has been said many times, resides in the whole object in its whole situation.

We mourn the death of a loved one in the abrupt ceasing of relationships. The importance of an automobile lies in the extension of space relationships it brings into the life of the owner. A thing or a situation has importance (to something or somebody) only in terms of its relationships. Human evaluating depends upon the discovery and study of the relationships which influence us and others. The difficulty throughout the ages of human struggle has been in the lack of awareness of most of those influences, the great mass of relationships of which we are ignorant. The task of the researcher is constantly to push back the curtains of ignorance to bring these influences into awareness.

This paper attempts, first, to strengthen the rationale of the researcher concerning the nature of the Universe as a great complex of relationships, with order in uncountable levels of process, with a functioning together of countless events, along with a structure which underlies the surface appearance of chaos. And second, we wish to explore briefly the hazards of elementalism which have been inherited in our Aristotelian tradition. We hope the research designer will be helped to avoid the tendency to chop off relationships as he evaluates his object of research and formulates and carries through his research design.

Relatedness Lies in the Being of Reality

The exchange of signals between the Tiros satellite and the earth which enabled Tiros to correct its course to and past the planet Venus, while millions and millions of miles out in space, has significance far beyond that of the flight itself. That such an exchange could be made demonstrated dramatically the physical linkages and

The Researcher and the Three "Laws of Thought" 237

connectedness of things, of the physical unity of the heliosphere, in which we conduct our human affairs. There are no gaps, no vacuums, no discontinuities in that universe (whether or not it has boundaries) with which we must cope and live. There may, however, be gaps and discontinuities in our perceptions and assumptions. The only "vacuums" are in our heads.

That which occupies the spaces between the changing objects in the heavens and that which occupies the spaces clear down into submicroscopic realms of the atom has been labeled with terms like gravitation electromagnetism, polarities, inductions, radiations, entropy. These invisible and inaudible factors refer to what we call "relations" and "influence." To some extent we have discovered and identified specific relationships, which in working together and maintaining themselves we call structures.

Relationship—the mode (manner) in which one thing stands to another, or the mode in which two or more things stand to each other; any sort of connection between two or more things. There must be at least two things; a thing has relations only with something else. This applies to the apple as it is pulled toward the ground (as in gravitation), to the attraction and repulsion of a piece of iron to another piece of iron as in magnetism and polarity, and in the interactions among organisms with their environments as in evolution, as the loss in fidelity of a message (sometimes called entropy) between what the receiver is responding to and what it transmits.

While the two things may be brought into relationship by direct physical contact, they may respond to each other at a distance, sometimes vast distances, as in the guidance of the Tiros satellite. In induction the transformation of energy into electricity does not require physical contact between the rotor and its shell; there is a crisscrossing of polarities between them.

And there seems to be a very powerful analogy in respect to communication when this is carried into the relationships of ideas within and among human beings. When two bodies of data are brought together, higher abstractions or new ideas may result, depending upon the similarities and the differences in the structures being compared. The generation of ideas and their transmission among persons seems in principle similar to a criss-crossing of electromagnetic fields. Radiation, likewise, depends upon two or more entities which are brought into relationship for the results which are obtained. There is no such thing as sun-tan without a person placing himself in exposure (a relationship) to the sun.

Certainly, it is not possible to define the exact limits of magnetic and polarizing influences. Does this not also apply to human communication, in the influences of persons and groups upon each other? There has never been built an absolute insulation of fields within either electrical or human networks.

In respect to one Universe, Dr. Frank Dickinson, Emeritus Professor of Philosophy at the University of Denver, has said that it may be inappropriate to describe its wholeness in materialistic terms. From the ancient Upanishads, "reality" is derived from the movements realized after a period of silence. The reply to "I want an answer" was "keep still, I am answering—you don't understand." Dr. Dickinson says that when you talk about the sub-conscious you are in the very nature of things shutting it off from further investigation. In fact, he goes somewhat further than Korzybski in claiming that all fact territories become distorted in our perceptions as soon as words are applied to them.

The notion of "reality" as a complex of relations instead of an aggregation of objects is implied in the assumptions and philosophical bases of general semantics. To bring about this relational orientation and to improve human evaluations Alfred Korzybski built general semantics as a methodology.

Korzybski never claimed to be the originator of the view of the Universe which this implies; nevertheless his documented sources directly encompass the sources of all of that now very deep stream of organismal, emergence, and evolutionary theory activated from so many areas since Darwin.

Korzybski's connection to this is further evident in the subtitle to his book, *Science and Sanity,* namely, an *Introduction to Non-Aristotelian Systems and General Semantics.*

This view of the Universe today is rapidly approaching flood proportions in all of the natural and behavioral sciences. In particular, it has become the basis for Space-Age developments, in the release of atomic and hydrogen power. Systems is now a by-word in the great military and industrial complexes.

Systems, systematics and cybernetics, information theory, games theory support a view of the Universe which is directly a continuation of what was underway as general semantics was being formulated and of which general semantics is a part.

There is just one attempt to encapsulate a non-Aristotelian view in a statement. Namely, the Universe, in terms of general semantics as extended by cybernetics, may be viewed as a vast expanding vibrating manifold, as a field of gravitational-electromagnetic-induction-relational forces in all of which flux there is a tendency toward a state of equilibrium. Equilibrium, a precarious balance of integrative and disintegrative forces (entropy), is maintained by negative feedback, the control and regulating principle. In the human realms the tendency toward entropy might be negated by consciousness of abstracting, the extensional orientation and the extensional devices, all of which reflect the negative feedback principle of cybernetics.

The equilibrium at any time would include an equilibrium of people with their environments, the correspondence of the language and semantic environments with the non-language environment. Within people there is a potential for changing their own environments if they bring about proper regulation and control of themselves. As they have developed better instruments to investigate nature they have dramatically modified their non-human environment of which at the same time they are a part.

Korzybski stressed that the older Aristotelian logic, Euclidian geometry, and Newtonian physics have been shown to correspond to only limited cases of the more general non-aristotelian, non-euclidian, non-newtonian systems; but that they are applicable in special circumstances: Aristotelian logic for mathematical reasoning, euclidian geometry for zero curvature of space-time, Newtonian physics for speeds much less than light. The prefix *non* carries the implication "beyond" rather than "anti." (Mayper, 1962).

Falsity Induced From the Laws of Thought

Distinction must be made between Aristotle (384-322 B.C.), and his followers, the Aristotelian establishment which dominates many areas today. It was his followers who imposed the so-called "Laws of Thought" upon our Judeo-Christian civilization. One statement with an analysis of each follows:[1]

1. *The law of identity.* Everything is what it is and not something else. Or, if a *proposition* is true, it is true. Dr. Dickinson notes that "In the common sense world who could deny this? Ingrained in us no assumption appears more true. But with a deeper consideration we must agree that in a world of relations everything is what it is plus everything else. Everything is what it is because of what it isn't. Everything has had its play in producing the it we abstract. I am what I am not as much as what I am. College is what it is for a student because of his leaving home as much as for what it was before he came to it. A thing does not exist by itself. In respect to the leather in my shoes, there would be no such thing if it weren't for the air the cattle breathe, and the grass they eat. Things are what they are for what they are not!"

Quoting Professor Dickinson again: "It is not true that everything is what it is and not something else!" The arrival of a callous on your hand is the result of complex interactions with other things, and the callous situation has these other relationships in it. A volcanic eruption forms a crust which requires an increased eruption to make a greater crust and higher and higher eruptions. Mt. Fujiama is more than it appears in its pictures.

Personality is not "personality"—a thing in itself; it grows in terms of its conflicts and the more we are agitated the more we grow.

"If a proposition is true, it is true." But Prof. Dickinson argues, "No proposition is true if what is meant is that it is true the next moment. This is not a static world. The more general you make it, the more true it is; on the other hand, the more false it is! As quick as you get into the general, the more you get into allness—the more general, the more abstract. The minute you 'know' something, you have already done some 'dirty work!' This is the human problem.

---

[1]The author is indebted to Dr. Frank Dickinson, Emeritus Professor of Philosophy, University of Denver, for suggestions and illustrations in this analysis of these laws.

It might help if we could induce a spirit of appreciation rather than 'knowledge'."

2. *The law of non-contradiction (or contradiction).* *An entity cannot both be a particular thing and not be a particular thing at the same time and same place.* Prof. Dickinson points out, "Being is greatly modified by non-being. The statement of this law does not hit the mark because it claims a thing cannot be and not be at the same time, but we cannot specify its beginning and ending. It requires an Aristotelian orientation to accept the statement (of this law). Non-being and being. You can say of this pencil it is a pencil because of what it isn't. It isn't a pen and it isn't something else. Everything that one says is the product of the sayer; the whole Universe is what it is for what it isn't. Too many people like to pigeon hole. The pigeon hole is the grave for a lot of things. They are in the 'hole.'

"If in any realm you refuse to consider things in terms of what they do, you have a narrow conception of reality, because by definition you have eliminated it altogether. Suppose you try to limit an auto you will no longer have an auto! That was why Korzybski wanted us to point to the specifics, or to index $Smith_1$ or $Smith_2$. This is a recognition that Smith is not contained in his own clothing."

3. *Law of excluded middle.* An entity either is or is not at a given time and place. Or : "Every *proposition* is either true or false when circumstances and definitions remain the same." Again quoting Prof. Dickinson, "Entity implies everything. It is everything that is. When you chop it up to call it entity, by the very nature of things you cut it from its relating elements. There are no entities. There is no 'is.' Everything is what it is because of what it was or will be. To start out with entities you almost declare there is no entity. You wreck whatever you chop up. Zero is about the only thing that remains the same.

"Propositions may be true in terms of words only. Propositions don't remain the same if they have any content. Maybe you can say things or something linguistically. A box is a box linguistically.

242   Elwood Murray

The word is itself if there is anything in itself. For practical purposes, since we are living beings and have to live from moment to moment, we can say this is reality, as *you look at a thing remain as it is*. But this is true only if you look at it through colored glasses. And this narrows our understanding of the Universe, it colors our thinking."

The Korzybskian Antidotes

To the extent that research today remains distorted if blocked by these laws of thought, some of the remedy lies in the three fundamental premises of general semantics: The map *is not* the Territory; the word *is not* the Fact. The map *does not say all;* the word *does not say all;* maps are *self-reflexive;* words are *self-reflexive*. (Maps and words are used to talk about themselves. Language must be used to talk about language.)

Available to apply these premises we have the whole general semantics methodology and orientation directly relevant to language behaviors; the extensional orientation, consciousness of abstracting, awareness of multi-ordinality, the extensional devices, and other general semantics formulations. These premises with their implementive formulations provide some safeguards on the use of language by researchers as well as others who could improve their evaluations.

In presenting these formulations Korzybski was aware of the difficulty which the researcher faces:

> Without the realization of the structural foundations emphasized in the present system, it is practically impossible not to confuse linguistic structural issues, which lead inevitably to semantic blockages. When we deal with doctrines or system-functions, it is of the utmost importance to keep them at first *strictly separated*; to work out each system by itself, and only after this is accomplished can we carry out an *independent investigation as to the ways they mutually intertranslate*. (Korzybski, 1958, p. 147.)

In respect to research dealing with the correction of research contaminated with the old assumptions we are told:

Let me again repeat, that the mixing of different languages, of different structures is fatal for clear 'thinking.' Only when a system is traced to its system-function, and the many implications worked out in their *unmixed* form, can we make a further independent investigation of the ways in which the different systems intertranslate. As a general rule, every new scientific system eliminates a great deal of spurious metaphysics from the older systems (p. 147).

For breaking through the old assumptions are these further suggestions:

In practice, the issues are extremely simple if one decides to follow the general rule; namely, either completely to reject or completely to accept *provisionally,* at a given date, a new system; use *exclusively* the structurally new terms; perform our semantic operations exclusively in these terms; compare the conclusions with experience; perform *new* experiments which the structurally new terminology suggests; and only then, as an independent enquiry, investigate how one system translates into the other. In those translations which correspond to the transformation of frames of reference in mathematics, we find the most important *invariant* characteristics or relations which survive this translation. If a characteristic appears in all formulations, it is a sign that this characteristic is *intrinsic,* belongs to the subject of our analysis, and is not accidental and irrelevant, belonging only to the accidental structure of the language we use. Once these invariant, intrinsic characteristics are discovered, and there is no way to discover them except by reformulating the problems in different languages (in mathematics we speak about the transformation of frames of reference), we then know that we have discovered invariant relations, which survive transformation of different forms of representations, and so realize that we are dealing with something genuinely important, *independent* from the structure of the language we use (p. 148).

In spite of the false assumptions internalized in the culture, research has made possible the fantastic progress of which the recent moon landing is only one example. It is the most dramatic example of time-binding we can cite. The specific help which general semantics has given these advances is difficult to measure. The crisis wherein similar advances must be made to bring human evaluations and communication into a similar effectiveness may find general semantics coming into its greatest usefulness.

REFERENCES

Barone, Francisco, 1958, "General Semantics: An Italian Philosopher's View," *Etc.,* 15 (4): 255-266.

Hayakawa, S. I., 1948, "What is Meant by Aristotelian Structure of Language?" *Etc.,* 5 (4): 225-230.

Hunnex, Milton D., 1961, *Philosophies and Philosophers,* San Francisco: Chandler Publishing Co., p. 4.

Korzybski, Alfred, 1958, *Science and Sanity, An Introduction to Non-Aristotelian Systems and General Semantics,* Connecticut: Institute of General Semantics, Lakeville.

Mayper, Stuart A., 1962, "Non-Aristotelian Foundations: Solid or Fluid," *Etc.,* 18 (4): 427-443.

Rolf, Ida P., 1963, "Structural Integration-Gravity, an Unexplored Factor in the More Human Use of Human Beings," *Systemics,* 1 (1): 66-77.

von Bertalanffy, L., 1962, "General System Theory, A Critical Overview," *Society for General Systems Research Yearbook, 1962,* p. 1-22.

CONCERNING THE CONFERENCE

AN EVALUATION OF THE CONFERENCE

JAMES E. ROEVER
Director of Research
Speech Association of America

When I accepted Elwood Murray's invitation to attend this Conference, I agreed to serve as an observer and evaluator. On the first day of the Conference, I overheard someone refer to me as an "outsider." Being an observer and an outsider, coupled with no previous history of participation in the International Society for General Semantics or the Institute of General Semantics, I believe that my role could properly be described as that of a "Peeker." If Charlotte Read's prediction during her presentation is correct, my remarks should therefore be "extensional."

Although I have a great temptation to discuss individuals and their ideas, I have satisfactorily rejected those notions in order to present a series of general observations and reactions concerning the persons who participated in this conference and the kinds of statements made by those persons.

It seems to me that four types of persons were in attendance:

1) those who needed *therapy*;

2) those who perceived themselves as *therapists*;

3) those who viewed themselves as *research methodologists*;

4) those who perceived themselves as *theorists of communication transaction*.

While each Conference participant probably exhibited behavior relative to each of these roles at one time or another, I am suggesting that each person was primarily motivated by a particular role. I, for example, was motivated by my interest in research methodology.

I tried to keep a flow chart of the types of statements which were made by the Conference participants. The following seven types of statements were the most common:

1) *Statements Repeating General Semantics Principles*—generally this was genuflection in the direction of Alfred Korzybski;

2) *Statements Attacking General Semantics*—generally these attacks were directed toward general semantics as a theory of human behavior, *not* toward general semantics as a research methodology;

3) *Statements of Hypotheses to be Tested*—these statements often related to general semantics principles and were offered with great redundancy;

4) *Statements Reporting Results of Research*—most research results reported were not based on "pure" or, for that matter, "impure" general semantics research. Although many of the research results probably could have been applied to general semantics, the interface generally did not occur;

5) *Statements about General Semantics Methods*—these statements could be classified as:
    a. Historical-Critical;
    b. Descriptive;
    c. Experimental;
    d. Phenomenological.

But, these are only labels for general methods. There was little discussion of the specifics of any particular method;

6) *Statements about Methods for Measuring Data*—two general categories were:
    a. the application of tests from "outside" general semantics. Discussion involved such things as physiological measurement and the application of psychological tests;

b. the application of general semantics formulations as methods of measurement, that is as dependent variables rather than independent variables.

There was little interface between those methods for measuring data which came from "outside" of general semantics and those methods for measuring data which came from general semantics itself;

7) *Statements about Research Design*—these statements were scarce. For the most part we did not consider research design, the stated purpose for this conference, because we really did not reach interface on the roles inherent in the preceding classification.

Because of the variety of roles and the variety of statements, our discussions often resulted in pseudo-arguments. Persons with *various roles* and *various motives* were discussing at different levels. We did not *identify our roles* in given situations (with few exceptions) and hence had few "real" arguments and discussions.

This lack of role identification was confounded by the use of many ideological statements. Professor Gustav Bergmann (1951) in his essay on "Ideology" defined statements of fact (which by definition are either true or false), statements of value (which by definition are neither true nor false, but represent states of mind which may represent positive aesthetic appreciation or moral approval), and statements of ideology (which are statements of value, consciously or unconsciously, used or interpreted as statements of fact). As Bergmann has written: "The motive power of a value judgment is often greatly increased when it appears within the rationale of those who hold it not under its proper logical flag as a value judgment but in the disguise of a statement of fact. A statement of this kind, that is, a value judgment disguised as, or mistaken for, a statement of fact, I shall call an 'ideological statement.' A rationale or an important part of a rationale that contains in logically crucial places ideological statements I shall call an 'ideology' ". (p. 310)). I would like to suggest that many of us in this Conference were bound up in our ideologies.

I believe that an example of ideology is found in many of the statements which related general semantics to Korzybski. Consider the following statements:

General semantics is a *good* therapeutic technique.
General semantics is the *best* method for behavioral analysis.
General semantics is the *best* theory for explaining human communication.

I suggest to you that many statements similar to these were made during this Conference as ideological statements; namely, they were made, or interpreted, as statements of fact rather than statements of value.

Now that I have made some of these distinctions, let me make several *value* judgments. I believe that one thing we must do is *recognize* our roles as receivers of therapy, as therapists, as research methodologists, and as communication theorists. We must *develop* new roles, *reject* old roles, or decide which roles we choose not to develop. We must *develop interface* among our roles. *THEN* we must develop interface with others and their roles.

I have often been critical of what I, and others, have called—perhaps ideologically—the "General Semantics Cult." In these three days I have observed, I have experienced (perhaps phenomenologically), and I hope I have analyzed. I conclude, in the terms of General Semantics Theory which was so eloquently presented by Dr. Podea, that general semantics has been a *closed system* for many years.

For the first time, or if not for the first time at least at a most salient time, general semantics during these three days has been given an opportunity to break out into an *open system* and it now has a tremendous opportunity to *reorganize.*

If you are content inside your *ideological world* and your *closed system,* then stay there.

If you have seen, as I have, the need to break out of the closed general semantics system into the confusion of an open system needing reorganization, then perhaps general semantics may once again be called a good and useful theory of human behavior and perhaps a useful methodology for studying human behavior.

If I may be permitted to close with an either-or-statement—Either you will use this Conference as a stimulus to break out of the closed system, or the system of general semantics will soon self-destruct.

REFERENCES

Bergmann, Gustav, 1951, "Ideology," reprinted from *Ethics,* 61 (April, 1951), 205-218 in *The Metaphysics of Logical Positivism,* New York: Longmans, Green and Company, (1954), pp. 300-325.

OBSERVATIONS

TITUS PODEA

Society for General Systems Research

There is no way of integrating, of putting together, without having a design, an image of "the whole." There has never been a bridge-builder on this side of the valley who by hook or crook did not have to imagine what the other side of the valley was. He took a rowboat or he went in a roundabout fashion over the "other bridge," or swam, and if he could not cross to the other side to test and measure where the footing of the bridge was going to end, he had to imagine it!

At this level of complexity, we deal always with models. We have good models or bad models. Complete models or incomplete models. We are in a continuous succession of cascading sequences of search and findings, of what the computer programmers like to say so much of the time: information in—information out, and much of the time waste in—waste out or "garbage in and garbage out" when the process is sterile. In information theory we call it "low entropy" and "high entropy."

Given a system (i.e. complex information with specific attributes of entivity within definite boundaries) we are also given a level of entropy. We start with low entropy. We go around seeking bits, fragments of imagery which have low entropy, pregnant with new information. We derive new meaning (knowledge) and in the process dump high entropy away. This is what man is: he consumes low entropy and discards high entropy *in all of his creative activities.* Man is an image-maker, a model-builder. In the process he becomes a symbol-user or tool-maker. I believe there is no such thing as legitimate literature, legitimate art, moral or immoral literature. There is good or bad literature. There are good or bad models. There is good theory and bad theory. There are good hypotheses and there are bad hypotheses. In our search for new knowledge we do an awful lot of discarding.

This is the time for the general semanticist to stop and take a critical look at what he must discard. This is a crossroad and he must decide how to meet the "crisis", i.e. close the gap. There is a need perhaps to rework some of the basic assumptions of general semantics and make them explicit. There is an awful lot of intellectual waste that must be brought back and reworked. There is much that general semantics has to offer at this time.

In the long run, civilized man, modern man, the would-be rational man, needs and must formalize two basic theories: a fundamental theory of *organization*—and there are scholars trying to do that—and a basic theory of *action*. I submit that there is room for a fundamental theory of *communication,* to work between organization and action. I think that the way the general semanticist must confront this problem is with a new degree of awareness, the problem must be embedded into a larger frame, a "new whole." That's how new creative notions will arise. The whole is more than the sum total of the parts. There must be "a better than" re-arrangement of the whole. There must be discovered some new *interfaces* between the established disciplines and general semantics, i.e., more explicit proximities to the adjacent sciences. *Inter-disciplining* will surprise and bring new meanings.

I think that the hard sciences as much as the soft sciences need *communicators*. This is a serious crisis. We need better communicators. This requires not only knowledge of the process of communication, i.e., a theory of communication, but the general knowledge that fits appropriately into what is now known as a theory of *general systems*. The general semanticist should take it upon himself to bring his specific contributions to inter-disciplinary studies within the schema of a general system.

I read Korzybski in 1949. He was then in the stream of the prevailing winds of the "quantifiers" of the early thirty's. The historical schools had seen the turning of the tides and the word was quantification. I have been engaged for 20 years in econometrics and operations research and I neglected this field. I am back with this particular group after many years.

Perhaps there was a traffic jam, a queue, a congestion of too many new ideas with unknown and unforeseen implications; perhaps what was needed was time, more performance and activity in the various scientific fields before the implications could be made explicit, the new applications fully realized; perhaps the computer had to be developed; perhaps statistical applications and the management sciences with their operations research had to do their part. Now that we have arrived at a new crossroad, I foresee an opportunity for a new thrust in research activities. Much of your past research is so minute, i.e., deals with micro-systems, and the data so quantitatively large that for the first time it becomes practicable and manageable to approach research in general semantics in a "systematic" way. The computing machine is available. What was not possible and manageable with paper and pencil in the last 20 years might now be tractable. We have a new extension. This is a gadget of the mind, of course, and I believe in gadgetry, i.e., instruments. Research creates instruments (methods) and formalizes their uses. It reduces the complex to the simple. It gives you tools of simplicity to tinker in complexities.

There are simultaneously two inverted movements. We move all the time from the simple to the complex; from generalities toward the specific. These are like two spinning cones. Imagine two conic movements. One that is spiraling outwards, ever enlarging, opening the horizon, and another conic movement that sort of drills inward. This is what we call an "explosive" and "implosive" activity because it is pregnant with potential creative power. Formally it is a general recursive system. We must bring things together in a new design! Make new adaptations. I am saying you have to *cross lines*. There has to be some kind of a marriage here between the general semanticist and the other scientists! This can only be done by delibeate design. In the last analysis this is the purpose of research.

SUMMARY SESSION
Transcribed from a tape recording

QUESTION: If we are going to do another conference like this I would like to ask Irwin Berger how he would suggest it be improved.

IRWIN BERGER: This conference has been based primarily on people reading their reports, and there are all kinds of advantages to doing it that way. But there are some alternatives. One is to plan a conference a long time in advance. Invite papers well in advance. Have them printed and distributed to all the participants, so that when they come to the conference they are prepared to question and to interact with the person who gives it. It might be too difficult to do because of the logistics, but it is worth a try.

Another alternative is to go to lower levels of abstraction. We have been working at very high levels of abstraction. People have been talking primarily about the principles of their research: they apologize every time they give a concrete example, as if to say, "I just have to mention at this point what took place in Chicago. But that has nothing to do with principles of what I am talking about, because what I'm saying is applicable to any city." Why shouldn't we have a conference that is on the concrete level, where the people invited to participate give demonstrations of specific activities? Like the sensitivity demonstration we had. There are many other specific things which can be done by people coming to the conference from so many different fields. Then allow us to generalize how this can be applied to the universe. This can be done through interaction. Moreno was mentioned a great deal—why not have a psychodrama and act it instead of just talking about it?

258 Summary Session

ELWOOD MURRAY: May I ask a question about that? Are you talking about a research conference on designs of general semantics, or are you talking about the teaching of general semantics?

BERGER: I meant to be general. It could apply to either one.

MURRAY: How could we introduce more of that into a research conference?

BERGER: Why not invite people to come to the conference the same way you're invited as a graduate student to a seminar on research techniques? We are asked to bring in a proposal for a research design. We present it to the group as a specific one—this is an experiment, or this is a study I wish to do. Then the group can criticize it and see if it holds water. That does not have to be the entire conference, but I think it would be a useful part of the conference.

JAMES ROEVER: The Speech Association of America has just been funded by the National Council of Humanities to have a national development project on rhetoric. It took us about six months of work to get the proposal in a form that it went in. It took another three or four months until funding. The way the conference is set up speakers will now be picked for the first conference. The papers will be sent out and later the reactions to those papers will be written up and sent out. The people will come to the first conference to establish the priorities and the issues that ought to be discussed at the second conference, which is comparable to this one. Then the second conference will come to pass. That whole process will take about two years. What I'm suggesting is that I think it is a good plan to have an invested interest, but you really have to plan on spending time in preparation if you're going to do it that way. That's the way I would suggest you do it, however.

—————: We had a one-week conference on speech communication last February and it was all structured at the beginning. People were randomly assigned to groups. But after the first day people got together and said, "This just doesn't work. Let's let people go off in their own groups and formulate concepts in the areas in which they have the most interest." And that's how we got productivity. Throw the structure out. Let people migrate to their own interests and let them come up with recommendations. It worked.

——————: People have argued whether there could be research in general semantics or not. It seemed to me that this particular meeting is a milestone in saying, "Yes, there is interest; yes, there are some possibilities; here are some actual studies in general semantics." And for us to be able to come and express our interest and concerns—I think is a necessary first step. Now perhaps out of this meeting can come some directions for future meetings. I didn't really see this as a research meeting as such. I didn't think we were ready for that.

GERALD PHILLIPS: By way of a defense of the whole operation here, I have the feeling that it is being attacked by people whose gluteus maximus hurts from sitting. It occurs to me what has happened here is that a lot of people who didn't even know each other had a chance to meet. There was a kind of compulsion to sit and listen. It was not like the traditional Speech Association convention where you listen to your friend's paper and spend the rest of the time at the bar—which is fun, but hardly edifying. We sat and we listened. We made acceptances. We made rejections. We made some evaluations. I think everybody had some good ideas about what we can do for the next conference.

But I think we could visualize this thing as kind of a hot box operation where the people representing a pretty wide range of views were put together under enforced conditions. We had to hear each other out. This, I think, was the essentially useful feature. I think anybody who listened carefully cannot help but to go home with nine or ten good ideas of things to try out. I'm not prepared to accept that if an idea worked for "A" it's going to work for me, too. But at least there are some things in my head that seem to be worth playing with.

The next time you have a conference I'll be happy to send my paper in advance and have it critiqued and I'll bring a demonstration and the Mt. Nittany Normal College girls' drill team and the Mormon Tabernacle Choir, if you want, but there was a kind of an absence of the dilettante atmosphere that you usually get at conferences. So, on this basis, I would say that this is highly useful. We could have had more time to mill around, you know, and make talk.

BERGER: I'm reminded of the mother who brings her son two ties—a blue one and a red one—and the next time he sees her he wears one of his ties. Whereupon his mother says, "What's the matter, you didn't like the other one?" There was no way to satisfy that situation without wearing both ties. I wanted to say in making my suggestions as to how this conference might have been otherwise, that I enjoyed the conference and I got a great deal out of it—the way, in fact, it was. But there is always room even with a successful and worthwhile activity to think of alternatives, and that's what I meant with my suggestion.

DONN BAILEY: I have two observations. First, I'm concerned that the speakers were not able to defend their positions, or to elaborate on certain points that were a bit obscure to some of us. I think we owe the speaker that kind of relationship. They went to a lot of trouble in preparing talks and I, for one, would like to react to some of the things that I agreed with or disagreed with.

Second, presenters of papers were all white. I think it is about time that the academic community understood the thrust of the revolution and one of the things that that thrust is suggesting to community people—be they non-academic or academic people—is the fact that the time has passed when white people can sit and make certain kinds of decisions exclusive of the black input. And there was not a black input here. I would like to have seen something regarding racism in research design. I think we spoke all around it but hardly anyone used the term "racism." I think this is awfully significant when we think in terms of this being an Institute of General Semantics.

HARRY MAYNARD: I would like to ask a question. We have been

deeply concerned in the New York Society with the fact that we don't get more Negroes or more black people at our meetings and we try various strategies, but we just are not too successful. Could you give us some advice on this problem?

BAILEY: Well, in a three-day conference something approaching the most crucial for this country's survival takes place on the last day and the fast-approaching "getaway" time for all of us, so I think that says something about the concern of this group for the black/white encounter. I think the black/white encounter is looked upon by most whites as being something superfluous and I think that's far from the truth. It is most crucial and if we recognize that it is crucial, we would place it on the agenda or structure the conference in such a way to give validity to that belief. There seems to be a lack of black participants. The question arises are the blacks capable of coming here and presenting their thoughts to you? I think they are. I think the blacks are ready. I have a list of about 50 people who could have contributed a great deal to what was going on here.

MURRAY: May I ask you about a related effort? We are trying to put on a workshop in this area, an introductory one, called the "encounter," and every militant leader that we asked turned us down so fast it's not funny. How can we get them involved? I wanted to get the 50 most influential "militant" and the 50 most influential "racists" and 50 of our people who thought they could communicate a little bit. We were going to lock them up until everybody began to act decently toward each other and listen to each other. But we got scared to do that. We had to modify it and we are trying to work out a new way. Do you have any suggestions?

BAILEY: If I understand your thinking, that black militants are not now addressing themselves to white groups, I would like to caution you about an allness statement. There are some of us who are quite militant in our stance but who have not really written off white people as a body to address and as a body to persuade. The black community is not monolithic. There are a number of people who would view with much favor coming to a group such as this to provide this essentially white group their perspective, and I cannot agree with the idea that militants—all black militants—are not willing to share their concerns and their perceptions with others. I'm here. I'm not as militant as some of my brothers on the street corners. But when you listen to Dr. Walker and some of his statements about the unrest on this campus, perhaps in this context I might be considered a militant. But I haven't written off talking to white people and there are others like me. I was not asked to participate. I'm not suggesting that I should have been asked. I had a number of other things to do, but I think there are a number of black speakers available who could have provided this conference with additional input.

MURRAY: You're suggesting that we can go at it one by one.

BAILEY: No, I'm not. In fact, that's the one issue that I wish to bring up with Dr. Sheldon. He indicated that perhaps individual interaction is what we need. I disagree. I think perhaps maybe a greater and bigger map, a more accurate map, can be constructed not by individual interaction but by groups interacting. Racism in this country is built on group action. We cannot resolve the problems stemming from this by interacting individually. I'm suggesting that perhaps we have black groups and white groups and begin to interact as a group. There are those groups, community action groups, who are willing to do just that—come in, in sixes and sevens, and make their presentations and have the whole group react to that presentation.

CHARLOTTE READ: In that setup you have a group of blacks and a group of whites. Could it be that they could all be together and have a common problem, without reference to black or white or separate groups?

BAILEY: I don't quite follow. You're saying not to recognize it as a black/white issue? To have blacks and whites together?

READ: Not to approach it with the feeling that the blacks are staying in their group, addressing the whites from their group, and speaking from their group to the other group. But rather that they are all together talking about the problem together.

BAILEY: I'd like to get to that stage in our development in this country, but right now we are talking me to you, is that right? It is still a confrontation. It's still verbal posturing coming from black and verbal posturing coming from white. Until we penetrate that kind of barrier, it will remain right there in that stage of development. And I think the only way we can move an organization like this is to address it in our program and build it into the kind of program that we see as being a step in the right direction, in the direction of co-existence. Right now we are not doing too much toward this.

CECIL COLEMAN: What meaning did you have in mind when you used that word "confrontation"? Whenever two people speak together, it is a confrontation in the very specific definition of the word. But did you mean it with more of an antagonistic approach?

BAILEY: I don't particularly like the word "antagonistic."

COLEMAN: No, that's too strong.

BAILEY: No, it's not strong enough.

COLEMAN: Oh. I thought it was too strong.

BAILEY: If we view what has been happening here for the last few days as an example of confrontation, then we are operating on a wholly different conception of it. "Confrontation," as far as I'm concerned, is to speak what's on our mind. It is giving the chance to ask questions, to respond to questions.

————: Some of the criticism that has come out was of the sort: "Well, gee, why don't we come down and do something real with this meeting instead of talking about research today; why don't we get out of the clouds?" It seems to me that the purpose of the meeting was research rather than confrontation. It was billed as a research meeting rather than as a confrontation meeting. I think that the structure of the meeting itself had a lot to do with what we talked about while we were here. Am I right, Dr. Murray?

MURRAY: Well, that is the theme. That's right.

BAILEY: My point is that in dealing with research designs, if we consider ourselves a part of this society as a whole, and if we are members of our society, then the research designs that we are foisting on our students, that we are ventilating to our colleagues, are in essence racist in some of their aspects. So what I'm suggesting is not to throw away the idea of a research design conference, but talk about aspects of research design that could be racist in orientation.

PHILLIPS: I will take umbrage—well, mild umbrage, anyway—at the notion that a research design, which is kind of a neutral methodolgy, can be classified as racist and non-racist. Its applications may be so. Sometimes a research design can be used to justify a set of premises that are racist both in and out of context, and on that basis it is the premises of the study and also the research that have to be challenged and questioned. The agenda of this Conference seemed to focus specifically on methodologies for testing, evaluating, and utilizing the principles of general semantics, which I also regard as neutral things. We are trying to figure out how to plug them in. Broadening the contributions would be useful.

It occurred to me that nobody talked at all at this meeting about certain Oriental approaches of obtaining insight into human behavior and intuiting certain scientific propositions, and this might have been very helpful. One of the rigidities that we Westernized researchers get ourselves onto is that we block out possibilities for other kinds of data because we talk only to each other. So, maybe that should go on the critique list for the next conference. But it also occurs to me that as far as it went this conference represented a kind of significant broadening, ranging from orthodoxy—if Mrs. Read will let me so classify her because she comes directly from the fountainhead—to peripheral and marginal characters like myself. This was kind of a beginning of an ecumenical movement in a great many ways. We saw each other. We confronted each other. We discovered that we neither frothed at the mouth nor bit, although some of us were boring at frequent intervals. This way, maybe not a great leap forward, but at least a good solid step.

DONALD WASHBURN: I think we do have a basic question here. I think that what you are indicating is we turn this into a movement for the purpose of eliminating racism. I cannot go that route. I don't really see where that position is anymore acceptable to me than Mayor Daley's. I'm not sure I agree with Dr. Phillips, however, that designs cannot be intrinsically racist. I think there are some basic operational assumptions we make that eliminate areas of consideration that we can talk about.

READ: I'm not very keen about being classified as orthodox. Orthodoxy seems awfully rigid to me. I personally am very much intrigued with Eastern philosophy and what it has to offer. I like to branch out. I feel that if people who are using Korzybski's work go out from there or change it, they should know what they are doing. That's all. And be clear cut. "I don't agree because of this" or "I want to change it because of this," etc. Simply know what they are doing and state it.

RACHEL LAUER: I'm just wondering what general semantics has to offer to the black/white encounter at this stage of its history. This is a stage of history where there is resistance to meeting together and increasing polarity and confrontation. How, then, can general semantics contribute at this stage? As a general semanticist and as a black man, you might have some ideas on that.

BAILEY: I have some. I think first of all we have to recognize where the resistance comes from. I'm not so sure that you can say it is the blacks who are resisting communication or dialogue. Witness what took place here in the last few days. The blacks did not on a wholesale basis decline from presenting their thoughts to this group. I have not been advised as to how many blacks have been contacted, but I doubt very seriously if 100% turned this group down.

LAUER: Now, that to me is an answer. You are saying one contribution this organization or *any* organization can make is an extra effort to include blacks as participants. That's an organizational thing. That is, open the doors, make room, go out of our way. That's not specific to GS, but it is a good idea.

BAILEY: I think we could probably do something about this whole "cultural disadvantage" syndrome—the label which, as far as I'm concerned, maintains the superior/inferior relationship of plantation owner/slave mentality that still exists in this country in a number of areas including the world of academia. I think Dr. Phillips speaks on a number of occasions about the verticality and horizontality of relationships and I think the insistence that black people are disadvantaged simply keeps intact the white myth that pervades our educational institutions. And I think that as people concerned with semantics, we should take a very hard look at that and help set the record straight.

MURRAY: Why couldn't we put on a conference of whites and blacks on this subject? Would you help us organize such a conference? Would you get us in contact with those that would come in?

BAILEY: Sure.

MURRAY: It would be a very important thing if we could work that out.

BAILEY: I'm available. I'm trapped right here on campus.

MURRAY: Phillips, you remember this. We have gotten a link. You are in good communication with Dr. Phillips, aren't you?

BAILEY: I think so. He is the chairman of my committee.

PHILLIPS: I think this would be a superb idea because Donn just finished a general semantics class this last term which had some significant things happen in it that I think support the truth of the premises that he is laying down here. What was intriguing to me was how ineffective the training in general semantics often is when emotions start running. I'm still trying to figure out what happened that evening because it was all wrong. It should never have happened if anybody had learned anything. So, maybe our first-hand experience is fairly important.

MAYNARD: I don't know just where it ought to be on the agenda, but one of the things that did strike me is that several people implied that there has been quite a bit of research in general semantics. But it has not been cataloged and pulled together in one place. I have found this out because so many people are approaching the General Semantics Foundation for grants for research and we already have given money for seven or eight projects. I'll just give a concrete example. In his opening remarks, Al Goldberg made the point that he wanted to see a piece of research which talked about, "Should general semantics be taught inductively or deductively?" Well, this piece of research has been finished for six months. Ray Arlo of NYU did it for his Ph.D. Thesis, "The Relative Effectiveness of Inductive and Expository Teaching of Principles of General Semantics Upon the Critical Reading Ability of 9th Grade Students." Irwin Berger, in my opinion, did one of the greatest Ph.D. theses I have ever read it. It is readable. And Howard Livingston did another. But a gentleman gave a paper right from New York City, the very area where these people live and work, and he was not even aware of the research that these two people had done. Both of them had gotten their Ph.D. as a result of this research.

Elwood Murray has been promising me for the last two years that he is going to find a bright M.A. candidate who will pull together all of the M.A.'s and Ph.D.'s in Denver and in many other universities around the country that have been done explicitly related to general semantics. I can see that at a conference like this, if we held it again, the very first thing we would do would be to pass out an inventory of the research that *had* been done. The offer is out! Anybody who will do this kind of basically library research, already has a grant from the General Semantics Foundation.

This is not to negate the essential point made by a lot of people here: *that there has not been enough research in the field of general semantics.* If I have my way and I can raise the money for it, there will be a hell of a lot more. But I do think almost every speaker I listened to was not aware that there is anywhere near as much research as has actually been done. I might add as far as future meetings go, similar to this, I generally found the response very favorable to this meeting.

PHILLIPS: Back in twelve hundred and something Petrus Ramus found that everything that Aristotle wrote was wrong. He did not really do much to Aristotle, who went merrily rolling along, and lots of researchers since Ramus have continued to be Aristotelian. I don't know that Korzybski has destroyed Aristotle either, but thinking horizontally, he has certainly given us another set of premises.

I guess I was firing too many rhetorical cannons at this meeting, but one of the ideas that I was trying to plant was the notion that it seems to me to be a waste of time to sit and test the formulations of general semantics which in my mind have considerable analogy to the formulations of Aristotle. We now have an alternate mode, an alternate set of propositions which we can use to examine, if you will, the same realities. There are some investigators who will go at it in essentially an Aristotelian fashion; some that will go at it in a general semantics fashion; and some that will try to combine the two, which is not so difficult to do. I think the experiences that we have had here and the exposure to the wide range of approaches and the use of the technical terminology indicate fairly clearly that there is a viable and substantive body of theory and methodology available to us. One need not accept everything that Korzybski wrote any more than one need not accept everything that Aristotle wrote or that anyone else wrote. But one certainly has available a pretty wide source of premises that could be used to investigate many, many phenomena.

If a Foundation is interested in spending some money, I think it would be money well spent to devote it to the teaching of general semantics principles on a number of levels so that greater numbers of people will have the opportunity to utilize them in the kind of work that they do. What I mean by many, many levels—I mean the devising, for example, of a course in general semantics or an approach to general semantics usable to the terminal students in a community junior college. We have been experimenting with the teaching of general semantics in the second and third grades—I think with a reasonable degree of effectiveness. There are great numbers of places where teaching methodologies can be developed and in a sense this is a kind of pragmatic sort of research because a good teacher, immersed in the act of teaching, can intuit from the experience the kinds of propositions that are effective with the students and those that are ineffective.

I would like to read somewhere—even better I would like to see on film or live—some of the work done by the significant teachers of general semantics. The films for example, that Irving Lee made many, many years ago are still widely used by many teachers that never heard of Korzybski, never heard of a structural differential, but are captivated by the fundamental logic and appeal of the developments that Lee had in those films. I think that taking some of Donn's premises would provide us with another useful approach. Is it possible to improve the human dialogue between the races by utilizing some of the general semantics principles? We cannot do a formal research study because—this is a point I have not made yet—I think the act of doing human research on human subjects is essentially undignified, no matter who the human being is. But we can certainly try teaching it and see how it works.

MAYNARD: Right to your point, Gerry, we have a standing offer from the board of the Foundation to do a study of the effectiveness or ineffectiveness of general semantics in the improvement of interracial communication. We have an academic advisory board of several excellent people who have done significant research in the field of general semantics and we have spent a great deal of time on this very subject. Let's bring together some of the people who by example, one way or another, have done outstanding jobs in teaching general semantics and let them perform and give examples of their teaching and perhaps indicate where general semantics could make a contribution to interracial communication.

PHILLIPS: Well, let me make a direct request, by golly. Here goes the hustle in public with all of the witnesses looking at it. We are working in elementary schools in Appalachia—Donn and two other men from Penn State are about to go into some intercity areas. Much of what we are doing there is basic general semantics. How would you like to produce some films?

MAYNARD: Send me your script and we will look it over.

PHILLIPS: No! No script. Live action on the scene!

MAYNARD: I meant your request for a grant.

PHILLIPS: I'll catch you before you go home.

LAUER: I would like to propose that general semantics is not a discipline, that general semantics is not a theory, and that typical research is not appropriate to general semantics. If it is not a theory, and if it is not a system, then the type of effort which says let's set up research designs to test basic general semantics principles is not appropriate. I think it is not. I am inclined to go along with the gentleman this morning who described general semantics as an integration of many other disciplines which have been drawn from experimental methods. The whole structural differential, in a sense, all of Korzybski's book, is a different interpretation of knowledge that has been abstracted from various other sciences. This is not something to be tested. You do not test statements such as "The word is not the thing." Do you? That's not a testable hypothesis. That is not based upon a theory. That's a statement of something based upon observations that are in turn a reflection of the Einstein theory, a reflection of different ways of describing what is going on in the world. To me, it is a false hope to seek research designs on general semantics *principles*. The research to make is in the area of how do you get people to change from the view that A is A to the view that A is not A. And when you get them to change, how do you get them to integrate it into behavior? I don't think it's a question to test A is not A.

MAYNARD: As I understood Glynn Harmon's comments, he felt that general semantics should not spend a lot of time on doing research on minutiae. If I read him correctly, he implied that if we just look outside the field of general semantics, much of this work has already been done. We should look for the integrative factors rather than grinding down narrow pieces of behavioral research which might either disprove or prove some of the working hypotheses of general semantics.

MURRAY: You should know that Harry Maynard and the General Semantics Foundation were principal donors to this conference. The President of the Institute of General Semantics, Robert Strauss, was a substantial donor, as were S. I. Hayakawa and Pennsylvania State University.

MAYNARD: Two other people should be mentioned. One is Torey Browald who is Vice-Chairman of the Nobel Foundation and he feels deeply about the importance of general semantics. He is one of Sweden's most important bankers. He was the Ambassador to the United Nations for many years. He got interested in general semantics because we hold most of our meetings right next to the United Nations building in New York City, The Carnegie Peace Foundation. Another man—Ed Walther—also gave some money for this get-together. And I want to thank Penn State University for being such wonderful hosts. I think that Elwood Murray, particularly—he has had a dream of doing this sort of a conference for many years—deserves our deep appreciation.

MURRAY: I believe it is time to bring this conference to a close. 1 took the position of Director of the Institute of General Semantics for two years and it terminates September first. My successor, Dr. Christopher Sheldon, is here. My number one goal as director was to open up the methodolgy called general semantics to scrutiny and research. I wasn't afraid for that to happen. I taught general semantics long enough to know that I don't care if all the battalions of scientists in all the world go after it. It will stand. You come to know that in what happens in your students and your results. But in my environment, the academic life I lived in, the situation was very, very unsatisfactory, because we were not building the image which an academic establishment has got to have. So I was worried that we might never get this Conference off the ground. But you see what happened. Last November the Board of Trustees made this possible. And this Conference is going to make possible many others. We now know a level at which research can be conducted. Incidentally, I do not care if general semantics as we know it won't stand up to the research; it will just have to go to hell or it will have to modify itself. But I don't think it will go to hell, in spite of all hell being turned loose on it. I think it has a terrific future. We've got the opportunity, but there are forces that are pulling it back. But I can say this to the Board of Trustees: I don't think you would permit that to happen. So thank you, former students, colleagues, and the Board of Trustees. Thank you very much.

READ: Thank you, Elwood.

NAME INDEX

Ackoff, R. L., 178.
Aiken, H. D., 141, 142.
Alexander, F., 177.
Alliance for Progress, 143.
American Documentation Institute, 179.
American Society for Information Science, 179.
American Sociological Association, 80.
Annual Review of Information Science and Technology, the, 181.
Applebaum, Ronald, 160.
Argyle, Michael, 79.
Aristotle, 77, 85, 116, 140, 239, 268.
Arlo, Ray, 267.
Aron, Raymond, 232.
Asch, Solomon, 5, 79.

B

Bacon, Francis, 141.
Bailey, Donn, 260ff.
Barbour, Alton B., 77.
Barnlund, D. C., 96.
Barrett, W., 140.
Barzun, J., 142.
Bateson, Gregory, 41.
Becker, Ernest, 157.
Becker, Samuel L., 162, 163.
Behavioral Research Council, 177.
Bentham, J., 142.
Berelson, Bernard, 51, 78.
Berger, Irwin, 257ff.
Berman, Sanford, 50.
Bermann, Gustav, 249.
Bettinghaus, Erwin P., 162.
Black, Edwin B., 7, 161.
Black, Max, 165.
Bloomfield, Leonard, 178, 185, 188.
Bois, J. Samuel, 26, 38, 50.
Borden, George A, 205, 206.
Borgatta, E. F., 81, 82.
Bourland, D. David, Jr., 217, 226.
Briggs, Asa, 142.

Broadus, James M., 229.
Browald, Tore, Pref., 271.
Brown, Roger W., 8, 163.
Buckley, W., 97.
Burke, Kenneth, 114, 116.
Burrow, Trigant, 48, 50.

C

Cabot, Richard C., 120.
Calhoun, John C., 142.
Carpenter, C. R., 157, 160.
Carterette, Teresa, 92.
Case Western Reserve University, 175.
Caspari, Ernest W., 63.
Center for Theoretical Biology, 61.
Chase, Stuart, 3.
Chicago, University of, 49, 213.
Chomsky, Noam, 185, 186.
Coleman, Cecil J., xii, 16, 263.
Combs, Arthur W., 157, 162.
Comte, Auguste, 141.
Concerned Citizens of Cicero and Berwyn, 99.
Condon, John C., Jr., 193.
Condon, W. S., 61.
Cottrell, L. S., Jr., 96, 99.
Criswell, J. R., 82.
Croft, Wilfred F., 16.
Cuadra, C. A., 180, 181.
Cummings, E. E., 126ff.

D

Daley, John, 265.
Dark, Raymond, 157, 160.
Darling, C. M., 179.
Darwin, 182, 238.
Defense Department, 212.
Denver, University of, xii, 3, 77, 125, 238.
Deutsch, Martin, 231.
Deutsch, Morton, 90, 92.

Name Index

De Vito, Joseph A., xii, 35, **185**, **193**, 199.
Dewey, John, 176.
Dickinson, Frank, 238ff.
Dulles, John Foster, 169.

E

Edinboro State College, 109.
Edwards, A. E., 69, 70.
Edwards, Allen L., 91.
Ehninger, Douglas, 165.
Einstein, Albert, 210, 270.
Else, G. F., 140.
Erickson, Erik H., 231.
Ervin-Tripp, Susan, 194.
Eysenck, Hans, 160.

F

Fearing, F., 96.
First International **Congress for the** Unity of Science, 176.
Force, Maryane, 166.
Force, Roland W., 166.
Ford Foundation, 177.
Francis, Roy G., 32.
Viktor Frankl, 207.
Friedman, Neil, 13.
Fulbright, William, 169.
Fulkerson Memorial Scholarship, 62.

G

General Semantics Foundation, **Pref.**, 267ff.
Gerbner, George, 162.
Germino, D., 140, 142.
Giffin, Kim, 51, 89, 92.
Glaser, Barney, 96.
Glorfeld, Louis E., 3, 16, 55.
Goffman, W., 176.
Goldberg, Alvin A., 3, 16, 55, 267.
Goode, H. H., 221.
Gregg, Richard B., 161.
Gronlund, N. E., 82.
Guilford, J. P., 69.

H

Hall, Edwin, 160.
Haney, William, 55.

Handy, R., 177.
Hansen, Helen M., 16.
Harmon, Glynn, 175, 270.
Harvard University, 213.
Harvey. O. J., 11.
Harvey-Gibson, R. J., 176.
Hayakawa, S. I., Pref., 3, 14, 155, 175, 195, 271.
Headstart, 158.
Hempel, C. G., 70.
Herndon, William, 160.
Hertzler, Joyce, 8.
Hexter, J. H., 140.
Hilgartner, Andrew, 30, 61.
Homans, George C., 78, 83.
Hope-Wallace, Philip, 131.
Humboldt State College, 95.
Hunsinger, P., 125, 175.
Hunt, D. E., 11.

I

Illinois Institute of Technology, 211, 214.
Illinois, University of, 69.
Information Research Associates, Inc., 217.
Institute for the Future, 179.
Institute of General Semantics Pref., 62, 235, 247, 260, 271, 272.
International Institute of Bibliography, 179.
International Society for General Semantics, 8, 247.

J

Jackson, Jesse, 99.
Jacobson, Lenore, 13.
Jennings, Russell W., 95, 99, 101.
Jobs or Income Now, 103.
Johnson, F. Craig, 23.
Johnson, Kenneth G., 16, 23, 32, 33.
Johnson, Robert G., 119.
Johnson, Wendell, 15, 16, 27, 28, 31, 69ff., 202.

K

Kansas, University of, 89.
Kassoway, Walter, 160, 167, 168.
Katter, R. V., 181.
King, Martin Luther, 99.

Name Index 275

King, William A., 23.
Klare, George R., 23.
Klinzing, Dennis, 160.
Kluckhohn, Clyde, 198.
Koopman, B. O., 221.
Korzybski, Alfred, xi, 3, 8, 10, 15, 18, 23, 29, 30, 34, 37, 38, 39, 47, 50, 62, 69, 71, 83, 84, 98, 113, 114, 115, 116, 119, 122, 137, 142, 151, 178, 180, 181, 185, 196, 197, 199, 208, 209, 217, 218, 219, 224, 230, 231, 241, 242, 248, 250, 254, 265, 268, 269, 270.
Kozol, Jonothan, 160.
Kurtz, P., 177.

L

Latin American Defense Organization, 103.
Lauer, Rachel, 16, 34, 202, 265, 270.
Lee, Irving J., 3, 12, 50, 195, 269.
Leighton, Dorothy, 198.
Lerner, Daniel, 231.
Lindzey, G., 81, 82.
Livingston, Howard, 55, 267.
Locke, John, 141.
Lorenz, Konrad, 157, 160, 175.
Lucas, Robert, 99.

M

McCroskey, James C., 162.
McManus, R. P., 226.
MacLiesh, Archibald, 127.
Maloney, Martin, 185, 188.
Marwell, Gerald, 13.
Marx, Karl, 141.
Maslow, Abraham, 31, 47, 50.
Masserman, Jules, 160.
May, Rollo, 160.
Maynard, Harry, Pref., 260, 267ff.
Mayper, Stuart A., 239.
Meerloo, Joost A. M., 193.
Mellinson, J. R., 90.
Mental Health Research Institute, 8.
Meredith, Patrick, 212.
Messick, David M., 93.
Meyers, Russell, 27.
Michigan, University of, 8.
Middleton, D., 224.
Miller, Arthur, 119ff.
Miller, George, 142.
Mills, John Stuart, 142, 143.

Minter, Robert L., 41.
Minor, Gene, 3, 12, 16.
Minteer, Catherine, 202.
Mitchell, Francis Henry, 49.
Moodie, Catherine, 71.
Moreno, J. L., 80, 84, 257.
Morris, Charles, 178, 213.
Murphy, Gardner, 96, 120.
Murray, Elwood, Pref., 175, 235, 247, 258ff.

N

Nash, R. T., 224.
National Aeronautics and Space Administration, 61.
National Council of Humanities, 258.
National Institute for Neurological Diseases and Blindness, 75.
National Science Foundation, 213.
National Society for the Study of Communication 41.
Newcomb, Theodore M., 90.
Newill, V. A., 176.
Newton, Isaac, 182.
New York, City University of, 185, 193.
New York Society for General Semantics, 261.
Nieman, Gilbert, 127.
International Conference of General Semantics, Ninth, 65.
Nobel Foundation, 271.
Norman, Charles, 130.
Nunnally, Jum, 30.

O

Oglesby, Carl, 167, 168.
Ogston, W. D., 61.
Operation Breadbasket, 99, 103.
Operation Headstart, 143.
Osborn, Michael M., 165.
Osgood, Charles, 14, 70, 142.

P

Pace, Thomas J., Jr., 95, 99.
Payne, Buryl. 27.
Pelligrini, John, 99.
Pennsylvania State University, Pref., 149, 161, 205, 269, 271.
Pepinsky, P. M., 81, 82.

Name Index

Peters, Henry N., 3, 12.
Phillips, Gerald M., 31, 149, 259ff.
Piaget, Jean, 120.
Podea, Titus, 250, 253.
Poincare, J. H., 217.
Prather, Elizabeth M., 73.

Q

Queens College, C.U.N.Y., 139.

R

Ramus, Petrus, 268.
Randolph, John F., 65.
Rapoport, Anatol, 3, 4, 8, 92.
Read, Charlotte, 47, 247, 262ff.
Rees, A., 179.
Richards, I. A., 142.
Rivett, P., 178.
Roby, Thornton B., 92.
Rochester, University of, 65.
Roever, James E., 247, 258.
Rokeach, Milton, 31.
Roosevelt, Franklin, 166.
Rosenblith, Walter, 129.
Rosenfield, Lawrence W., 139, 140.
Rosenthal, Robert, 13.
Ruesch, Jurgen, 41.
Rusk, Dean, 169.

S

Sapir, Edward, 8, 178.
Saporta, Sol, 194.
Saracevic, T., 179.
Schroeder, H. M., 11.
Schultz, D. G., 181.
Schuchardt, Charlotte, 51.
Scott, Robert L., 161.
Senate Foreign Relations Committee, 169.
Shannon, C., 23, 177.
Sheldon, Christopher, 262, 272.
Shera, J. H., 181.
Sherman, Dorothy, 71.
Shriner, T., 71.
Shutz, William C., 77, 78, 83.
Silverman, Franklin H., xii, 29, 69, 71.
Skinner, B. F., 157.
Slobin, Dan, 194.
Smith, Donald K., 161.
Snell, B., 139, 143.

Snygg, Donald, 157.
Society for General Systems Research, 253.
Sondel, Bess, 211.
Southern Christian Leadership Conference, 99.
Southern Illinois University, 95, 103.
Speech Association of America, 247, 258.
State University of New York at Buffalo, 61.
Steiner, Gary, 51, 78, 163.
Stelzner, Hermann, 166.
Stephenson, William, 168.
Stevens, S. S., 69.
Stigen, A., 140.
Strauss, A. L., 96.
Strauss, Robert, 271.
Struik, D. J., 176.
Students for a Democratic Society, 103.
Suci, G. J., 70.
Suttie, Ian D., 52.

T

Temple, University, 41.
Terwilliger, Robert, 163ff.
Thayer, Lee, 3.
Theler, Herbert A., 120.
Thorndike, Edward L., 232.
Thorngate, Warren B., 92.
Thurstone, L. L., 91.
Tolela, Michele (Myers), 17.
Torrance, E. P., 55.
Trainer, Joseph C., 16.
Transylvania College, 229.
Triandis, Harry C., 89, 90.
True, Sally R., 16, 55.

U

United Nations, 271.
Upward Bound, 158.
Urban Renewal, 143.

V

Van Meter, D., 224.
Van Velsen, J., 96.
Vick, Charles, 17, 41.
Von Bertalanffy, L., 97, 178.

W

Wallace, Karl, 141.
Walther, Ed., Pref., 271.
Washburn, Donald, 109, 265.
Wayne State College, 119.
Weaver, W., 23, 177.
Weinberg, A. M., 181, 193, 202.
Weinberg, Harry L., 3.
Weiss, Thomas, 3, 55.
Westley, Bruce H., 28.

White, David Manning, 33.
Whitman, Walt, 131.
Whorf, Benjamin Lee, 8, 69.
Wiener, Norbert, 177, 178.
Wilson, Susan Vance, 92.
Winters, Dennis E., 95, 99.
Winthrop, Henry, 50.
Wisconsin-Milwaukee, University of, 23.
World Future Society, 178.

SUBJECT INDEX

absolutistic thinking, 56, 121.
abstract, 214.
abstracting, 11, 84, 180, 181.
abstracting, consciousness of, 10, 12, 17, 18, 27, 30, 34, 50, 71, 98, 109ff, 181, 219, 239, 242.
abstracting, relational, 37f.
abstraction, 121, 226, 230.
abstraction, levels of, 7, 14, 15, 24, 32, 47, 89, 93, 119, 132, 135, 181, 229, 257.
abstraction, process of, 26, 29, 119.
abstractions, higher and lower order, 24, 31, 33, 34, 52, 84, 113, 135, 181, 237.
academic advancement, 154.
achievers, high/low, 11.
aesthetics, 126.
affection, 77.
allness, 7, 10, 11, 49, 71, 109, 111, 219.
All My Sons, 119ff.
alpha waves, 48.
ambiguities, 164, 169.
analogy, 112, 117, 119.
analysis of variance, 152.
analytical procedures, 101, 141.
animal behavior, 157.
animal psychology, 33.
anxiety, 17, 63, 64, 200.
Appalachia, 269.
appeals, emotional, 162.
appeals, logical, 162.
Aristotelian assumptions, 67, 236.
Aristotelian logic, 239.
armchair speculation, 140.
Art of Awareness, The, 38.
assumptions, 4, 29, 32, 42, 63, 64, 125, 167, 230, 237, 254.
assumptions, conscious, 218.
assumptive sets, 101.
attitudes, 29, 31, 89.
attitude change research, 140.
attitude scales, 92, 159.
audio-tape, 70, 105.

authorititis, 221, 223.
authoritarianism, 55, 56.
autokinetic, 79.
awareness, level of, 33.
axiomatic system, 65.

B

behavior, defensive, 48.
behavior, impaired/unimpaired, 66.
behavioral analysis, 250.
behavioral differential, 89.
behavioral distortions, 63.
behavioral hypotheses, 64.
behavioral sciences, 176, 177, 180, 182, 193.
behavioral sequences, 61.
behavioral technicians, 143.
behaviorism, 42, 140, 141, 143.
bionics, 178.
biological sciences, 207, 211.
Birth and Death of Meaning, 157.
bisociation, 112.
blacks, 260, 261, 265.
black/white encounter, 261, 265.
brainwashing, 164, 165, 169.
brain waves, 47, 48.
breathing rate, 29.

C

case histories, clinical, 160.
case studies, 9.
causality, 28, 231.
cause/effect, 28, 212.
cepts, 127ff.
chemical changes, 47.
chi-square, 152.
civil rights activists, 99.
client-centered counseling, 49.
client-therapist relationship, 49.
closed-mindedness, 11.
codability, 163.

code, 186.
cognitive dissonance, 30.
cognitive structure, 208.
college teachers, survey of, 16.
communication behavior, 161.
communication chain, 32.
communication, definition of, 41.
communication, effective, 202.
communication ideologies, 139.
communication, man-computer, 181.
communication theory, 140, 177, 186, 208, 247.
community junior college, 268.
computer, 30.
computer simulation, 206.
conditional statements, 49.
conditioning, 34, 156, 200.
conference, 247ff.
conference groups, 10.
confession, 164.
conflict, 85.
conformity, 11, 78, 79.
confrontation, 105, 262.
connotative meanings, 14.
conservatives, 155.
constructs, 154.
content analysis, 30, 181.
context, 205.
control, 77.
coping behavior, 102.
cotention, 48, 50.
counseling, 10.
counteraction, 101, 102.
creativity, 55, 127.
critic, 109, 120, 125ff.
criticism, 119ff.
Crucible, The, 119ff.
" cultural disadvantage " syndrome 266.
cybernetics, 177, 206, 239.

D

data, demographic, 100.
dating, 18, 48, 56, 132, 202, 230.
Death of a Salesman, 119ff.
decision making, 10, 206.
decision theory, 97, 101.
decoding, 194, 196, 197, 199, 202, 207.
deep structure, 189.
deductive, 17.
deficiency-motivated, 47.
demoralization, 71.
determinism, linguistic, 8.
deviants, 11.

Subject Index 279

dialogue, 131.
dictionary, 11, 44.
direct magniture-estimation, method of, 72, 73.
discoveries, simultaneous, 176.
ditention, 48, 50.
dogmatism, 11, 16, 29, 55, 121, 200.

E

Eastern philosophy, 265.
econometrics, 255.
ego involvement, 201.
" either-or " syndrome, 11.
elementalism, 219, 235, 236.
emotive, 114.
empathy, 47, 157.
encoding, 194, 196, 197, 199, 202, 207.
encounter, 66.
English Utilitarians, 142.
entropy, 239, 253.
environment, 42, 43.
epistemology, 117.
equal-appearing intervals, 71.
esteem, 79.
etc., 18, 132, 134, 201, 202, 230.
ETC.: A Review of General Semantics, 195.
ethologists, 157.
ethos, 13.
Euclidian geometry, 239.
evaluation, 13, 114, 115, 195, 208, 217, 219, 238.
evaluation, proper order of, 10.
evaluational rigidity, 69, 71.
evaluation, theory of, 119.
events, 26.
Evidence and Inference, 231.
evidence, role of, 162.
evocative images, 166.
exhibitionism, 201.
experience, 45.
experimental conditions, 28.
extended-case study, 95ff.
extensional, 12, 29, 31, 71, 232, 239, 247.
extensional devices, 15, 17, 30, 34, 230, 239, 242.
extensional man, 50.
extensional methods, 52.
extensional orientation, 6, 30, 47ff, 151, 155, 239, 242.
eye movements, 29, 48.

F

fact-territory, 6, 109, 238.
factor analysis, 12.
faith healers, 14.
feedback, 26, 31, 32, 221, 239.
feedback, effects of, 32, 206.
feed forward, 132.
field studies, 9, 160.
film, 6, 61, 66.
Finian's Rainbow, 151.
formative mode, 213.
frame of reference, 13, 29, 112.
freshman composition, 16.
frustration, 71.
fully functioning, 51.
function, 115, 219.
futurology, 179.

G

galvanic skin response (GSR), 14, 28, 29.
game theory, 177, 239.
gatekeepers, 32.
General Semantics Bulletin, xiii, 195.
general semantics courses, xii.
general semantics, descriptive, 199.
general semantics, effectiveness of, 4.
general semantics formulations, scalability of, 74.
general semantics, pertinence of, 139.
general semantics, prescriptive, 34, 196, 201.
general semantics principles, integration of, 55.
general semantics, teaching of, 258, 268.
general semantics, training in, 84.
general systems theory, 175, 177, 254.
gestalt, 128.
gestures, 47.
grammar, 44, 187, 188.
Grammar of Motives, A, 116.
group, discussion, 7, 63.
group dynamics, 140, 209.
group formation, 77, 78.
group norms, 78, 79.
group objectives, 79.
group psychotherapy, 209.
groups, community-action, 95, 97, 99.
groups, control, 16, 17, 58.
groups, dissident, 99.
groups, economic, 44.
groups, ethnic, 44.
groups, experimental, 16, 17, 58.
groups, geographic, 44.
groups, minority, 31.
groups, primary, 44.
growth, 47.

H

hate, 152.
Heisenberg principle, 154.
heuristic value, 27, 194.
historica-literary-critical, 144.
historio-graphic methods, 152.
holistic, 52, 152, 169.
homeostasis, 157.
hostility, 64.
human interaction, 149, 151, 157, 160.
human psychodynamics, structure of, 65.
human uniqueness, 159.
humanistic investigations, 139, 150.
humanistic psychologists, 47.
humanistic thinking, 140.
humanists, 150.
Humanity of Words, 213.
hyphen, 18, 132, 136, 230.
hypothesis-falsification, 63, 64.
hypothesis, metalinguistic, 8.
hypostatization, 159.

I

idealism, 71ff.
identification, 10, 12, 18, 37, 49, 84, 121, 219.
ideologist-behaviorist, 142.
ideology, 139ff, 249.
inclusion, 77.
indexing, 8, 10, 48, 56, 84, 111, 116, 132, 181, 202, 230.
Individual Behavior, 157.
individual differences, 45.
inductive, 17, 237.
inference, 55, 56, 125, 201, 232.
information, 32, 211, 225, 226.
information science, 175, 176, 179, 180, 182.
information systems, 181, 225, 226.
information theory, 23, 152, 177, 239, 253.
innate ideas, 141.
innovation, 79.
input-output continuum, 211, 221.
intangible, 47ff.

Subject Index 281

integration, 102, 270.
integrative disciplines, 175ff.
integrative factors, 271.
integrative research, 180.
intelligence, 152.
intensional orientation, 6, 12, 13, 47ff, 151, 232.
interdisciplinary approach, xi, 205ff, 254.
interpersonal communication, 41, 78.
interpersonal encounter, 89ff.
interpersonal relationships, 64, 67, 77, 80, 83, 84, 85, 152, 154.
interpersonal trust, 89ff.
interracial communication, 269.
interview, 31, 101.
intrapersonal transactions, 64.
invariance under transformation, 32, 98, 112.
invariant structures, 38.
IQ scores, 13.
is of identity, 121.
Is of Identity Test, 55.
isomorphism, 5, 112, 180.

J

journalism, 29, 31, 32, 160.
judges ratings, 71.

K

Korzybskian antidotes, 242ff.
Korzybskian models, 23ff.
Korzybskian premises, 45.
Korzybskian theory, 66.

L

language-as-known, 186.
language-as-used, 186.
language behavior, 8, 11, 17.
language competence, 186, 190.
language, distrust of, 141.
language, experimental, 9.
language-fact relationships, 190, 195.
language habits, 12.
language performance, 186, 190.
language structure, 29, 30, 31, 34.
languages, other than English, 8, 198.
language universals, 190.
law of excluded middle, 241.
law of identity, 240.
law of non-contradiction, 241.
laws of thought, 235ff.
leadership, 79.
level of significance, 58.
lexical patterns, 167.
liberals, 155.
library research, 267.
Lickert-type questionnaires, 14.
linearitis, 221, 223.
linguist, 45.
linguistic analysis, 140, 166.
linguistic competence, 208.
linguistic correlates of judgments, 31.
linguistic habits, 8.
linguistic patterns, 110, 193.
linguistic relativity, 197.
linguistics, 8, 177, 185ff, 208.
literary criticism, 132.
literary research, 125ff.
logical calculus of behavior, 66, 67.
logotherapy, 207.
love, 47, 152, 154.
loving behavior, 50.

M

maneuvers, contact-avoiding, 66.
map/territory, 5, 7, 132, 136, 158.
mass media, 100, 168.
mathematics, 123, 187.
maximitis, 221, 223.
meaning, intended, 42.
meaning, obtained, 42.
meaninglessness, 188.
means-ends, 212, 213.
measurement problems, xii, 69ff, 152, 159.
mechanitis, 221, 223.
mediation, 10, 42.
medicine, 212.
"medium is the method," 149.
memory traces, 44.
mental health, 143.
mentally ill, 10, 18.
mentally ill, language behavior of, 12.
message, 131, 186.
message variables, 31.
messianic humanism, 142, 143.
metalanguage, 34, 187, 193ff.
metalinguistic competence, 199.
metalinguistic position, 8.
metalinguistic statements, 34.
metaphors, 109, 116, 154, 165.
metaphysics, 140, 143.
methodolatry, 150.

282 Subject Index

methodologies, of Moreno and Korzybski, 83.
methodology, xii, 15, 69, 70, 84, 95, 119, 149, 163, 229, 235, 247, 250.
micro-language, 8.
militants, 261.
mixed media, 122.
model, heuristic value of, 27.
models, 23ff, 109, 253.
models, mathematical, 221.
motivation, 29.
multi-level analysis, 43.
multiordinality, 109, 111, 132, 137, 152, 159, 242.
multivalued orientations, 14.

N

natural order, reversal of, 33.
need for achievement, 201.
negative premises, 37.
Negroes, 260, 261, 265.
neo-Aristotelian assumptions, 161.
neurotic, 202.
news values, 29.
Newtonian physics, 239.
non-Aristotelian, 31, 219, 239.
non-Aristotelian logic, 181.
non-Aristotelian methodology, xi.
non-Aristotelian system, 23.
non-elementalistic, 111, 119.
non-euclidian, 239.
non-identity, 55, 113.
non-linear approach, 17.
non-newtonian, 239.
normative statements, 140.
null-hypothesis, 66.

O

object language, 187, 198.
objective level, 37, 43.
objectivity, 114, 140, 156, 158, 160, 230.
observers, panel of, 70.
OG Principle of Research, 30, 149ff.
onomatopoeia, 111.
open and closed minded 31.
operational statements, 230.
operations research, 178, 255.
opinionation, 16, 55.
organism-as-a-whole-in-an-environment, 47, 114, 209.
Oriental approaches, 264.
Oxford English Dictionary, 128.

P

patterned signals, 211.
patterns, 213, 214.
peak experiences, 50.
Pearl Harbor, 166.
people-oriented, 11.
perception, 6, 7, 44, 45, 141, 162ff, 237.
perception, selective, 26, 29.
perceptual analysis, 167.
perceptual approach, 161ff.
perceptual change, 165, 169.
perceptual efficiency, 29.
perceptual images, 162.
perceptual world, 167, 168.
Personality, A Biosocial Approach, 120.
personnel managers, 31.
phenomenological psychologists, 162.
philosophy, 140, 144.
phonetics, 110, 187.
phonology, 188, 189.
physiological measurement, 51, 248.
physiological variables, 67.
playwright, 120.
poetry, 110, 126.
Poetry Magazine, 127.
polarity, 237.
positivism, 141, 156.
potentialities, 52.
predictability, 28.
prejudice, 31, 159.
pre-literary experience, 126.
premises, 52.
prisoner, 164.
Prisoner's Dilemma, 33.
problem solving, 7, 14, 221.
program-generating function, 212.
progress, 128.
projecting, awareness of, 29.
pseudo-arguments, 249.
pseudo-science, 150.
psychiatry, 31, 160, 207.
psychodrama, 257.
psychogalvanometer, 48, 152.
psycholinguistics, 42, 140, 188, 193ff, 207, 208.
Psycholinguistics: A Book of Readings, 194.
psychological profiles, 85.
psychological reality, 188.
psychological scaling techniques, 69ff.
psychological tests, 167, 248.
psychology, 13, 33, 42, 199.
psychometry, 81.
psychophysiological reactions, 218.

Subject Index 283

psychotherapy, 64.
psychotic, 202.
publish or perish, 154.
pulse rate, 29.
puns, 112.

Q

Q-sort, 167, 168.
questionnaire, 12, 159.
quotes, 132, 136.

R

racial tension, 95ff.
racism, 261, 262, 264, 265.
racism, in research design, 260.
ranking, 78, 80.
rating scale, 82.
rationalization, 157.
reactions, delayed, 10, 34, 71.
reactions, higher order, 34.
reality, 236, 238.
recording procedures, 48.
redundancy, 226.
referent, 6.
reifications, 158.
relations, 111, 236.
relativity, 8.
relaxation, 71.
relavance, 112.
reliability, 58, 71, 82.
replication, 28.
reporters, high fidelity, 32.
research designs, xi, 119, 264.
research, empirical, 3ff.
research, experimental, 3ff., 16.
research-generating terms, 195.
research, literary, 109ff.
research methodology, 84, 247, 248, 264.
research process, 217ff.
research technique, 157.
results, biased, 13.
rhetoric, 113, 139ff., 161ff., 208, 258.
rhetoric of confrontation, 161.
rhetorical analysis, 162, 167, 169.
rhetorical transaction, 163.
rigidity, 12, 55.
risk, 90.
roles, 97, 101.

S

safety devices, 197, 199.
sanity, 4, 12.
Sapir-Whorf-Korzybski hypothesis, 89, 163, 165, 197.
scaling methods, psychological, 69ff.
schizophrenics, language of, 12.
Science and Sanity, xi, 62, 116, 137, 229, 238.
science news, 31, 32.
science of man, 18.
sciences, pure, 211.
scientific documents, 211ff.
scientific method, 122, 143.
scientistic terms, 142.
scores, Minnesota Multiphasic Personality Inventory, (MMPI), 12.
segregation, de facto, 99.
self-actualizing, 31, 50, 51.
self-awareness, 232.
self concept, 17.
self-paralyzing maneuvers, 64.
self-reflexiveness, 13, 98, 116, 121, 132, 136, 197, 242.
semantic amgibuity, 188.
semantic analysis, 120, 181.
semantic differential, 14, 89, 168.
semantic environment, 115, 181, 239.
semantic factors, 217ff.
Semantic Interaction Test, 34, 55ff.
semantic reactions, 26 28, 69ff, 77ff, 109, 114, 132, 180, 187, 189, 217, 226, 227.
semantic reactions, higher order, 30, 33.
semantic reactions, structure of, 61ff.
semantic reactor, 26.
semantic structures, 41ff.
seminar-workshops, xi, 62.
semiotics, 208.
sensitivity sessions, 31, 49, 156, 257.
set-theory notation, 65.
short-run effects, 162.
signal-symbol reactions, 10, 15, 18, 69.
Signs, Language and Behavior, 213.
Silent and Verbal Levels diagram, 23ff.
sincerity, 47.
situational analysis, 95ff.
social approval, 200.
social atom, 81.
social interaction, 43.
social psychology, 209.
social similarities, 45.
sociogram, 81, 84.
sociology, 16, 209.
sociomatrix, 80, 81, 84.
sociometric measures, 77ff.
sociometry, 78ff.
source credibility, 13.

Subject Index

space, metric, 224, 225, 226.
space, semantic, 224, 225, 226.
space-time, 38.
Speech Behavior and Human Interaction, 206.
Stanford-Binet, 56.
statistics, 158.
status, 78, 79.
stimulus-response research, 33.
Stroop Test, 12.
structural assumptions, 219.
structural design, 211.
structural differential, 23ff, 37ff, 181, 269, 270.
structural similarity, 25, 28, 224.
structure, 111, 237.
subjectivity, 114, 141, 156, 160.
submicroscopic, 38.
summated rating scales, 89.
surds, 127ff.
surface structure, 189.
surveys, 11.
survival, 4, 15, 157.
symbol, 166, 180.
symbolic equivalences, 113.
symbolic interactionism, 97, 99, 101.
symbolic structures, 226.
symmetry, 39.
syntax, 110, 188.
system, 239, 253.
system of systems, 206, 208.
system, closed, 250.
system, open, 250.
systematics, 239.
systemic mode, 213.
systems, 111, 206.
systems analysis, 78.

T

tactical approach, 162.
tape recording, 10, 13.
taxonomies 152.
tele, 80, 81, 83.
test performance, 17.
test-retest, 82.
T-Group training, 18, 209.
thematic analysis, 101, 102.
theology, 140.
theoretical analysis, 142.
theoretical models, 152.
theory, 3, 139, 143.
therapeutic technique, 250.
therapeutic value, 17.
therapy, 247.
time binding, 52, 56, 123, 180 233.

Time Magazine, 128.
titles, 214.
traits, 5.
transaction, 64.
transactional model, 152.
transference, 80, 81, 83, 85.
Trobrianders, 14.
trust, 47, 51, 89ff, 100.
two-valued orientation, 14.

U

unconscious, 114.
unconscious assumptions, 218, 221.
unconscious response, 164.
Uncritical Inference Test, 55.
undefined terms, 38, 230.
unity of science movement, 176.
universe, 236, 238, 239.
urban communication, 95ff.
urban tension, 99.
utility values, 92.

V

validation, empirical, 153.
validity, 58, 82.
value judgment, 166, 167, 249.
values, 78, 126.
variable, dependent, 17, 205, 208, 249.
variable, extralinguistic, 186.
variable, independent, 16, 205, 208, 249.
variable, personality, 31.
verbal/non-verbal, 47, 67, 197.
verbal behavior, 42, 49.
Verbal Cocoons, 72.
verbal influence, 165.
verbal output, 31.
videotape 6, 50, 61, 66, 67, 70, 105.
Vietnam, 166, 169, 181.
voodoo practitioners, 14.

W

warmth, 47.
Watson-Glaser Test, 55.
Wechler Intelligence, 56.
Whorfian hypothesis, 8, 9, 163, 165, 197.
wisdom, 160.
witch doctors, 14.
word-association, 45.
words, four letter, 14.
words, multiordinal, 11.
working devices, 197, 199.
World War II, 166.